"Seasoned theologians Jared Ortiz and Daniel Keating here introduce the Creed in a book that would make a great textbook for introductory theology classes as well as for study groups. What shines forth is the sheer reasonableness of Christian faith. They also draw a link between faith and hope, both vitally needed in our culture of despair. Deeply rooted in Scripture and the Church Fathers, this book exemplifies what Christian instruction at its best can be."

—**Matthew Levering**, Mundelein Seminary

"This splendid book provides a brilliant presentation of the Nicene Creed that is richly historical but accessible, and conceptually profound but clear, so that readers can understand why Christianity teaches and professes what it does. The book functions both as an excellent introduction to Christianity and as a reference for the pursuit of deeper understanding of the Catholic faith. In a world where many who are nonreligious have a creed of some kind that remains unstated, this statement of the Christian creed invites all to reflect on what is ultimately true and suggests plainly how true knowledge of God orients the human being toward happiness."

—**Thomas Joseph White, OP**, Pontifical University of St. Thomas (Angelicum)

"In the introduction, we hear that 'the creeds are precisely the medicine we need' because of their 'densely packed summaries of the Christian faith.' One could say the same of this book, which commends itself as a wonderful tool—indeed, a treasure trove—for those prepared to follow the authors in unpacking these rich phrases that Christians have recited for centuries. Here is a powerful antidote that helps us to 'overcome our contemporary allergy to truth' as we lean deeply into the Nicene Creed, understanding how it addressed the problems of its day and continues to speak powerfully to our own age."

—**Edith M. Humphrey**, Pittsburgh Theological Seminary (emerita)

"The Nicene Creed is the most widely accepted confession of faith among all Christian people. This superb exposition of the Creed, written by two faithful Catholic scholars, shows how this classic statement has practical relevance for believers of all confessions. A true treasure for the Lord's people everywhere!"

—**Timothy George**, Beeson Divinity School, Samford University; cochair of Evangelicals and Catholics Together

"An extremely well-thought-out introduction to the Nicene Creed, this book explains the Cree͏   In an age impatient with

T0339290

complex truths and truth itself, this is no small feat. Demonstrating that the Creed is far more than a list of Christian beliefs, this book connects the Creed to both Testaments, church history, the words of the Church Fathers, the *Catechism of the Catholic Church*, and the prayers of the church in a way that not only teaches but also deepens faith. The faith of the church shines through in this text as the living, dynamic reality of unfathomable depth that it is, providing welcome clarity in our moment of deep confusion about the most basic Christian truths. More than an excellent teaching tool, this book is a great companion for prayer and for doing 'the work of God,' which is 'to know the one he has sent' (John 6:29)."

—**Jonathan J. Reyes**, Knights of Columbus

The

NICENE CREED

A SCRIPTURAL, HISTORICAL,
AND THEOLOGICAL COMMENTARY

JARED ORTIZ
and DANIEL A. KEATING

Baker Academic
a division of Baker Publishing Group
Grand Rapids, Michigan

Published by Baker Academic
a division of Baker Publishing Group
Grand Rapids, Michigan
BakerAcademic.com

Printed in the United States of America

Library of Congress Cataloging-in-Publication Data
Names: Ortiz, Jared, author. | Keating, Daniel A., author.
Title: The Nicene Creed : a scriptural, historical, and theological commentary / Jared Ortiz and Daniel A. Keating.
Description: Grand Rapids, Michigan : Baker Academic, a division of Baker Publishing Group, 2024. | Includes bibliographical references and index.
Identifiers: LCCN 2023009231 | ISBN 9781540965110 (paperback) | ISBN 9781540966834 (casebound) | ISBN 9781493442850 (ebook) | ISBN 9781493442867 (pdf)
Subjects: LCSH: Nicene Creed.
Classification: LCC BT999 .O69 2023 | DDC 238/.142—dc23/eng/20230419
LC record available at https://lccn.loc.gov/2023009231

Nihil Obstat	Imprimatur
Reverend Lam T. Le, S.T.L.	Most Reverend David J. Walkowiak, J.C.D.
Censor Deputatis	Bishop of Grand Rapids
May 4, 2023	June 9, 2023

Contents

Acknowledgments   vi
A Note on Texts and Translations   vii
Abbreviations   viii
The Nicene Creed in English   x

Introduction   1

1. Belief   15

2. God the Father   37

3. God the Son Divine   74

4. God the Son Incarnate   103

5. God the Holy Spirit   141

6. Life in the Trinity   172

Appendix 1: Three Creeds Compared   211
Appendix 2: The Nicene Creed in Latin and Greek   214
Glossary   216
Suggested Resources   220
Index of Sidebars   223

Acknowledgments

The authors would like to thank Dave Nelson for first pitching the idea of a commentary on the Nicene Creed, as well as our editor, Anna Gissing, for so ably and encouragingly bringing the manuscript to completion. We are grateful to Nathan Betz, David DeJong, Abigail Favale, Angela Franks, and Jacob Wood for ad hoc consultations on key points and to Eric Boldiszar, Nathan Gilmore, Dustin Gordon, Bryan Harr, Bryan Noonan, and Denium Roman for their careful reading and astute suggestions.

A Note on Texts
and Translations

Unless noted otherwise, all translations of Scripture come from the Revised Standard Version.

The English text of the Nicene Creed comes from the standard translation approved by the United States Conference of Catholic Bishops: https://www.usccb.org/beliefs-and-teachings/what-we-believe.

The Latin and Greek texts of the Creed come from Heinrich Denzinger, *Compendium of Creeds, Definitions, and Declarations on Matters of Faith and Morals*, ed. Peter Hünermann, 43rd ed. (San Francisco: Ignatius, 2012), §150.

Abbreviations

General

†	Indicates that the definition of a term appears in the glossary
ANF	*Ante-Nicene Fathers*
CCC	*Catechism of the Catholic Church*, 2nd ed. (New York: Doubleday, 2003)
cf.	*confer*, compare
ESV	English Standard Version
FOTC	Fathers of the Church
LXX	Septuagint
NAB	New American Bible
NABRE	New American Bible (Revised Edition)
NPNF¹	*Nicene and Post-Nicene Fathers*, Series 1
NPNF²	*Nicene and Post-Nicene Fathers*, Series 2
NRSV	New Revised Standard Version
NT	New Testament
OT	Old Testament
para.	paragraph
PPS	Popular Patristics Series
Roman Missal	*The Roman Missal*, Amended Third Typical Edition (Collegeville, MN: Liturgical Press, 2011)
RSV	Revised Standard Version
RSV-2CE	Revised Standard Version, Second Catholic Edition
WSA	The Works of Saint Augustine

Books of the Old Testament

Amos	Amos	Eccles.	Ecclesiastes
Bar.	Baruch	Esther	Esther
1–2 Chron.	1–2 Chronicles	Exod.	Exodus
Dan.	Daniel	Ezek.	Ezekiel
Deut.	Deuteronomy	Ezra	Ezra

Gen.	Genesis	Mal.	Malachi
Hab.	Habakkuk	Mic.	Micah
Hag.	Haggai	Nah.	Nahum
Hosea	Hosea	Neh.	Nehemiah
Isa.	Isaiah	Num.	Numbers
Jdt.	Judith	Obad.	Obadiah
Jer.	Jeremiah	Prov.	Proverbs
Job	Job	Ps(s).	Psalm(s)
Joel	Joel	Ruth	Ruth
Jon.	Jonah	1–2 Sam.	1–2 Samuel
Josh.	Joshua	Sir.	Sirach
Judg.	Judges	Song	Song of Songs
1–2 Kings	1–2 Kings	Tob.	Tobit
Lam.	Lamentations	Wis.	Wisdom
Lev.	Leviticus	Zech.	Zechariah
1–2 Macc.	1–2 Maccabees	Zeph.	Zephaniah

Books of the New Testament

Acts	Acts	Mark	Mark
Col.	Colossians	Matt.	Matthew
1–2 Cor.	1–2 Corinthians	1–2 Pet.	1–2 Peter
Eph.	Ephesians	Phil.	Philippians
Gal.	Galatians	Philem.	Philemon
Heb.	Hebrews	Rev.	Revelation
James	James	Rom.	Romans
John	John	1–2 Thess.	1–2 Thessalonians
1–3 John	1–3 John	1–2 Tim.	1–2 Timothy
Jude	Jude	Titus	Titus
Luke	Luke		

The Nicene Creed
in English

I believe in one God,
the Father almighty,
maker of heaven and earth,
of all things visible and invisible.

I believe in one Lord Jesus Christ,
the Only Begotten Son of God,
born of the Father before all ages.
God from God, Light from Light,
true God from true God,
begotten, not made, consubstantial with the Father;
through him all things were made.
For us men and for our salvation
he came down from heaven,
and by the Holy Spirit was incarnate of the Virgin Mary,
and became man.
For our sake he was crucified under Pontius Pilate,
he suffered death and was buried,
and rose again on the third day
in accordance with the Scriptures.
He ascended into heaven
and is seated at the right hand of the Father.
He will come again in glory
to judge the living and the dead
and his kingdom will have no end.

I believe in the Holy Spirit, the Lord, the giver of life,
who proceeds from the Father and the Son,
who with the Father and the Son is adored and glorified,
who has spoken through the prophets.

I believe in one, holy, catholic and apostolic Church.
I confess one Baptism for the forgiveness of sins
and I look forward to the resurrection of the dead
and the life of the world to come. Amen.

Introduction

Why Creeds Today? A Medicine for Our Times

Why would we bother with creeds in our day?[1] Aren't they just relics from a past age? People today are less and less concerned with truth, and no one seems inclined to follow any authority, especially if that authority is *imposed* on them from the outside. We could say that our age has taken aim at truth and wants either to obliterate the idea of truth or render it so weak that it has no force in our lives. To recite a creed—to make a common confession of faith that is already worked out and defined—just doesn't fit with our desire to go our own way as individuals and to establish our own truth. We are told that people today are hungry for stories—for narratives—not for statements and declarations that seem detached from real life. In a sense, everything connected to the idea of a creed seems out of step with the drift and direction of our culture.

Our view is that these apparently unfavorable conditions are exactly what make the creeds so crucial for our times. Through their densely packed summaries of the Christian faith, the creeds are precisely the medicine we need. *Because* we live in an age that doubts the very reality of truth, and *because* we are trained to go our own way and encouraged to craft our "own truth," we need more than ever an anchor of Truth—given, tested, and secure—not just as individuals but together as the Church. To our culture, the creeds implicitly say, "These things are true and real. Here is the genuine narrative of our world. And this is true for *everyone*."

1. By referring to "creeds" in the plural, we are referring not only to the Nicene Creed of 381 (the subject of this book) but also to the Apostles' Creed and the Athanasian Creed, both originating within the Western Christian tradition, as well as to many other local creeds in circulation in the early Church.

What are the core truths that the creeds announce as true? That God has made the world and all that is in it—and that it is good; that Christ, true God and true man, has come to redeem the world and to bring forgiveness of sins; that the Spirit of God is alive and real, acting in the Church and in the world; that there will be an end to the world, when we will experience the resurrection of our bodies and life eternal with God. From its origins, Christianity was inescapably concerned with "truth," with a right understanding of the gospel of Jesus Christ. "The early Church was from the start a believing, confessing, preaching Church."[2] If we are to overcome our contemporary allergy to truth, the creeds will play a critical role.

But the creeds are not only an antidote for minds that doubt the very reality of truth. By requiring a vocal, public *confession*, the creeds also supply another important remedy for our times. We live in a world that loves to hedge its bets. We want to try things out and experiment with options, but we are reluctant to commit ourselves to anything definitively. The creeds invite and summon us to confess: "Here I stand, this is my conviction, and I will put my life on the line for this truth." When we confess the creeds, we commit ourselves both to God and to the truths that the creeds contain. In a very real sense, we have not really made the truths of the creeds our own possession until we *confess* those truths and *commit* ourselves to them. In a marriage covenant, the public profession of commitment secures the love of the spouses and strengthens them to live out that commitment against all the challenges that may come. So it is with the creed—by confessing our beliefs, we pin our lives to the truths we acknowledge. We don't hedge our bets; we put our lives on the line. Strikingly, the confession of the creeds is a kind of rehearsal for martyrdom. What we do each week by committing ourselves to the truths of the faith prepares us to make good our confession of faith should the call of martyrdom come our way. For some people, even today, this martyrdom will mean shedding their blood for the faith, but for all of us it means dying to ourselves daily and living a life in accord with the truth.

We see two further benefits of creeds for our day. The first is that the creeds keep us in balance. By presenting a short summary of the main outlines of our faith, the creeds steer us away from focusing on just one thing. They place before our minds the full narrative arc of God's saving action through Christ, from the creation of the world to eternal life in the age to come. For many

---

2. J. N. D. Kelly, *Early Christian Creeds* (London: Longmans, 1949), 7. Frances Young concurs, observing that "Christianity is the only major religion to set such store by creeds and doctrines" (*The Making of the Creeds* [Harrisburg, PA: Trinity Press International, 1991], 1).

of us, there is a temptation to focus on those truths of our faith that we find most congenial and comforting. Like sheep wandering in the fields, we migrate toward what we perceive as "good food" for our soul and shy away from things we don't understand or that seem threatening. The regular confession of the creeds helps to keep us balanced and open to the fullness of our faith.

For instance, I may be utterly amazed by the grace of Christ and the work of the cross that brought me forgiveness of sins. This is excellent and worthy—but I shouldn't neglect the created order and the life in the Spirit that follows from Christ's work. Or I may be overjoyed by the goodness of creation and desire to steward it well. This is wonderful and praiseworthy. But I can't be attached to the created order without recognizing the "fall" in the created order, the need for redemption, and the fact that we are really looking forward to the new and everlasting creation. Or I may be thrilled by the action of the Holy Spirit in my life and in the life of the Church. This is beautiful and worthy of full attention. But we also believe in the Father and the Son, and I need to integrate my love for the Holy Spirit with a full trinitarian understanding of our destiny.

Certainly, creeds do not make any claim to be thorough; they are only a digest of the primary truths of our faith. The *Catechism* is the main resource provided by the Catholic Church to open up and explain all the elements of our faith in a detailed and ordered way. But the creeds, by moving us briskly from the beginning to the end and by ordering what we believe around the trinitarian God in whom we believe (Father, Son, and Spirit), keep our faith—and our lives—in balance.

Finally, the creeds function like a treasure chest, waiting to be opened and explored. The creeds are not meant to reduce our faith to simple facts; they are not intended to drive away mystery and complexity. Rather, the creeds secure a framework for the whole of our faith, *so that* we can freely go and explore the riches of the mystery in each part and in the whole. Every line and phrase contains within it an astonishing "world" to explore. Of course, we cannot explore everything at once, just as we cannot explore a large and beautiful country all at once. We have to take things in turn, even as we keep the whole in view. To say this differently, we are not meant to stop with the creeds. Just as the creeds are condensed summaries of biblical revelation, so they ought to lead us back to the great wealth of riches revealed in the Scriptures. They ought to lead us further into the rich treasury of the liturgy and inspire us to explore the deep dogmatic foundations of our faith. All this, in turn, opens up for us the treasure of our common prayers and hymns and directs us to the witness of the saints, who embody the truths of the creeds in their lives. The creeds, then, secure an ordered confession of the central mysteries of our faith *so that*, as the redeemed sons and daughters of God, we may pursue the riches of our faith and become more fully "conformed to the image" of Christ (Rom. 8:29).

When and Why Did Creeds Originate?

The creeds arose because of a felt need for a short confession of the basic truths of Christian belief. We can detect in the New Testament short formulas of faith—creedal *elements*—that function as summaries of what is believed. One example comes from Paul when he is presenting his teaching on the resurrection. He begins by describing how the faith was handed down to him: "For I delivered to you as of first importance what I also received, that Christ died for our sins in accordance with the Scriptures, that he was buried, that he was raised on the third day in accordance with the Scriptures, and that he appeared to Cephas, then to the Twelve" (1 Cor. 15:3–5). Paul sums up here the basic teaching on Christ's death, burial, and resurrection in a short formula that he is "passing on" to the church in Corinth. It functions as a short statement of faith on Christ's passion and resurrection.

Another example occurs in Paul's First Letter to Timothy (3:16). Summing up what he calls "the mystery of our religion," Paul offers this poetic hymn to Christ:

> He was manifested in the flesh,
> vindicated in the Spirit,
>   seen by angels,
> preached among the nations,
> believed on in the world,
>   taken up in glory.[3]

This short narrative "hymn" to Christ refers to the incarnation, resurrection, and ascension of Christ but also includes the preaching of the gospel to all the nations. The apostolic writings in the New Testament already show evidence of short creedal statements that capture the heart of Christian belief.[4] "There is plenty of evidence in the New Testament to show that the faith

---

3. In the original Greek, each phrase begins with a verb that has an identical ending, giving this hymn a poetic quality that does not appear in English translation.

4. For other passages in the New Testament that function as short creedal statements, see Rom. 1:3; 1 Cor. 8:6; Phil. 2:6–11; 1 Tim. 2:5; 2 Tim. 2:8; 1 Pet. 3:18–22.

was already beginning to be formed into conventional summaries. Creeds in the full sense were yet to come, but the movement towards formulation and fixity was under way."[5]

The next stage on the road toward fixed creeds occurred in the second century when the internal needs of the churches combined with various external challenges to create the conditions for the development of creeds. What were the internal needs? By the second century, the Church was primarily evangelizing gentiles ([†]pagans) who had little or no contact with Judaism or the revelation given in the Old Testament. Catechumens, therefore, needed more time and further instruction to prepare to live successfully the life in Christ into which they were being baptized. To serve this longer process, short summaries of the faith, normally delivered in the form of questions and answers, were created to help new believers grasp and confess their newfound faith. "The creeds took the form they did in response to the situation in which they arose, namely the context of catechesis and baptism."[6]

At the same time, the Church was confronted with popular teachers and movements who presented a plausible but false version of the gospel. We identify many of these groups today as "[†]Gnostics" (and the teaching they gave as "[†]Gnosticism"). In fact, they were a diverse and varied set of movements that possessed certain common tendencies. Most notably, these groups typically rejected the Old Testament as the work of an inferior God, and they often rejected the material creation itself as marked by sin and evil. Salvation, according to this view, comes through a "flight" from the material world by means of a secret "knowledge" (gnosis). Further, these movements often denied the true incarnation of the Word, claiming instead that the Word only *appeared* to take on human flesh, a teaching that we call "[†]Docetism."[7] Coupled with this claim was a denial that Christ actually suffered and died on the cross, as he could hardly do so if he did not really assume our flesh. And so the Church in the second century was faced with various movements that repudiated the goodness of creation, rejected the Old Testament, and denied the incarnation, the passion, and the resurrection of Christ.

Faced with these considerable deviations in teaching, the Church needed to find a way to communicate and confess effectively the true faith received from the apostles. One response was the development of what we call "the [†]rule of

---

5. Kelly, *Early Christian Creeds*, 13.

6. Young, *Making of the Creeds*, 6.

7. The name "Docetism" derives from the Greek verb *dokein*, "to seem" or "to appear"; according to this view, Christ only *appeared* to be a true human being but did not really assume our human nature.

faith" (or "the rule of truth").[8] This was a short creed-like statement, typically organized around the three †persons of the †Trinity (Father, Son, and Spirit), that briefly summed up the Christian faith. Saint Irenaeus of Lyons, writing between 180 and 200, presents one of the clearest examples of such a rule:

> And this is the order of our faith, the foundation of [the] edifice and the support of [our] conduct: God, the Father, uncreated, uncontainable, invisible, one God, the Creator of all: this is the first article . . . of our faith. And the second article: the Word of God, the Son of God, Christ Jesus our Lord, . . . by whom all things were made, and who, in the last times, to recapitulate all things, became a man amongst men . . . in order to abolish death, to demonstrate life, and to effect communion between God and man. And the third article: the Holy Spirit, through whom the prophets prophesied . . . and who, in the last times, was poured out in a new fashion upon the human race, renewing man, throughout the world, to God. For this reason the baptism of our regeneration takes place through these three articles.[9]

Irenaeus offers this remarkable summary of the narrative of our faith in three "articles" governed by the Father, Son, and Spirit, and he concludes by linking the recitation of this faith with baptism. We can see here the general shape of the formal creeds that will soon appear.

Fixed creeds likely began to appear in local churches by the last decades of the second century, but the first literary evidence we have is from the early third century.[10] What purposes did these fixed creeds serve? Scholars often point to many contexts in which creeds—and creedal statements—functioned in the early Church, but these can be summed up under three main headings:

- in the catechesis and baptism of new members
- in preaching and teaching (to local congregations and in written treatises)
- in the communal worship of the liturgy

8. For the role of the rule of faith in relation to Scripture and the creeds, see Everett Ferguson, *The Rule of Faith: A Guide* (Eugene, OR: Cascade Books, 2015).

9. Irenaeus, *Demonstration of the Apostolic Preaching* 6–7, in *On the Apostolic Preaching*, trans. John Behr, PPS 17 (Crestwood, NY: St. Vladimir's Seminary Press, 1997), 43–44. Writing from Carthage in the early third century, Tertullian offers a similar rule of faith, organized into the same three articles centered on the Father, the Son, and the Holy Spirit (see *Against Praxeas* 2).

10. Kelly (*Early Christian Creeds*, 145) proposes that the first version of the Old Roman Creed (the precursor to the Apostles' Creed) appeared around 175–80. Young (*Making of the Creeds*, 2) places the origin of written, fixed creeds at the turn of the third century: "All these different credal formulae, including the Old Roman Creed as well as Eastern forms, emerge around the turn of the third century, and cannot be traced in earlier Christian literature."

In the early Church, the primary form of the creed used in catechesis and especially in baptism was *interrogatory*—that is, it was delivered through questions and answers: *Do you believe in God, the Father almighty? . . . Do you believe in Jesus Christ, his only Son, our Lord?* We encounter this interrogatory form of the creed today in the renewal of baptismal promises during the Easter Vigil. Creeds used in preaching, teaching, and worship were typically *declaratory* in form—that is, they confessed the faith through a declaration of the truth: *I believe in God, the Father almighty*, and so on.

How and Why the Nicene Creed Came to Be

The story of how the Nicene Creed came to be written is a long and complicated tale.[11] Here we can offer only a short summary of the main stages. In the commentary that follows, we will develop some of the specific historical circumstances in greater detail.

The story begins with the teaching of a priest in Alexandria named Arius in about the year 318. In reaction to his own bishop (i.e., Alexander), Arius began to teach publicly that Jesus, the Son of God, was a kind of semidivine *creature* brought into existence by the Father (who is the only *true* God) and sent into the world to redeem it. For Arius, the Son was not fully and truly God; he was the first and highest creation of the Father. Brought into existence before the creation of the material world (and so before time), the Son was not, in Arius's view, eternal. Famously, he claimed that "there was when he was not."[12] In a similar way, Arius also denied that the Holy Spirit was truly God. This teaching—that Jesus the Son of God was a creature—stirred up a roiling controversy that spilled out from Alexandria to surrounding regions.

One cause for the controversy's quick spread was the recent legalization and acceptance of Christianity by the Roman Empire. Periodically persecuted and consistently marginalized, the Church got a surprising boost in prominence when Constantine attributed a key military victory to the Christian God. From 312 onward, Constantine favored the Church and saw in it a way he might unify a faltering empire. In 325, Constantine called a worldwide

11. For a detailed study of the development of the Nicene Creed and its theology, see Lewis Ayres, *Nicaea and Its Legacy: An Approach to Fourth-Century Trinitarian Theology* (Oxford: Oxford University Press, 2004). Ayres offers his own brief summary of how to understand the development of the faith confessed in the fourth century on pp. 430–35.

12. See appendix 1 for our translation of the condemnations of Arian statements in the Creed of Nicaea.

council of bishops to gather in Nicaea to settle this controversy about the true identity of the Son.

The bishops who met together in that first ecumenical council produced what is called "the Creed of Nicaea" (see appendix 1 for the English text of this creed). This statement of faith rejected the claims of Arius by confessing that the Son was "†begotten, not made," and that he was "God from God, Light from Light, true God from true God." In order to strengthen this confession, the Creed made use of nonscriptural terms to describe the Son's relationship with the Father, saying that the Son was †consubstantial (in Greek, †*homoousios*, "one in being") with the Father. The end result of this council was that Arius's views were condemned, and it seemed as if the Church could now be at peace on this issue.

But in fact, not all the bishops fully understood or were in full agreement with this confession of faith from Nicaea. It seemed to some of them to go too far by endangering the distinction between the Father and the Son. Though only a minority of bishops supported Arius's radical conclusions, others sought a mediating position that (in their view) more effectively guaranteed the priority of the Father and the personal distinction between the Father and the Son. And so a decades-long contest ensued between various competing positions, with Constantine's successors often supporting positions at odds with the confession of the Creed of Nicaea. Many local councils and synods were convened, and many mediating "creeds" were produced in the hope of reaching a consensus. To complicate matters, a group of bishops who readily confessed the full divinity of the Son denied the divinity of the Spirit. And so a new front in the battle was opened, with the need to explain and confess the full divinity of the Holy Spirit.

In the end, those who championed the teaching and the language of Nicaea prevailed. Figures such as Athanasius, Basil the Great, Hilary of Poitiers, and Gregory of Nazianzus, among many others, played crucial roles in helping the Church explain and defend "the faith which was once for all delivered to the saints" (Jude 3). The years of controversy were not wasted; the Church attained greater clarity about its own confession of the divine Trinity (the Father, Son, and Holy Spirit). In the year 381, the emperor Theodosius called a council to meet in Constantinople to discuss and clarify the faith expressed at Nicaea in 325. The result of this council is what we now call (somewhat confusingly) "the Nicene Creed," which presented an updated and expanded version of the Creed of Nicaea. In a short time, this creed of 381—the subject of this book (hereafter often referred to simply as "the Creed")—became the most authoritative ecumenical confession of the Christian faith for both the East and the West.[13]

The teachings of the Creed were widely accepted, but the Creed itself was not universally used. In the fifth century, for example, Augustine was still using the †Old Roman Creed (a precursor to the Apostles' Creed) when preparing catechumens for baptism. It was in the seventh century that the Nicene Creed (the 381 version) became a standard part of the weekly liturgy. It was (and is) professed—and was often sung—after the sermon, and it is worth pondering why the Church placed it there. The Creed serves as a fixed rule of faith, a measuring stick of what we as Christians believe. It helps us to interpret the Scriptures we just heard, to confirm the orthodoxy of the sermon just preached, and to unite our minds and hearts in confession of what we believe. It is the culmination of the Liturgy of the Word and serves as the hinge that leads us into the Liturgy of the Eucharist. Similar to its role in baptism, the profession of the Creed serves as the doorway to the sacraments. It is a public demonstration of our right belief and our desire for communion with God and his Church. Indeed, the Creed, in a sense, opens the door to communion with the God and the Church we profess.

Creeds and Belief: An Overview of the Mystery

The Nicene Creed briefly articulates the central mysteries of our Christian faith: the Trinity, the †incarnation, and our redemption in Christ. The commentary that follows will explore every phrase of this Creed, but it will be helpful to have a brief and clear summary here in order to situate the specific teachings within the whole and to provide a rough map of the more intricate terrain we will explore in the coming chapters.

The Creed uses certain technical terms that became further refined and then normalized in the following centuries. With the Council of Chalcedon (451), the theological language became largely fixed in the East and the West. It will be helpful to grasp the basic meaning of these developed terms, even if they weren't systematically in use at the time of Nicaea, since they will allow us to explain things with more conceptual clarity.

---

13. The Apostles' Creed also functions in the Catholic Church (and for many Protestants) as an authoritative creed. Developing organically from the Old Roman Creed (late second or early third century), the Apostles' Creed probably reached its final form in the 600s. For the stages in the development of the Apostles' Creed, see Kelly, *Early Christian Creeds*, 368–434.

When speaking about the Trinity, we are speaking about a "tri-unity," a "three and one." The *Catechism of the Catholic Church* admirably summarizes the tradition:

> The Church uses (I) the term "substance" (rendered also at times by "essence" or "†nature") to designate the divine being in its unity, (II) the term "person" or "hypostasis" to designate the Father, Son, and Holy Spirit in the real distinction among them, and (III) the term "†relation" to designate the fact that their distinction lies in the relationship of each to the others.[14]

Using the terms above, we can say that God is one substance or one divine nature and three divine persons. The oneness of God refers to *what* God is—that is, it names his divine nature or (to use the more technical philosophical term) substance. The threeness of God refers to *who* God is—that is, to the three divine persons: the Father, Son, and Holy Spirit. The divine persons are not one-third of the Godhead, nor are they separate beings. The threeness of God does not violate his oneness, a truth expressed in the well-known hymn: "Holy, holy, holy, merciful and mighty! God in three persons, blessed Trinity!"[15]

Augustine was a great teacher of the Trinity and often summarized the mystery in concise ways. In *The Trinity*, he writes, "Let us believe that the Father and Son and Holy Spirit are one God, maker and ruler of all creation; and that the Father is not the Son, and the Holy Spirit is neither the Father nor the Son, but that they are a Trinity of persons related to each other, and a unity of equal being."[16] Taking our lead from Augustine, we can articulate three basic rules for thinking about the Trinity in a fitting way:

1. There is only one God.
2. The Father is God, the Son is God, and the Holy Spirit is God.
3. The Father is not the Son, the Son is not the Father, and the Holy Spirit is neither the Father nor the Son.

These rules are paradoxical, and it is surprisingly difficult to keep all three in mind at the same time. To deny any one of them is to fall into some heresy: to deny the first is to fall into †polytheism (that there is more than one God); to

---

14. CCC 252.

15. Reginald Heber, "Holy, Holy, Holy! Lord God Almighty!," Hymnary.org, accessed January 25, 2023, https://hymnary.org/text/holy_holy_holy_lord_god_almighty_early.

16. Augustine, *The Trinity* 9.1.prologue, trans. Edmund Hill, WSA I/5 (Hyde Park, NY: New City, 1991), 271.

deny the second is to fall into †subordinationism (that the Son and the Spirit are ontologically inferior to the Father); and to deny the third is to fall into †modalism (that there is no distinction of persons, and so the Father is the same person as the Son and the Spirit).

When speaking about the mystery of the incarnation, we can say that Jesus Christ is one divine person (the Son) in two natures (divine and human). Jesus Christ is true God and true man, fully God and fully man. He is not a hybrid or a third thing or a half-and-half combination of divine and human. The Jesus Christ who walked on earth is the same eternal Son of God through whom the Father †created all things. In the incarnation, this eternal Son of God (and not the other persons of the Trinity) takes on a human nature in the womb of Mary. So when we encounter Jesus, we must confess that he is one divine person (the Son) who is divine (because he is God) and human (because he is born of Mary).

The claim that God is three and one or that Jesus is fully God and fully man at the same time is an expression of the mystery of God. It is not a logic puzzle to be figured out. That God is one and three at the same time means that we are dealing with a reality not of this world. That Christ has two natures at the same time means we are dealing with a transcendent reality that goes beyond our common and even advanced ways of thinking. It might be likened to a kind of Zen koan, meant to train us not to fall back on usual patterns of thinking but to open our minds to go beyond what we can capture easily with our thoughts. The rules and pithy formulations given above, simple to articulate but difficult to understand, are not meant to reduce God to a formula. They are meant to help us maintain the paradoxical truths about God revealed to us in Scripture.

Plan of the Book

This volume was originally conceived as a companion to Baker Academic's Catholic Commentary on Sacred Scripture. Like that series, our book is directed primarily to preachers, teachers, and other thoughtful Christians who enjoy studying as a way to deepen their understanding of what to believe and how to live a Christian life. Our intent is not to break new ground in research or interpretation but to present the faith in a winsome, compelling, and helpful way. To that end, we have a number of useful aids: glossary terms (marked with † on first appearance in the text, as you may have already noticed), a variety of sidebars, Scripture and *Catechism* references for each article, and the relevant section of the Creed in three languages at the start of each section.

The book is divided into six chapters. The first chapter is devoted to a discussion of what it means to believe, which in itself turns out to be a defining feature of Christianity. The remaining chapters deal with the mysteries of the Creed. Chapter 2 is devoted to the article on the Father. Chapters 3 and 4 treat Christ in his divine and human natures and his redemptive work. Chapter 5 focuses on the Holy Spirit, whereas chapter 6 treats the final articles of the Creed, which we have summarized as "Life in the Trinity."

In each chapter, we try to do three basic things: situate the particular teaching in its historical context; show the teaching's biblical foundations and logic; and, finally, articulate the teaching in its developed form. By doing this, we hope to show what is at stake with the formulation of each doctrine. Often, Christians take the teachings of the Creed for granted, but each word and phrase is carefully chosen and excludes a number of other real possibilities. Why was the teaching of *one* God so radical (and difficult)? Does God need to be creator of *all* things? Why should we believe that Jesus was fully God and fully human, not part God and part man? Is the Holy Spirit really divine? And so on. We want readers to feel the weight of the alternative choices so they can appreciate the achievement of the Creed.

We use three kinds of sidebars: "Witness to the Tradition," "Lex Orandi," and "Contemporary Issues." A brief comment on each. In the "Witness to the Tradition" sidebars, we highlight voices from the early Church that articulate or extend the article of faith under consideration in a particularly apt or beautiful way.

In the "Lex Orandi" sidebars, we draw on the Church's life of prayer to show how Christians express their faith in worship and song. The term †*lex orandi* literally means "the law of praying." It comes from the ancient formula *lex orandi, lex credendi*, which can be loosely translated "What the Church prays reflects and determines what she believes."[17] The Church was baptizing and worshiping "in the name of the Father and of the Son and of the Holy Spirit" (Matt. 28:19) long before there was a full articulation of the Trinity. But the reverse of the ancient phrase is also true: *lex credendi, lex orandi*. What the Church believes—and articulates in official councils—comes to be the law and standard for prayer and song. We use examples from all periods of the Church in order to highlight some of the beautiful expressions of our faith in the liturgy.

17. Literally, "the law of praying is the law of believing."

In the "Contemporary Issues" sidebars, we address important questions that would not have arisen in the ancient world, such as questions about evolution, gendered language for God, and ecumenism. These were not burning questions in the first thousand (or even most of the second thousand) years of Christianity. But they are important questions for us today, and we believe that the Creed can speak to them in compelling ways. The commentary seeks to focus on explaining the doctrines of the Church within the historical context in which they were written, but these sidebars will show how those ancient answers can illumine contemporary questions.

Finally, we have tried to weave a theological thread throughout each chapter so that the volume is more than a compendium of individual articles (as helpful as that may be!). We want to show that the Creed serves the narrative purpose of God in salvation. Much of this will be accomplished in our "Living the Mystery" sections, which are devoted to showing how the doctrines illumine our Christian lives. And so we have placed the Creed within the overarching narrative of our divine adoption as sons and daughters of God, leading to our glorification and †deification.

We hope that your study of the Nicene Creed will be illuminating and will draw you more deeply into the mysteries of our faith.

CHAPTER 1

BELIEF

Introduction

When we think about what it means to believe, we are immediately met with a difficulty. The term "belief" and the corollary term "faith" mean almost exactly the opposite today from what they meant in the early Church. Today, faith is generally understood to be a personal assertion of what is true, a strong feeling about what should be, and something that is held tenaciously in the face of contrary evidence. On this account, faith is a private choice, is in tension with reason, and resides almost exclusively in the subjective realm. It may be meaningful, personally fulfilling, and felt to be true, but it cannot have a claim outside of one's own sphere. Believing deals with opinions, not facts. Many people today would agree with the pithy quote attributed to Richard Dawkins, "Faith is belief without evidence and reason," even if not all would agree with what follows: "coincidentally that's also the definition of delusion."[1]

Nothing could be further from how early Christians understood faith. Writing in the second century, Saint Irenaeus outlines the essential elements:

1. The actual origin of this quote is unknown, but it is ubiquitous on the internet and quite accurately summarizes Dawkins's own view, which is evident in his many writings, talks, and interviews. For example, in his book *The God Delusion* ([Boston: Houghton Mifflin, 2008], 28, emphasis added), he says,

> The dictionary supplied with Microsoft Word defines a delusion as "a *persistent false belief* held in the face of strong *contradictory evidence*, especially as a symptom of *psychiatric disorder*." The first part captures religious faith perfectly. As to whether it is a symptom of a psychiatric disorder, I am inclined to follow Robert M. Pirsig, author of *Zen and the Art of Motorcycle Maintenance*: "When one person suffers from a *delusion*, it is called *insanity*. When many people suffer from a delusion it is called Religion."

We must keep the rule . . . of faith unswervingly, and perform the commandments of God, believing in God and fearing Him, for He is Lord, and loving
Him, for He is Father. Action, then, comes by faith, as "if you do not believe,"
Isaias says, "you will not understand" [Isa. 7:9]; and the truth brings about faith,
for faith is established upon things truly real, that we may believe what really is,
as it is, and believing what really is, as it is, we may always keep our conviction
of it firm. Since, then, the conserver . . . of our salvation is faith, it is necessary
to take great care of it, that we may have a true comprehension of what is.[2]

According to Irenaeus, faith is not a subjective opinion but is based on objec-
tive reality. Faith is not about feelings but concerns both action and morality.
Faith is not contrary to reason but is the only path to true understanding.
Faith is not a mere personal preference but gives us access to the ground of all
reality since it recognizes "what really is, as it is." So, far from being a delusion, faith "is established upon things truly real." Faith leads us to the solid
ground of truth on which we can stake our lives, for it is faith that enables "a
true comprehension of what is" and leads to eternal salvation.

Every time we profess the Creed, we plant our flag anew on this solid
ground. We boldly proclaim the truth about ultimate reality and the reality of
all things. But more than just declaring our beliefs, we enter into the realities
we profess. In this chapter, we explore the first words of the Creed: in Latin,
credo in (I believe in), and in Greek, *pisteuomen eis* (we believe in). We hope
to show why the Christian emphasis on faith is unique, interesting, and necessary for salvation and for coming to the truth about God. We do this first by
exploring the biblical witness and the terms or language of faith. Then we
engage some early controversies that challenged not just particular Christian
beliefs but belief itself. Finally, we will look at how the Creed employs various
kinds of belief in its profession of the faith.

Scripture and the Language of Faith

I believe in . . .	Credo in . . .	Πιστεύομεν εἰς . . .

OT: Deut. 32; Ps. 131; Isa. 7:9; Hosea 2:20; 4:12
NT: Mark 16:16; Rom. 1:5; 10:17; 1 Cor. 13:12; 2 Cor. 5:7; 6:16; Gal. 3:23–27; 2 Thess. 3:2–3
Catechism: faith, 142–84

2. Irenaeus, *Demonstration of the Apostolic Preaching* 3, in *On the Apostolic Preaching*,
trans. John Behr, PPS 17 (Crestwood, NY: St. Vladimir's Seminary Press, 1997), 41.

Theological Exposition

When we say "I believe" or "We believe," what are we doing? What kind of declaration is this? What dimensions of the human person are involved? In this section we address the question "What is faith?" by looking at the witness of Scripture and the wisdom of the way different languages have named the act of faith.

"Faith" in Hebrew

In the Old Testament, the most common Hebrew word for "faith" is *'emunah*, which is related to the word for "amen." The range of meaning of this word is really quite beautiful: it can mean "faithfulness, trustworthiness, steadfastness, allegiance," and at its root it is related to words for "truth" and "upholding." The word primarily describes the dependability of God, who is "the Rock. . . . A God of faithfulness [*'emunah*] and without iniquity, just and right is he" (Deut. 32:4). God's fidelity is often contrasted with the infidelity of his people, who are not just and right but who have "sacrificed to demons which were no gods" (32:17) and who have been "unmindful of the Rock that begot [them]" (32:18), for "they are a perverse generation, children in whom is no faithfulness [*'emun*]" (32:20). God calls his people to faithfulness, to be upheld by his own faithfulness, but time and again they abandon the stability of union with God for the instability of adultery with idols (see Hosea 4:12).

"Faith" in Greek

While the †Septuagint (LXX) sometimes translates *'emunah* and its related terms with the Greek *pistis* (faith, faithfulness), the New Testament settles on this word to name what the Old Testament meant by *'emunah*. Paul employs these terms in the traditional sense when he says, "Pray . . . that we may be delivered from wicked and evil men; for not all have faith [*pistis*]. But the Lord is faithful [*pistos*]; he will strengthen you and guard you from evil" (2 Thess. 3:1–3). God is steadfast in his faithfulness to us; those who abandon God are without faith; and we become faithful like God when he gives us a share in his own fidelity.

Still, the Greek term *pistis* introduces a new range of meaning and associations. It derives from the word *peithomai* (the passive of *peithein*), which means "to obey" or "to be persuaded." Paul picks up on the former meaning when he speaks of "the *obedience* of faith" (Rom. 1:5), and he picks up on the latter when he says, "Faith comes from what is heard, and what is heard comes by the preaching of Christ" (10:17). The one who has *pistis*, then, has heard something persuasive from someone. The believer *hearkens* to the speaker and *trusts* that what he hears is reliable—that is, he has confidence that what is said or the one who says it is trustworthy. Ultimately, faith comes from listening to those who listened to Christ. The proper response is obedience.

The consequences of this expanded range of meaning become clearer when we think of the proper contrasts to *pistis*. In the Old Testament, the faithful love of God is contrasted with the unfaithful idolatry of the people. This sense is retained in the New Testament, but we also have a different contrast that arises from the Greek context: faith is now contrasted with knowledge or sight. "We walk by faith, not by sight," Paul says to the Corinthians (2 Cor. 5:7). These are not necessarily opposites, but they are naturally contrasted ways of knowing. For Paul, faith is the incomplete way we know God in this life, but in the next, we will know him fully: "For now we see in a mirror dimly, but then face to face. Now I know in part; then I shall understand fully, even as I have been fully understood" (1 Cor. 13:12). Faith is a kind of light, proper to this side of heaven, which enables us to see otherwise inaccessible divine realities. This is why the early Christians never tired of quoting Isaiah 7:9: "If you do not believe, you will not understand."[3] Only through the light of faith can we come to a true understanding of reality.

We see a similar sense of faith as a way of knowing in the Letter of James: "Faith [*pistis*] by itself, if it has no works, is dead. . . . You believe [*pisteueis*] that God is one; you do well. Even the demons believe [*pisteuousin*]—and shudder" (James 2:17, 19). "Faith" in these verses cannot mean "allegiance to God" or "sharing in God's fidelity." It must signify some kind of assent to the truth that can (to our peril) be separated from a corresponding way of life. Clearly, for James, *true* faith means recognizing the truth about God with our intellect *and* giving our allegiance to God with our will, both of which necessarily entail doing the works of God. The goal is the same as what Paul aptly describes as "faith working through love" (Gal. 5:6).

---

3. This translation represents Isa. 7:9 LXX, which made its way into early Christian thought, as we saw in the Irenaeus quote at the beginning of this chapter. The Hebrew is usually translated, "If you will not believe, surely you shall not be established." The Hebrew words for "believe" and "established" are both related to *'emunah*. Believing leads to being made firm. In English, the word "understand" has something to do with getting at the reality that "stands under" what we are investigating.

LEX ORANDI

Faith and Works

A beautiful collect for the Christmas Mass plays with the image of light and shows the integral relation of faith and life:

Grant, we pray, almighty God,
that, as we are bathed in the new radiance of your incarnate Word,
the light of faith, which illumines our minds,
may also shine through in our deeds.
Through our Lord Jesus Christ, your Son,
who lives and reigns with you in the unity of the Holy Spirit,
God, for ever and ever.[a]

a. *Roman Missal*, 174 (modified).

"Faith" in Latin and English

While not part of the original languages of the Bible, the Latin and English words for "belief" are also very interesting and reflect important meanings present in the biblical witness. In Latin, two words are used for "faith": the noun *fides* and the verb *credere* (from which we get our word "creed"). *Fides* comes from a root that means "bind" or "trust." It is related to the Greek *pistis*, and it generally has the same range of meanings. *Credere* means "to put faith in something or someone," but in common usage it originally meant "to give as a loan" or "to commit or entrust something." Only later, figuratively, did it come to mean "to trust," "to believe," and "to give credence to." *Fides* and *credere* complement one another: together they convey a sense of binding oneself in some kind of mutual exchange that requires fidelity over time. One moving example of this is the image of adoption. "In Christ Jesus," Paul says, "you are all sons of God, through faith" (Gal. 3:26). Therefore, we can be "like a child quieted at its mother's breast; like a child that is quieted is my soul" (Ps. 131:2). To be a believing person means to entrust oneself exclusively to God in a binding exchange.

This insight is augmented by the English word "belief," from the Germanic *lief*, related to the word "love." It means "beloved" or "dear" as an adjective and "a beloved, dear person," "a friend," or "a wife" as a noun. The prefix "be-" generally denotes a sense of association, similarity, or mutual relation. "Be-lieving," we might suggest, involves a mutual relation of love. It means friendship with God and may even introduce a "spousal" dimension to it. The prophet Hosea communicates this sense of "be-lief" beautifully: "I will espouse you in faithfulness ['*emunah*; LXX: *pistis*]; and you shall know the Lord" (Hosea 2:20 RSV-2CE). God faithfully pursues his errant bride. Faith is the proper loving response to our bridegroom. This leads to knowledge. Hosea uses the same word as in Genesis 4:1, "Adam *knew* Eve his wife," to name the fruit of our espousal to God. Clearly, our knowing God will not be sexual. The word "know" in Scripture is a euphemism for intimate, legitimate, and rightly ordered union. This is what faith gives us.

Faith and Baptism

In the New Testament, faith cannot be separated from baptism. Paul says we are "justified by faith. . . . For in Christ Jesus you are all sons of God, through faith. For as many of you as were baptized into Christ have put on Christ" (Gal. 3:24, 26–27). Baptism is the sacrament of faith: it represents faith and is our entrance into the life of faith. Faith and baptism are necessary for salvation. Jesus says, "He who believes and is baptized will be saved; but he who does not believe will be condemned" (Mark 16:16). Why is this the case? How do faith and baptism lead to our salvation?[4]

Faith saves us by grafting us onto Christ through baptism (Rom. 11:17–24) and giving us his divine life (2 Pet. 1:4). In baptism, we are incorporated into the Body of Christ and so put on Christ. We have become "sons in the Son." Faith and baptism mean that we are members of Christ himself, and so we share in the things that are Christ's. We share in his sonship and his relationship to the Father. "And because you are sons, God has sent the Spirit of his Son into our hearts, crying, 'Abba! Father!'" (Gal. 4:6). We now have a divine source of power animating our lives. In Christ, we have his Holy Spirit who transforms us into his divine likeness and gives us a more perfect communion with the Father. Faith saves us by enabling us to share in the trinitarian divine life (see Matt. 28:18–20).

Faith makes us children of God. This is first and foremost a gift, a grace we receive from God through others (who teach us the faith and who baptize us). Faith is also what later tradition will call a "theological virtue." A virtue is a stable habit or firm disposition ordered toward doing good: "Every sound tree bears good fruit" (Matt. 7:17). A *theological* virtue is a grace that "adapts man's faculties for participation in the divine nature . . . [and]

---

4. See the sidebar on p. 21 for Augustine's account of how infants have faith.

Augustine on the Faith of Infants

Augustine explains how an infant can be said to have faith:

> To believe, however, is nothing else than to have faith. And for this reason when the answer is given that the little one believes, though he does not yet have the disposition of faith, the answer is given that he has faith on account of the sacrament of the faith and that he is converted to the Lord on account of the sacrament of conversion, because the response itself also pertains to the celebration of the sacrament. In the same way the apostle says of baptism, *We were buried together with Christ through baptism into death* (Rom. 6:4). He did not say, "We signified burial," but, *We were buried*. He, therefore, called the sacrament of so great a reality by the word for the same reality.
>
> And so, even if that faith that is found in the will of believers does not make a little one a believer, the sacrament of the faith itself, nonetheless, now does so. For, just as the response is given that the little one believes, he is also in that sense called a believer, not because he assents to the reality with his mind, but because he receives the sacrament of that reality. But when a human being begins to think, he will not repeat the sacrament, but will understand it and will also conform himself to its truth by the agreement of his will. As long as he cannot do this, the sacrament will serve for his protection against the enemy powers, and it will be so effective that, if he leaves this life before attaining the use of reason, he will by this help for Christians be set free from that condemnation which entered the world through one man, since the love of the Church commends him through the sacrament itself.[a]

a. Augustine, *Letter* 98.9–10, in *Letters 1–99*, ed. Roland Teske, WSA II/1 (Hyde Park, NY: New City, 2001), 431–32.

disposes Christians to live in relationship with the Holy Trinity."[5] Through the theological virtue of faith, God increases our understanding of him and conforms our will to his so that we do the works God prepared for us (Eph. 2:10). In other words, faith understood as a theological virtue means growing in sonship, growing in the excellences of what it means to be a child of God.

5. CCC 1812.

Summary of Faith

In this section we surveyed "faith" language as well as what the Bible means by "faith." What we discovered is that faith is polyvalent. Faith means God's faithfulness. It means our allegiance to God founded on his fidelity to us. It involves obedience. Faith comes by listening to others. It is the way of knowing or seeing divine things appropriate to this life. It can (but should not) be merely intellectual. Faith is an exchange of persons involving love. It is covenantal. After Christ, faith is inseparable from baptism. Faith is a theological virtue we grow in through grace. Finally, faith saves us by transforming us into children of God and increasing God's divine life in us.

Challenges to Faith: Philosophical, Gnostic, and Pagan

| I believe in . . . | Credo in . . . | Πιστεύομεν εἰς . . . |

NT: Rom. 1:19–25; 10:9–11; Gal. 5:6
Catechism: faith, 142–84; the authority of the Church, 748–975

Theological Exposition

Contemporary atheists today are not the first to criticize Christians for their emphasis on faith.[6] In the early centuries, Christian faith was belittled by philosophers, attacked by Gnostics, and compromised by pagans. From the philosophically minded, Christians were charged with †fideism, a gross rejection of reason and a blind following of superstition. This criticism was picked up and modified by Gnostic Christians who articulated a two-tiered Christianity, one for the fleshly commoners who lived by faith and one for the spiritual elect who lived by knowledge. Christians also were surrounded by a pagan culture that was often content to separate practice from belief and pressured Christians to follow suit. In meeting these challenges, early Christians defended and developed their unique understanding of the centrality of faith for daily life, knowing the truth, and being saved.

---

6. For an excellent exploration of how ancient pagans viewed their Christian neighbors, see Robert Louis Wilken, *The Christians as the Romans Saw Them*, 2nd ed. (New Haven: Yale University Press, 2003).

Faith and Philosophy

Galen, the renowned second-century physician and polymath, dignified Christianity by considering it a school of thought; he just thought it was a rather mediocre one. For Galen, Christians were the default example of unthinking fideists. "If I had in mind people who taught their pupils in the same way as the followers of Moses and Christ teach theirs—for they order them to accept everything on faith—I should not have given you a definition."[7] Christians, according to Galen, did not investigate the truth but were commanded to swallow whatever their teachers fed them, even the most irrational doctrines. Christianity was an "unreasoning faith," as the philosopher Porphyry summarized it a few generations later.[8]

Celsus, a late second-century philosopher, echoes the same criticisms. He compares Christians to "the begging priests of Cybele and soothsayers, and to worshipers of Mithras and Sabazius"—that is, to the adherents of superstitious cults who "do not even want to give or to receive a reason for what they believe."[9] Christians are taught to use expressions like "Do not ask questions; just believe."[10] These uneducated, unreasoning Christians were, according to Celsus, drawn from the lowest strata of society—"woolworkers, cobblers, laundry-workers, and the most illiterate and bucolic yokels"—yet they claim to teach with the greatest authority.[11] Even though they have no formal training, these Christians tell their followers (and would-be followers) not to listen to their schoolteachers and fathers, but to follow Christianity instead if they want to discover the happy life and become perfect.[12] These Christians do not dare speak their views in front of elders or other educated people, Celsus says, but seek out "children in private and some stupid women" before whom they parade their wild and unexamined opinions.[13]

---

7. Quoted in R. Walzer, *Galen on Jews and Christians* (London: Oxford University Press, 1949), 15. This quote comes from Galen's work *On the Prime Mover*, which is now lost, so that we have only fragments. Walzer has collected and translated the relevant fragments on Jews and Christians.

8. Porphyry's work is lost to us, but this criticism is recorded by Eusebius in *Preparation for the Gospel* 1.3.1.

9. The anti-Christian treatise of Celsus is lost to us, but it is quoted extensively in Origen's *Against Celsus*, a work that aims to refute Celsus line by line. The quote comes from Origen, *Against Celsus* 1.9, trans. Henry Chadwick (Cambridge: Cambridge University Press, 1980), 12.

10. Origen, *Against Celsus* 1.9 (Chadwick, 12).

11. Origen, *Against Celsus* 3.55 (Chadwick, 165).

12. Origen, *Against Celsus* 3.55 (Chadwick, 165–66).

13. Origen, *Against Celsus* 3.55 (Chadwick, 165).

There are certainly some elements of truth in these criticisms: Christian churches often were made up of uneducated lower classes, and very likely there were some stubborn fideists among them. Still, it is important to see how early Christian apologists turned these philosophical criticisms on their head. Christianity was not merely some fledgling school of philosophical thought, they argued, but *the* true philosophy. The faith that philosophers derided gave Christians access to the very truths and way of life that the philosophers themselves sought but could rarely find. Moreover, Christianity was more successful than any other philosophical school in passing on truth and morality to a wide and varied range of people all over the world.

For the ancients, philosophy was not something merely studied, but something lived. The word "philosophy" means "the loving pursuit of wisdom." It was generally understood as a way of life ordered toward attaining knowledge of ultimate things. For true philosophers, there was a requisite cultivation of virtue that made possible the contemplation of higher realities. With this understanding, it becomes clearer how Justin Martyr, who studied all the available schools of philosophy in his time, could say of Christianity, "I found this philosophy alone to be safe and profitable."[14]

Christ was the true philosopher and Christianity the true philosophy. Christ *is* "the wisdom of God" (1 Cor. 1:24) who came to earth as man to reveal to us the mind and heart of the invisible God. Irenaeus makes this point beautifully:

> For in no other way could we have learned the things of God, unless our Master, existing as the Word, had become man. . . . Again, we could have learned in no other way than by seeing our Teacher, and hearing His voice with our own ears, that, having become imitators of His works as well as doers of His words, we may have communion with Him, receiving increase from the perfect One, and from Him who is prior to all creation.[15]

Christ is the *Logos*—the Word or Mind of God, who was with God and was God prior to creation (John 1:1)—and only he can teach us the truth about ultimate reality. God understood our human weakness and, like a good teacher, met us at our level in order to bring us up to his own. The invisible God became visible so we could hear, see, look upon, and touch with our hands the Word of life (see 1 John 1:1–2). As the incarnate Word, Christ teaches us the hidden mysteries of God as well as the way of life that leads

14. Justin Martyr, *Dialogue with Trypho* 8 (*ANF* 1:198).
15. Irenaeus, *Against Heresies* 5.1.1 (*ANF* 1:526).

us into those mysteries. Only by hearkening to his words and imitating his deeds—and not as detached outsiders—can we enter into communion with God. We are then enabled to "look at everything from His point of view," as Origen says,[16] so that we make progress in understanding the mystery. Only from the "inside" of truth, as it were, can we learn the truth.

Christianity, Origen argues, brings people to the very goal of philosophy: a virtuous life that allows us to see the truth about God and the world. Origen speaks of Christian teachers

> who try to elevate the soul in every way to the Creator of the universe, and who show how men ought to despise all that is sensible and temporary and visible, and who urge them to do all they can to attain to fellowship with God and contemplation of intelligible and invisible things, and to reach the blessed life with God and the friends of God.[17]

Philosophers toil to attain these truths, and even if they attain them, which is not common, they are rarely able to pass them on to many others. Christianity, on the other hand, has taught more people than any other philosophy in the world the basic truths about ultimate reality and the good life. Even Galen, who criticized Christian intellectual life, recognized that Christians cultivated the virtue of true philosophers. He writes,

> For their contempt of death and of its sequel is patent to us every day, and likewise their restraint in cohabitation. For they include not only men but also women who refrain from cohabiting all through their lives; and they also number individuals who, in self-discipline and self-control in matters of food and drink, and in their keen pursuit of justice, have attained a pitch not inferior to that of genuine philosophers.[18]

Origen argues that Christians are taught the most profound metaphysical truths, and the critic Galen admits that Christians attain the same virtue as "genuine philosophers." Galen cannot grasp, as Origen can, that it is the work of Christian faith that accomplishes this.

To better understand the power of faith (and the philosophers' critique of it), we need to think about faith and knowledge together. We have faith when we

16. Origen, *Against Celsus* 3.57 (Chadwick, 167).
17. Origen, *Against Celsus* 3.56 (Chadwick, 166).
18. Galen, *Summary of the Platonic Dialogues*, fragment quoted in Walzer, *Galen on Jews and Christians*, 15.

learn something from another; we have knowledge when we see something for ourselves. Almost everything we think we know, we in fact *believe* on the testimony and authority of others. We believe our parents are our parents, though only our mother knows who our father is and only those attendant at our birth can confirm our mother.[19] We believe most things our friends relate to us about their lives and experience, though we often have not witnessed these things firsthand. We believe the history, geography, and science our teachers teach, even though we were not present at the events, have not visited the places, and cannot verify the science. Due to time, inclination, or ability, it is impossible to investigate every question for ourselves. It is completely reasonable, then, to have faith in most areas of our life. We could not operate our daily lives without it.

Having faith gives us access to all sorts of truths about our origins, our family and friends, history, and the world. Faith also gives us access to divine truths that otherwise we would not be able to discover. It is true that a handful of philosophers have attained insight into divine things, but they are only a handful. God does not want just a handful of people to come to the truth, but everyone. In heaven, we will all see the truth for ourselves, but for now we live by faith, which gives us access to the same truth we will eventually know firsthand.

In *The Advantage of Believing*, Augustine argues that, before we "are capable of gazing on the truth that is perceived by a pure mind," we must "accept the authority of the Catholic faith and by believing [be] strengthened and prepared for the God who will bestow light."[20] Due to original and personal sin, our minds are clouded and our wills are compromised, so it is virtually impossible for most people to come to the truth about God and his world on their own. By believing, we find and hold on to the truth, even if we do not see it clearly or understand it fully. "When you do not have the ability to appreciate the arguments," Augustine says, "it is very healthy to believe without knowing the reasons and by that belief to cultivate the mind and allow the seeds of truth to be sown."[21] By believing true things, we dwell with the truth and allow it to penetrate our minds. We get used to the truth, which heals our minds of error and the wounds of sin. Faith accustoms the eyes of the soul to see into the depths of God and the things he has made.

19. Students often object, "What about DNA tests?" Of course, none of them has had a DNA test, and they still firmly believe their parents are who they say they are. Moreover, even were they to have a DNA test, they would have to trust the lab technicians who performed it and the science behind it, which most of them do not understand and so must take on faith to be reliable.

20. Augustine, *Advantage of Believing* 1.2, in *On Christian Belief*, trans. Ray Kearney, WSA I/8 (Hyde Park, NY: New City, 2005), 116.

21. Augustine, *Advantage of Believing* 14.31 (Kearney, 141).

The philosophers were wrong to criticize the Christian reliance on faith. Faith is necessary in this life for coming to the very truth the philosophers sought. Faith is not unreasonable or unreasoning, but the only thing that can heal our reason so that it can embrace the truth it was made for.

Faith and Gnosticism

Perhaps the most persistent danger to Christian faith in the first centuries came from the Gnostics.[22] Like the philosophers, Gnostic Christians belittled ordinary Christians for their faith. According to the Gnostics, weak Christians believed in the fleshly tales of the Old Testament, with its crude stories of a god who created the material universe, of polygamous patriarchs bent on reproducing in this world, of circumcision, bloody animal sacrifices, and other things unworthy of a spiritual person. Worse, common Christians believed in the incarnation, the mixing of the unclean material world with a divine being. The Gnostics, on the other hand, presented a superior Christianity, one purged of materiality, which embraced the invisible world alone. The goal was to escape this material world to attain the spiritual. This was done by rejecting common faith and embracing a superior gnosis, a knowledge of the superior invisible realm.

Early Christians responded in a number of ways to the Gnostic challenge. They pointed out the irony that for all their emphasis on *knowledge*, Gnostics were compelled to *believe* all sorts of things. They had to accept with blind faith the wild stories of the gods and their genealogies and their struggles and falls. They had to trust the leader of whichever Gnostic sect they followed (e.g., Valentinus, Marcion, Mani) and had to believe that this man truly had received a private revelation worthy of devotion. No matter how much they denied it, Gnostics had to rely on faith just as much as other Christians did.

Early Christians also rejected the idea that there are fundamentally different kinds of Christians distinguished by the way or content of what they believe. Irenaeus argues that while it is certainly true that some Christians are more learned or eloquent than others, "the Catholic Church possesses one and the same faith throughout the whole world."[23] Even though our abilities differ,

---

22. For good introductions to Gnosticism, see David Brakke, *The Gnostics: Myth, Ritual, and Diversity in Early Christianity* (Cambridge, MA: Harvard University Press, 2010), and Christoph Markschies, *Gnosis: An Introduction*, trans. John Bowdon (London: T&T Clark, 2003).

23. Irenaeus, *Against Heresies* 1.10.3 (*ANF* 1:331). Today, many scholars advocate talking about "early Christianities," a trend that rightly acknowledges the diversity of the early Christian thought and experience. Still, this language often presupposes other ideological commitments, especially seeing all things in terms of power dynamics, winners and losers. While

"the faith being ever one and the same, neither does one who is able at great length to discourse regarding it, make any addition to it, nor does one, who can say but little, diminish it."[24] The faith is one and the same for everyone.

The Gnostic challenge made acute another question related to faith: If believing means trusting the word and witness of another, whom should we trust? Irenaeus articulated the Christian answer that would become standard. We cannot see Jesus for ourselves, so we must rely on those who did see him. Indeed, we should trust those whom Jesus himself chose and lived with and to whom he passed on his teachings—namely, the apostles. We should also trust those whom the apostles authorized: the bishops and other leaders who preserved the traditions of the apostles both in worship and in writing. It is worth quoting Irenaeus at length here:

> We have learned from none others the plan of our salvation, than from those through whom the Gospel has come down to us, which they did at one time proclaim in public, and, at a later period, by the will of God, handed down to us in the Scriptures, to be the ground and pillar of our faith. . . . For, after our Lord rose from the dead, [the apostles] were invested with power from on high when the Holy Spirit came down [upon them], were filled from all [His gifts], and had perfect knowledge: they departed to the ends of the earth, preaching the glad tidings of the good things [sent] from God to us, and proclaiming the peace of heaven to men, who indeed do all equally and individually possess the Gospel of God.[25]

These apostles knew Jesus, and none of them taught what the Gnostics teach. Neither in their writings nor in the traditions of the churches they founded can one find the secret gnosis of the various Gnostic teachers (who, after all, do not agree among themselves!). The teachings of the apostles were all deposited into the one Church that Christ founded. The apostles, "like a rich man [depositing his money] in a bank, lodged in [the Church's] hands most copiously all things pertaining to the truth."[26] This truth is one, and it is found altogether in one place. We will discuss the authority of the bishops and the Church in more detail in chapter 6, but for now we should note that, for early Christians, the true faith is one and can be reliably learned from the Catholic Church.

---

power dynamics certainly play a role in any movement and institution, Irenaeus and others show that it is not superior power but fidelity to the biblical witness and theological coherence that "win" in the end.

24. Irenaeus, *Against Heresies* 1.10.2 (*ANF* 1:331).
25. Irenaeus, *Against Heresies* 3.1.1 (*ANF* 1:414).
26. Irenaeus, *Against Heresies* 3.4.1 (*ANF* 1:416).

Augustine on the Authority of the Catholic Church

For nine years, Augustine belonged to a Gnostic Christian sect called the †Manicheans. His conversion to the Catholic Church raised the question of which authorities are trustworthy. In the text below, he articulates why he should trust the authority of the Church over the Manicheans.

> Perhaps you will read the gospel to me, and will attempt to find there a testimony to Manichaeus. But should you meet with a person not yet believing the gospel, how would you reply to him were he to say, I do not believe? For my part, I should not believe the gospel except as moved by the authority of the Catholic Church. So when those on whose authority I have consented to believe in the gospel tell me not to believe in Manichaeus, how can I but consent? Take your choice. If you say, Believe the Catholics: their advice to me is to put no faith in you; so that, believing them, I am precluded from believing you;—If you say, Do not believe the Catholics: you cannot fairly use the gospel in bringing me to faith in Manichaeus; for it was at the command of the Catholics that I believed the gospel;—Again, if you say, You were right in believing the Catholics when they praised the gospel, but wrong in believing their vituperation of Manichaeus: do you think me such a fool as to believe or not to believe as you like or dislike, without any reason?[a]

a. Augustine, *Against the Epistle of Manichaeus Called Fundamental* 5.6 (*NPNF*[1] 4:131).

Faith and Pagan Religion

Religion was ubiquitous in the Roman Empire. The whole empire was littered with deities, shrines, festivals, and private and public devotions. People in the empire were expected to show due reverence for the official gods of the city, but otherwise they enjoyed a rather broad freedom to worship whichever gods they preferred. These public and private rituals were the glue that kept society and families together. They were believed to bring good fortune to the empire and blessings to the family. Perhaps similar to Christmas dinners among nominal Christians today, it did not matter much whether one "truly believed" in the god being honored. What mattered was that everyone participated. Christians were unique—and problematic—in their categorical refusal to participate in pagan worship. It was a public and private offense, one that threatened the very fabric of society and family life.[27]

The Martyrdom of Polycarp is a remarkable document from the early second century that brings to the fore the challenge pagan religion posed to Christian faith. Polycarp, a bishop and disciple of John the apostle, is betrayed and arrested. The pagan authorities, respecting his age and quiet life, attempt to persuade him to just offer a pinch of incense to the emperor. "What is the harm in just saying, 'Caesar is Lord,' and offering incense, and so forth, when it will save your life?"[28] After these persuasions fail, they physically abuse Polycarp and bring him to the governor, who also tries to persuade him. Polycarp finally responds to their entreaties, "If you still think I am going to swear by Caesar's Luck, and still pretend not to know what I am, let me tell you plainly now that I am a Christian."[29]

The pagan authorities saw nothing wrong with Polycarp believing one thing and practicing another. They did not want to "convert" him but to make sure he conformed to the civic practices conducive to the well-being of the empire. The important thing was "orthopraxy." It did not matter that Polycarp was not truly devoted to the pagan gods; it did not matter that his heart was not really in his action; what mattered was the action. Roman religion was civic religion, and participating was required for everyone. It was part of their responsibility for the maintenance of the empire.

Polycarp, though, insists that he cannot pretend. "I am a Christian," he declares. This means that he cannot dissemble; he cannot have one thing on his lips and another in his heart. Faith is an act of the whole person and demands the integrity of the whole person. It involves mind and heart, as well as the actions of the body. All of them must speak the same true language about God. The Christian must believe in his heart and confess with his lips (Rom. 10:9–11), but faith must also work through love (Gal. 5:6). The whole person must confess the truth. Polycarp cannot pretend. He knows who he is. He is a Christian.

This consistency between faith and praxis is one of Augustine's arguments for why Christianity is the true religion.[30] In *City of God*, Augustine draws

27. For a thorough discussion of the tensions created in the Roman world by Christian exclusivity, see Larry W. Hurtado, *Destroyer of the Gods: Early Christian Distinctiveness in the Roman World* (Waco: Baylor University Press, 2016), especially 37–76. For the Jewish refusal to worship the pagan gods, see p. 39.

28. *The Martyrdom of Polycarp* 8, in *Early Christian Writings: The Apostolic Fathers*, trans. Andrew Louth (London: Penguin, 1987), 127.

29. *The Martyrdom of Polycarp* 10 (Louth, 128).

30. See, for example, Augustine, *On True Religion* 1.1–5.8.

on the pagan philosophers' own extensive critiques of pagan religion in order to demonstrate its falsehood, perversity, and inconsistency. Yet these same philosophers worshiped the gods they denounced and promoted the worship they condemned. After quoting Seneca's criticisms of pagan worship for some pages, Augustine says, "With regard to the rites of the civic theology, the role that Seneca chooses for the wise man is to exclude them from the religion of his soul but to pretend to go along with them in his actions." Then Augustine quotes Seneca himself: "The wise man will observe all these rites not because they are pleasing to the gods but because they are enjoined by law."[31] Over and over again, Augustine applies Romans 1 to pagan philosophers: "Although they knew God they did not honor him as God" (Rom. 1:21). They knew the truth but did not worship in truth. They dissembled. Christians, on the other hand, had the courage of their convictions. They taught about the true God and worshiped the same true God. They could not pretend. They obeyed a higher law than the imperial one. Christians worshiped as they believed and believed as they worshiped. Their faith and their worship were one and the same.

Kinds of Belief in the Creed

I believe in one God . . .	Credo in unum Deum . . .	Πιστεύομεν εἰς ἕνα Θεόν . . .
I believe in one Lord Jesus Christ . . .	Et in unum Dominum Iesum Christum . . .	καὶ εἰς ἕνα κύριον Ἰησοῦν Χριστόν . . .
I believe in the Holy Spirit . . .	Et in Spiritum Sanctum . . .	καὶ εἰς τὸ πνεῦμα τὸ ἅγιον . . .
I believe in one, holy, catholic, and apostolic Church.	Et unum, sanctam catholicam et apostolicam Ecclesiam.	Εἰς μίαν ἁγίαν καθολικὴν καὶ ἀποστολικὴν ἐκκλησίαν.
I confess one Baptism . . .	Confiteor unum baptisma . . .	Ὁμολογοῦμεν ἓν βάπτισμα . . .
and I look forward to the resurrection of the dead . . .	Et exspecto resurrectionem mortuorum . . .	Προσδοκῶμεν ἀνάστασιν νεκρῶν . . .

OT: Deut. 7:9; Jer. 29:5–11
NT: Matt. 7:21; Rom. 6:3–11; Gal. 2:20; Eph. 2:12; Heb. 11:1
Catechism: on faith, 142–84; on faith and hope, 1812–29

31. Augustine, *City of God* 6.10, in *City of God, Books 1–10*, trans. William Babcock, WSA I/6 (Hyde Park, NY: New City, 2012), 204.

Theological Exposition

When we profess the Creed, we are assenting to the doctrines contained therein, but we are also entrusting ourselves to the truths they proclaim. Still, a close reading reveals that there is nuance in how the Creed presents the act of faith itself. There seem to be different kinds, levels, or meanings of faith operative in the Creed. First, there is the difference between the Greek and Latin versions, which say "We believe" and "I believe," respectively. Second, there is a subtle shift in language (marked differently in the Greek and Latin, though obscured in the English translation) when we profess our faith in the Church. How is our faith in the Church the same as and different from our faith in the Father, Son, and Holy Spirit? Finally, in the last part of the Creed, there is a shift from the language of belief to the language of "confession" (regarding baptism) and "looking forward to" (regarding our resurrection and eternal life). How do these terms relate to what we mean by "faith"? We will explore the content of these doctrines in subsequent chapters. Here we look at the different kinds of faith the Creed employs in speaking of different doctrines.

"We Believe" and "I Believe"

In Greek the Creed begins with "We believe," while in Latin it begins with "I believe." The Greek "We" may possibly point to the bishops who gathered in council to articulate the Creed, but more commonly it is understood to refer to the people of God gathered at liturgy. The Latin "I" may possibly refer to the Church as a whole, the Church as our Mother, confessing the faith, but more commonly it is understood to refer to the individual believer professing the faith. Generally, the "We believe" emphasizes the communal dimension of faith, whereas the "I believe" emphasizes the personal dimension.

In her wisdom, the Church has retained both "We believe" and "I believe." We must always remember that faith is a grace of God that we receive from the Church. The Church is our Mother who brings us to new birth through faith. Still, each of us receives the faith not from the universal Church directly but from certain people—our parents or friends or catechists—some portion of the people of God who pass on the faith to us. The "We believe" of the Church precedes the "I believe" of the individual believer. But the "I believe" also reminds us how important it is that we, individually, assent to the truths of the faith and conform ourselves to them. Each of us will come before the Lord and have to render an account for how we confessed his name (see Matt. 7:21).

The Faith of Your Church

Individual believers are incorporated into the community of believers, and together we are one confessing subject: the Church.
In the Roman Rite, the priest asks God not to keep record of our
many individual sins, but to consider instead the saving faith of the
one Church.

> Lord Jesus Christ,
> who said to your Apostles:
> Peace I leave you, my peace I give you,
> look not on our sins,
> but on the faith of your Church,
> and graciously grant her peace and unity
> in accordance with your will.[a]

a. *Roman Missal*, 666.

Believing the Church and Believing in the Church

There is a fruitful difference in the Greek and Latin versions of the Creed
regarding belief and the Church. The Greek version repeats the pattern seen
in the articles on the Father, Son, and Holy Spirit: "We believe *in* one God
. . . and *in* one Lord Jesus Christ . . . and *in* the Holy Spirit . . . *in* one, holy,
catholic, and apostolic Church." The Greek drops the "and" but keeps the
"in." The Latin does the opposite: it repeats the pattern, dropping the "in" but
keeping the "and," so that the Latin version more properly reads "I believe *in*
one God . . . and *in* one Lord Jesus Christ . . . and *in* the Holy Spirit . . . and
[I believe] one, holy, catholic, and apostolic Church." What is going on in this
seemingly small linguistic difference? Each version of the Creed is trying to
get at a different dimension of the truth about the Church.

The Latin version is signaling a distinction between how we believe in
God and how we believe in the Church. The Church is not God and does
not require the full assent of our being the way God does. We must love God
with all our heart and mind and soul and strength, and through faith we give
ourselves entirely to him. We do not owe the Church this kind of devotion.
Indeed, it would be idolatry. The Latin "I believe the Church" signals a distinction between Creator and creation. But it also declares that we trust the

Church as the authoritative and divinely instituted source of saving truth. As our Mother, we give the Church filial obedience.

The Greek version makes our belief in the Church roughly parallel to our belief in the Trinity. This signifies something important about the nature of the Church. The Church is not just an important human institution with authority, but a truly divine one. As *Lumen Gentium* says, the Church is "one complex reality which comes together from a human and a divine element."[32] The Church is the Body of Christ animated by the Holy Spirit. The Church is not God, but it does have a divine dimension. So there is a properly theological faith that is required to see the Church as she truly is. Without faith, we cannot grasp the true nature of the Church.

Confessing One Baptism

There is a linguistic shift when we come to what we profess about baptism: we shift from what we believe in or who we believe to what we "confess." The Greek *homologoumen* and the Latin *confiteor* both mean "to agree" or "acknowledge" that something is the case. *Confiteor* can also mean "to bring to light" or "to confess," especially before a tribunal or a court of law. We put our faith—the assent of our mind and the devotion of our will—in God and, in a qualified sense, in the one, holy, catholic, and apostolic Church. And we acknowledge publicly that this Church offers salvation through baptism. There are no other baptisms beside or after the one offered by the Church. We agree before all that there is only one baptism for the forgiveness of sins.

Faith and Hope

For the final articles of the Creed, the language shifts again. "*I look forward to* the resurrection of the dead and the life of the world to come." The final article deals with our hope for the future life. We have professed our faith in God and his Church, we have acknowledged the saving baptism the Church offers, and now we profess what this faith will win for us in the future. Faith leads to hope. Faith and hope are intimately related in biblical and early Christian thought. The Letter to the Hebrews famously says, "Now faith is the assurance [or substance] of things hoped for, the conviction of things not seen" (Heb. 11:1). Faith, in the rich sense discussed in this chapter, gives us an assurance of God's blessings in the future. We can look forward with

---

32. *Lumen Gentium* 8, quoted in CCC 771.

confidence to the divine rewards promised to us. In the Hebrews verse, the word "assurance" (*hypostasis*) can also be translated "substance." Faith is the content or heart of hope, for hope is faith directed toward the future. Faith is the substance, the seed from which the great promises of God will grow into full form. Already now, in faith, we live the resurrection and eternal life (see John 11:25–26). Faith makes these heavenly realities present already. Because their substance is present in this life through faith, we can hope with assurance that they will become a full reality in the next life.

Living the Mystery

The twenty-first century has so far proved to be a time of religious decline in the West. Almost universally among once Christian peoples, there has been a widespread loss of faith. Many of us have witnessed this in our friends and families, but it is also evident in the statistical rise of the "nones" or the "nonreligious" who, as of this writing, make up about a quarter of adults and a third of young adults in the United States. It is also evident in the suspicion of traditional Christian ideas, especially of Christian morality, that we see in many public discussions and policies. Concomitant with this loss of faith is a loss of hope (for faith is the substance of hope). Our society is not just increasingly faithless, but increasingly hopeless.

One sign of this hopelessness is our demographic decline. More and more people are not having children. Indeed, the birthrate in the United States is about half of what it was a hundred years ago, so that now it has dropped below replacement rate. The present seems too bleak, too terrible, too hopeless to make a human future. We are afraid to bring new life into this world. We are like the Ephesians before they knew Christ, "having no hope and without God in the world" (Eph. 2:12). Perhaps we are even worse off than the Ephesians since we live in a *post*-Christian society, a society that has known Christ and rejected him.

What are Christian believers to do in such hopeless times? In a beautiful speech entitled "On Creative Minorities," the late Rabbi Jonathan Sacks reminds us of the hopeful words of the prophet Jeremiah, who wrote to the utterly distraught Jews captive in Babylon.[33] These Jews had lost everything: their homes, their city, and, worst of all, the temple. Through Jeremiah, God offers these grieving captives some seemingly mundane advice:

33. Jonathan Sacks, "On Creative Minorities," *First Things* 239 (January 2014): 33–39, https://www.firstthings.com/article/2014/01/on-creative-minorities.

> Build houses and live in them; plant gardens and eat their produce. Take wives
> and have sons and daughters; take wives for your sons, and give your daughters
> in marriage, that they may bear sons and daughters; multiply there, and do not
> decrease. But seek the welfare of the city where I have sent you into exile, and pray
> to the LORD on its behalf, for in its welfare you will find your welfare. (Jer. 29:5–7)

Go about the business of living. Have children. Pass on the gift of life. Keep the
flame of faith alive in your own homes and pass it on to your children and your
children's children. Do not give into hopelessness: "Multiply there, and do not
decrease." Pray for your persecutors. Be good citizens in a wicked city. Having
children and being good citizens are acts of faith and hope. They declare that
life and new life are good and that this world is worth fighting for even as we
prepare for the next. By staying faithful in these life-giving practices, we till
the soil from which "creative minorities" might arise and make a difference.

Soon after the above passage, God offers a moving consolation: "I know
the plans I have for you, says the LORD, plans for welfare and not for evil, to
give you a future and a hope" (Jer. 29:11). Many Christians use this passage
as their "life verse" (a verse taken as an inspiration for daily living). God's
beautiful promise, though, is not for the current generation, most of whom
will likely not see God's redemption come to pass: "When seventy years are
completed for Babylon, I will visit you, and I will fulfil to you my promise"
(Jer. 29:10). God's promise will be realized in their grandchildren and great-
grandchildren. We who live in a time of "Babylonian exile" can take these
words to heart too. The acts of faith and hope we make now in obedience to
God may not bear fruit in our lifetime, but they may in future generations.
We may not see the promises come true, but we can be assured that God will
keep his promises.

Here, we might build on Jeremiah's prophecy in light of Christ. If we live
the way of faith and hope in our own seemingly hopeless times, we can have
hope that God's promises will be fulfilled not just for our grandchildren but
for us, too, in the next life. Our God is "the faithful God who keeps covenant
and steadfast love with those who love him and keep his commandments, to a
thousand generations" (Deut. 7:9). Because of God's fidelity, our acts of faith
and hope will redound through the centuries in ways we cannot even imagine.
Indeed, we should give thanks to those who came before us, whose faith and
hope, unknown to us, have blessed us with faith and hope. And all those God
blesses—those in past generations and those in future generations—will join
us in the ultimate blessing we hope for: the resurrection of the dead and the
life of the world to come.

CHAPTER 2

GOD *the* FATHER

Introduction

A significant part of the doctrine of the Father was worked out before the Council of Nicaea. In the face of challenges from Gnosticism and paganism in the second and third centuries, early Christians started to work out systematically what it meant that there is only one God, who is an almighty Father and the maker of all things. In light of the †Arian controversy of the fourth century, these doctrines took on a deeper meaning.

This chapter will have three main considerations. First, we will discuss the radical doctrine that there is one and only one God and how Christian belief in the Trinity does not violate God's oneness. Next, we will explore the meaning of "Father" in the Christian tradition and how "almighty" came to modify it in essential ways. Finally, we will explore the uniquely Christian understanding of *creatio ex nihilo* and how this doctrine necessarily follows from the belief in "one God, the Father almighty."

One God

I believe in **one God**, the Father almighty, maker of heaven and earth, of all things visible and invisible.	Credo in **unum Deum**, Patrem omnipotentem, factorem caeli et terrae, visibilium omnium et invisibilium.	Πιστεύομεν εἰς **ἕνα Θεόν**, πατέρα παντοκράτορα, ποιητὴν οὐρανοῦ καὶ γῆς, ὁρατῶν τε πάντων καὶ ἀοράτων.

OT: Exod. 3:1–15; Deut. 6:4; Pss. 86:10; 95:3; 96:5; 139; Isa. 44–45
NT: John 8:58; Acts 14:15; 1 Cor. 8:6; Gal. 4:8
Catechism: oneness of God, 198–231

Theological Exposition

To believe in one God seems so much like common sense that it is difficult for us to imagine serious alternatives. Yet the oneness of God was a hard-fought battle in the early Church, a battle fought on many fronts. What we take for granted was a minority position in the ancient world and a teaching forged in the crucible of controversy. It was a radical doctrine that was developed and refined as Christians defended it against external and internal critics. It was theologically and politically revolutionary and, at times, a truth to die for.

Early Christians articulated a distinctively Christian vision of God as one and three. They came to understand Christian belief in the Trinity as a species of monotheism. The ancient critics of the Christian doctrine of one God can be divided into two groups: those who thought Christian belief should be absorbed into some form of polytheism and those who wanted to avoid polytheism at all costs in order to preserve the oneness of God, though at the expense of the threeness of God. In the first category were groups such as pagan polytheists, †Marcionite dualists, and Gnostic emanationists. In the second category were modalists, like Noetus and Sabellius, and subordination-ists, like the Arians who inspired the Council of Nicaea. It will be helpful to contrast the teachings of the Nicene Creed with the alternatives presented by these critics. This will allow us to see more clearly what is at stake in the Christian doctrine of one God.

Pagan Polytheism

Christianity grew up in a Roman pagan culture populated by countless gods. There were gods of the home and the city, of places and occasions, and gods for particular needs and activities. Roman religion was both personal and civic—that is, it involved religious practices that were directly oriented toward the well-being of the practitioners (and their families) and the city. Worship of the gods, especially the state-sanctioned gods, was believed to lead directly to temporal benefits, like health, peace, prosperity, fertility, security, and the expansion of the empire.

Roman religion was in many ways generous and tolerant: as the Roman Empire expanded and conquered neighboring nations, the Romans imposed law and order, but in general they were happy to incorporate the gods of their neighbors into their pantheon while also sharing their more powerful deities with their conquered neighbors. The ancient Romans practiced a religious pluralism that many today would find appealing. At home, people would worship their own gods and the gods of the city. If they traveled to another city, they would see nothing wrong with worshiping the local gods there. It was not seen as betrayal or idolatry but rather piety and prudence to pay deference to the god who reigned in a particular area. While religion was a matter of the heart for some, it was a matter of civic duty and well-being for all.

Early Christians were expected to participate in this civic religion. They could worship Jesus as a god if they wanted, but they also had to recognize the gods of Rome. Jews were exempt from this worship because their religion was so ancient. Romans tolerated their monotheism as a kind of ethnic quirk, but Christianity was a new religion, not tied to ethnicity, and its adherents therefore had to play by the rules like everyone else. Indeed, the well-being of the empire was at stake.

One can see the threat that Christianity posed. A new religion that claimed it did not have to worship the state gods was dangerous and could set a dangerous precedent. With their religiously exclusivist claims, Christians were considered atheists and therefore traitors, a godless congregation who undermined the good of society. The Christian god(s) could be incorporated into the religious landscape, but for Christians to insist on worshiping their own god to the exclusion of others was an implicit attempt to overthrow familial and societal structures as well as the foundations of peace and security of the empire. That Christianity was spreading at a rapid rate only heightened the sense of its threat.

Some early Christians embraced the name "atheist," at least in a qualified sense. "Hence are we called atheists. And we confess that we are atheists," Justin Martyr boldly writes to the emperor, "so far as gods of this sort are concerned"—that is, the evil demons of pagan story and worship—"but not with respect to the most true God. . . . But both Him, and the Son . . . , and the prophetic Spirit, we worship and adore, knowing them in reason and truth."[1] Justin confesses that he does not believe in the state gods, for "all the gods of the nations are demons,"[2] as his Septuagint (and later the Latin Vulgate) translation of Psalm 96:5 says. There is one true God—Father, Son, and Holy Spirit—who cannot be situated within the plurality of deities in the surrounding culture. There is one God, creator of all things visible and invisible, and therefore the gods of the nations are merely created beings, not to be worshiped alongside the one true God. Christians, like their Jewish spiritual

---

1. Justin Martyr, *First Apology* 6 (ANF 1:164).
2. Justin Martyr, *Dialogue with Trypho* 73 (ANF 1:235); cf. *First Apology* 41: "All the gods of the nations are idols of devils" (ANF 1:176).

ancestors, were called to heed the command "You shall worship no other god, for the LORD, whose name is Jealous, is a jealous God" (Exod. 34:14).

Marcionite Dualism and Gnostic Emanationism

The invocation of the Old Testament raises the specter of another challenger to Christian monotheism: Marcion of Sinope. Marcion lived in the early second century and was a leader in the early Christian movement in Rome. He is usually categorized as a Gnostic. Although some scholars are wary of applying this term to Marcion, he does hold things in common with early Christian Gnostics. Marcion argued that the Old Testament bore witness to a different god than the one we discover in the New Testament. The god of the Old Testament was a wrathful tribal deity of the Jews, a †Demiurge³ responsible for making this evil material world we suffer in. The God of the New Testament was a God of love who came to save us and lead us to a superior spiritual world.

This may seem far-fetched to us, but some Christians today make similar claims. They view the God of the Old Testament as harsh, jealous, violent, and therefore inconsistent with the loving, accepting, and gentle God of the New Testament. This temptation—to pit the Old against the New Testament vision of God—is a perennial Christian temptation. Early Christians had to resist it vigorously (and so should we). For at stake are profound questions: Are the Scriptures that Christ and the apostles considered sacred still sacred for Christians? Is there one God who rules over all or different gods for different dimensions of life? And ultimately there is the question of salvation: Is the God who made us the same God who saves us?

For many Gnostic groups, there were numerous deities who emanated from each other. Gods begot other gods, often through some kind of divine sexual coupling. Among these deities, we find one that perversely gave rise to the Demiurge of the Old Testament who made the (evil) world. We also find the "divine Christ" sent from the Father to save us. In one version, the divine Christ appears as the snake in the garden of Eden who overcomes the jealous Demiurge in order to reveal to us the knowledge of good and evil so that we might become gods.⁴ In another version, the divine Christ possesses a

---

3. The word "Demiurge" means "craftsman" or "artisan," though etymologically it means "public worker." The idea of a Demiurge was made popular by the wide reading of Plato's *Timaeus* in the ancient world.

4. This suggestion comes from the second-century Gnostic text *Testimony of Truth*. The logic is perhaps not as crazy as we might think. Christ identifies himself in John 3:14 with the

human Jesus to teach us the way to knowledge, though when the crucifixion comes he flees back to the heavenly realm, leaving the poor human Jesus on the cross alone.[5]

These Gnostic beliefs, especially in some of their wilder variations, may seem strange to us today, but early Christians recognized them as an existential threat to the Church and Christian belief. And they are making a resurgence today. Gnosticism is attractive because it helps explain many things, such as the origin of evil and why we suffer. But it is also attractive because possessing secret knowledge that others do not have is a powerful temptation. It gives one a sense of belonging and importance, even a sense of superiority. It gives meaning and direction to life, a concrete orientation and something clear to guide one's life. Perhaps most importantly, it gives an account of how to be saved from this world of suffering.[6]

There are many problems with the Gnostic vision of God and the world, especially its anti-creation and, therefore, anti-incarnation and anti-sacrament sensibilities. But the key point for now is that Gnosticism offers an extrabiblical hierarchy of many gods into which the Father, Son, and Holy Spirit could be neatly subsumed.

Irenaeus of Lyons, the great second-century Doctor of the Church, articulated the key flaw in the Gnostic vision of God: it reduced the transcendent God to another being in the world. In his treatise *Against Heresies*, Irenaeus writes, "By their manner of speaking, [the Gnostics] ascribe those things which apply to men to the Father of all, . . . and they deny that He himself made the world, to guard against attributing want of power to Him; while, at the same time, they endow Him with human affections and passions."[7] Irenaeus makes a distinction between the being of humans and God, who is Being itself. While there is some analogy between God and human beings made in the image of God, there is a fundamental distinction that the Gnostics blur. Irenaeus continues,

> God is a simple, uncompounded Being, without diverse members, and altogether like, and equal to himself, since He is wholly understanding, and wholly spirit,

---

bronze serpent Moses held up in the desert. For the attentive Gnostic reader, it is a small step from there to seeing that Christ is the serpent in the garden who came to liberate and heal us through wisdom.

5. Irenaeus relates that the Gnostic Cerinthus held this view (*Against Heresies* 1.26.1; 3.18.5).

6. See David Brakke, *The Gnostics: Myth, Ritual, and Diversity in Early Christianity* (Cambridge, MA: Harvard University Press, 2010), 53.

7. Irenaeus, *Against Heresies* 2.13.3 (ANF 1:374).

and wholly thought, and wholly intelligence, and wholly reason, and wholly hearing, and wholly seeing, and wholly light, and the whole source of all that is good—even as the religious and pious are wont to speak concerning God.[8]

God is not limited or made up of parts, but he is simple and uncompounded. God is not just one more being among other beings in the world, not even the highest being. This is a fundamental category mistake.

Scripture on the Oneness of God

Irenaeus says that pious readers of Scripture will learn how to speak about the nature of God in the proper way. The consistent teaching of Scripture is that there is only one true God. In Deuteronomy, Moses instructs the Israelites to pray daily, "Hear, O Israel: The LORD our God is one LORD" (Deut. 6:4). The psalmist praises God, "For you are great and do wondrous things, you alone are God" (Ps. 86:10 RSV-2CE). God himself declares to Isaiah, "I am the LORD, and there is no other, besides me there is no God" (Isa. 45:5). Irenaeus not only distinguishes God's being from human being; he also calls God "simple, uncompounded Being" and uses the word "wholly" eight times in one sentence to show that God is not made up of parts. In this profound passage, Irenaeus is invoking Exodus 3:14, God's revelation of his name as "I AM."

In Exodus, God appears to Moses in a burning bush, which, though on fire, is not consumed (Exod. 3:2). God identifies himself as the same God who was with Abraham, Isaac, and Jacob (3:6), and then he reveals his name: "I AM WHO I AM" or, simply, "I AM" (3:14). These three things—the mode of revelation, the identification of God as the same God of Moses's ancestors, and the mysterious name—all tell us something profound about the oneness of God.

In the normal course of nature, when fire burns something, it consumes what it burns. But the wondrous, supernatural thing Moses sees is a fire that does not need or use the bush as fuel, but burns without consuming. The burning bush reveals that God does not depend on the world to exist. Without fuel, a fire would cease to be. It would burn out. But God does not burn out because he does not depend on the world. God is active—in medieval terms, he is *Actus Purus*, "Pure Act"—and he does not change or diminish as he burns. God is infinite power, activity, being.

God reveals his name as "I AM," which early Christians interpreted to mean that God *is*—simply and without qualification. All creatures exist in a

---

8. Irenaeus, *Against Heresies* 2.13.3 (*ANF* 1:374).

WITNESS TO THE TRADITION

Augustine on Anthropomorphic Language in Scripture

Scripture uses metaphors, images, and anthropomorphic language to talk about God. Augustine offers a traditional way for us to understand this biblical way of speaking about God, which at first seems unworthy of his transcendent nature.

> To raise us from the earthly and human meaning up to the divine and heavenly, the divine Scriptures have [themselves] come down to those words which even the most simple customarily use among themselves. And so those men through whom the Holy Spirit has spoken have not hesitated to employ in those books, as the occasion best demands, names of even those passions which our soul experiences and which the man who knows better already understands to be completely foreign to God. For example, because it is very difficult for a man to avenge something without experiencing anger, the authors of Scripture have decided to use the name *wrath* for God's vengeance, although God's vengeance is exercised with absolutely no such emotion. Again, since husbands are wont to protect the chastity of their wives through jealousy, the Scripture writers have used the expression *the jealousy of God* to indicate that providence of God whereby he admonishes the soul and seeks to prevent its corruption and, as it were, its prostitution through following after various other gods. In the same manner they also use the expression *the hand of God* for that power whereby he acts, *the feet of God* for that power whereby he perseveres in sustaining and governing all things, *the ears of God* or *the eyes of God*, for that power whereby he perceives and understands all things, *the face of God* for that power whereby he manifests himself and is known, and so on.[a]

a. Augustine, *Eighty-Three Different Questions*, no. 52, trans. David L. Mosher, FOTC 70 (Washington, DC: Catholic University of America Press, 1982), 88–89.

certain way (the way God made them), so their being is limited by what they are. The authors of this commentary are human beings; we have our being as humans. The same is true of all creatures: the squirrel, the moon, and the amoeba all exist in a particular way. But God is not a part of creation, so he does not exist in a certain way or as a certain kind of thing. God is "I AM."

He is unqualified Being or, as Irenaeus says, "simple, uncompounded Being" and "wholly" what he is. God simply is.

If God is "I AM," then there can be no other gods—at least, no other gods in the same sense. Divinity is not a pie that numerous divine beings share. If this were so, then God's being would be qualified in some way. There would be a limit: God's divinity would extend to the point of some other god's divinity. But God is "I AM" and therefore *the one true* God. This also means that nothing exists apart from God. If God is "I AM," then anything that has being has received its being from God. In the biblical logic followed by the early Christians, belief in one God is inseparable from belief in creation.

While the burning bush teaches that God is transcendent to the world, this does not mean that God is distant from the world. God is, after all, the God of Abraham, Isaac, and Jacob (Exod. 3:6); he loves individual people and is involved intimately in their lives; and God reveals his name to Moses so that Moses can know him and call upon him. Philosophically, we might put it like this: God's transcendence is not in opposition to his immanence and is, in fact, a prerequisite of it. To put it more simply, we can say that God is not a part of the world and that this allows him to be intimate to it without competition. He burns without consuming. He is present without interfering. We will discuss this more when we look at God as creator, but for now we can note that believing in one God means that God is far beyond all created things; he is the source of those created things and is intimately close to what he created.

Other chapters will explore how Scripture shows that the Son and the Spirit are also fully God. But we can note here that when Christ says, "Before Abraham was, I am" (John 8:58), he is claiming the divine name for himself. But if Christ is "I am" and the Father is "I AM," we cannot be speaking of two gods. The name "I AM," as we argued above, means that God is simple, absolute being and not limited or qualified in some way. The revelation that Jesus is God and, later, that the Spirit is God does not mean that each person of the Trinity is one-third of God. The revelation in the burning bush shows that this cannot be the case: God is simple and cannot be divided. Each divine person is fully God, and yet each person is not collapsible into the other persons. If the Son is divine and the Spirit is divine, then everything we have said about God as "I AM" applies equally to them.

False Oneness: Modalism and Subordinationism

The dangers to the Christian doctrine of one God came not only from attempts to absorb the Christian God(s) into an already existing pantheon,

LEX ORANDI

God, the I AM

The nineteenth-century American hymn "What Wondrous Love Is This" beautifully captures the unity of Father and Son in light of Exodus 3:14 and John 8:58.

> To God and to the Lamb I will sing, I will sing;
> to God and to the Lamb I will sing;
> to God and to the Lamb, who is the great I AM,
> while millions join the theme, I will sing, I will sing,
> while millions join the theme, I will sing.[a]

a. Anonymous, "What Wondrous Love Is This," Hymnary.org, accessed January 19, 2023, https://hymnary.org/text/what_wondrous_love_is_this_o_my_soul_o_m.

but also from internal Christian movements trying to preserve the oneness of God. We will briefly consider here two problematic ways of preserving God's oneness at the expense of his threeness: modalism and subordinationism.

Modalism is usually attributed to figures like Noetus and Sabellius, who were active in the third century. Modalism claims that God is not three distinct divine persons, since this would (seem to) make Christians polytheists; rather, God has three roles or three modes of interacting with the world. He has a Father mode (for example, when he is creating), a Son mode (for example, when he is saving), and a Holy Spirit mode (for example, when he is inspiring). The one God has three ways of being in the world, and there is no distinction of persons: Christ *is* the Father, and the same goes for the Holy Spirit. The persons of the Trinity are identified with one another. The popular version of this, heard even today in Sunday schools around the world, is the analogy of the human person who is, for example, a wife, a mother, and a teacher: one person with three roles just as the one God has three roles.

Subordinationism (literally, "ordering beneath") can take various forms, but it is most famously articulated by Arius. Subordinationists argue that God is one and that the one God is, properly speaking, the Father alone. The Son and the Spirit are subordinate to the Father, higher than the angels but less than God. In the Arian version, the Son and the Spirit are the highest things created by the Father. Therefore, there is an ontological distinction between the Father (who is the divine creator) and the Son and the Spirit (who are

LEX ORANDI

Undivided God

"Holy God, We Praise Thy Name" is a beautiful hymn, inspired by the fourth-century *Te Deum*, that powerfully expresses the Christian belief in the triune God:

> Holy Father, Holy Son,
> Holy Spirit, Three we name thee;
> While in essence only One,
> Undivided God we claim thee;
> And adoring bend the knee,
> While we own the mystery.[a]

a. Kelly Dobbs-Mickus, ed., *Worship*, 4th ed. (Chicago: GIA, 2011), no. 614, https://hymnary.org/hymn/WORS2011/614.

his most excellent creations). By subordinating the Son and the Spirit, Arius avoids tritheism and preserves the oneness of God. This subordinationist logic also has seemingly significant biblical warrant. When Christ says things like "The Father is *greater* than I" (John 14:28),[9] then it seems like Christ himself is declaring his inferiority to the Father.

Christians embraced the teaching about one God that they inherited from the Jews, but they rejected both the modalist and the subordinationist solutions to preserving the oneness of God. The primary weakness of these views is that they cannot account for all the data of Scripture, which gives evidence not only that there is one God, but that the Son and the Spirit are distinct persons and divine. It will be the task of other chapters to show how this is the case, but for now it will be helpful to remember the basic rules for thinking about trinitarian monotheism discussed in the introduction: (1) there is only one God (the denial of which leads to polytheism); (2) the Father is God, the Son is God, and the Holy Spirit is God (the denial of which leads to subordinationism); and (3) the Father is not the Son, the Son is not the Father, and the Holy Spirit is neither the Father nor the Son (the denial of which leads to modalism). We must keep each claim in mind as we speak and think about God.[10]

9. Italics in Scripture quotations have been added for emphasis, here and elsewhere.
10. While each person of the Trinity is fully God, this does not mean that there is no "order" within the Trinity. Early Christians understood the Father to be the eternal source of the Son,

Living the Mystery

In his *Confessions*, Augustine famously writes, "But you [God] were more deeply within me than the innermost part of my being, higher than what was highest in me."[11] This intimacy is only conceivable because of the Christian understanding of the one God who is "I AM." Because God is so transcendent ("higher than what was highest in me"), he can be intimately present in us ("more deeply within me than the innermost part of my being"). God is above *and therefore* deeply within.

To call God "I AM" means that God never changes. Some people think that this would mean that God does not respond to us or is indifferent to us. But it is just the opposite. "God is love," as Saint John says (1 John 4:8), and because God does not change, God is *unchanging* love. The Epistle of Saint James makes the connection between God's love and his changelessness explicit: "Every good endowment and every perfect gift is from above, coming down from the Father of lights with whom there is no variation or shadow due to change" (James 1:17). God is the giver of all good gifts, our lover whose love never changes.

That God never changes should be a source of great consolation. It means that God is the one stable reality we can always turn to. All created things are unstable. They change constantly. The seasons and weather change; political fortunes change; bodies change; our minds and hearts change; our families and friends and feelings change. We may promise others that we will "always be there" for them, but sometimes we are busy or asleep or unavailable or leave the ringer off or fail to live up to our promises. To call God "I AM" means that he *will always* be there for us.

This is a great comfort, especially for those of us with a checkered past (or present). We may try to draw away from God, but he does not draw away from us! As Augustine says, "You were with me, but I was not with you."[12] Psalm 139 is a moving expression of this reality (a prayer we might consider praying to help us live the mystery of the one God). I am transparent to God, who "knitted me together in my mother's womb" (Ps. 139:13).[13] He knows when I sit or stand, and he knows my thoughts (v. 2); he also knows what I am going to say even before I say it: "LORD, you know it altogether" (v. 4).

---

whom he eternally generates, and the Holy Spirit, whom he eternally spirates ("breathes forth"). The Father begets the Son; the Son does not beget the Father. The Father spirates the Spirit; the Spirit does not spirate the Father (see chap. 5 for a discussion of the Spirit proceeding from the Father and the Son).

11. Augustine, *Confessions* 3.6.11, trans. Thomas Williams (Indianapolis: Hackett, 2019), 35.
12. Augustine, *Confessions* 10.27.38 (Williams, 183).
13. Quotations from Ps. 139 here are from the RSV-2CE.

Though we may try to hide, God will always find us because he is always there. He is not limited to one place rather than another, like a local deity of pagan imagination. God is everywhere present. "Where shall I go from your Spirit? Or where shall I flee from your presence?" asks the psalmist (v. 7).

> If I ascend to heaven, you are there!
>   If I make my bed in Sheol, you are there!
> If I take the wings of the morning
>   and dwell in the uttermost parts of the sea,
> even there your hand shall lead me,
>   and your right hand shall hold me.
> If I say, "Let only darkness cover me,
>   and the light about me be night,"
> even the darkness is not dark to you,
>   the night is bright as the day. (Ps. 139:8–12)

God is always there, and all we have to do is turn to him—not physically, but with our minds and our hearts.

Father Almighty

I believe in one God, **the Father almighty,** maker of heaven and earth, of all things visible and invisible.	Credo in unum Deum, **Patrem omnipotentem,** factorem caeli et terrae, visibilium omnium et invisibilium.	Πιστεύομεν εἰς ἕνα Θεόν, πατέρα παντοκράτορα, ποιητὴν οὐρανοῦ καὶ γῆς, ὁρατῶν τε πάντων καὶ ἀοράτων.

OT: creator and ruler, Deut. 32:6; Job 33:4; Ps. 104; Isa. 64:8; 2 Macc. 1:25; maker and Father to humans and Israel, Gen. 1:26–27; Exod. 4:22–23; Hosea 11:1–4

NT: Father of only-begotten Son, Matt. 10:29–33; John 1:1–18; 5:16–18; 20:17; of the baptized, Matt. 6:9; Gal. 4:6; 1 John 3:1; almighty, Mark 10:27; Rev. 15:3

Catechism: the Father, 232–67; the almighty, 268–78

Theological Exposition

While there is ample testimony in Scripture that God is called "Father" and "almighty," there is no occurrence of these terms together.[14] God is called

---

14. The closest these two words get in the Bible is 2 Cor. 6:18, where Paul discusses God's promises to those who have become temples of God: "I will be a *father* to you, and you shall

"Father" seventeen times in the Old Testament and more than 250 times in the New. In the Greek translation of the Old Testament (the Septuagint), the term "almighty," *pantokratōr*, translates two different Hebrew terms, *'el shaddai* and *yhwh tseva'ot* (LORD of hosts), and occurs more than 150 times. *Pantokratōr* is used only nine times in the New Testament (eight of which occur in Revelation). It is likely that in some earlier formulation of the Creed, there was an understood comma between "Father" and "almighty": "I believe in one God, the Father, the Almighty." By the time of Nicaea, however, the terms had become a unit wherein "almighty" qualified "Father" in important ways.[15]

Drawing on Scripture, the early Christian tradition speaks about God as "Father" in six ways:

1. God is Father of the world in that he is its creator and its ruler (cf. Deut. 32:6; Isa. 64:8).
2. God is Father of all human beings, whom he made in his own image (cf. Gen. 1:26–27; Luke 3:38; Acts 17:28).
3. God is the Father of the nation Israel as a whole (Exod. 4:22–23; Deut. 1:31).
4. God is Father of the kings of Israel (2 Sam. 7:14; 1 Chron. 17:13; Ps. 2:7).[16]
5. God is the Father of Jesus Christ, his only-begotten Son (John 1:14; 5:16–18).
6. God is Father of those who are "baptized into Christ" (Rom. 6:3) and, therefore, adopted into his family, so that they become children of God who can call God "our Father" (Matt. 6:9; cf. Gal. 4:6; 1 John 3:1).

The thread uniting all these meanings is the notion of God as source. He is the source of creation, human beings, and the nation Israel and its kings; he is the eternal source of the Son, who offers us the chance to be born again from a divine source. In order of importance, the fifth meaning is primary: God is

---

be my sons and daughters, says the Lord *Almighty*." Paul writes this in a string of quotations from the Old Testament, though it is not clear what this line is in reference to.

15. The Apostles' Creed uses the term "Father almighty" two times, while the Gloria that Catholics sing at Mass uses the term "almighty Father" (*Roman Missal*, 521–22). Both the Apostles' Creed and the Gloria likely developed in the fourth or fifth century.

16. This can be understood in two ways. First, the king is the head and representative of the Israelite nation, so he stands in as "son" for the nation-as-son. Second, these texts are prophetic in that they point to Christ the King, the true Son of God (Heb. 1:5).

properly and eternally the Father of the Son. All other meanings and paternal relations to creation flow from this primary, eternal relation of Father and Son.

The term "almighty" also has a range of meanings in Scripture and Tradition. It translates the Greek word *pantokratōr* (ruler of all) and the Latin *omnipotens* (all-powerful). In Scripture, God is called "the Almighty" because he is the creator, sustainer, provident ruler, and judge of all the universe (Job 33:4; 2 Macc. 1:25; Rev. 15:3). His reign and power extend to everything that he has created. This first meaning of "almighty" coincides with—and eventually modifies—the first four meanings of "Father" listed above.

In the early Christian tradition, the meaning of "almighty" is deepened. God is almighty not only because he creates us from nothing, but even more so because he can re-create us after we have plunged ourselves into the deeper nothingness of sin. Eventually, God comes to be seen as almighty in an even more fundamental sense: God has power to beget a Son equal to him and one with him. This last meaning emerges especially in the Arian controversy, where "almighty" comes to modify "Father" in its primary †christological sense.

Over time, Christians came to see God as "the Father almighty." This coupling of originally distinct terms was an important development in understanding who and what God is. As usual, this development happened in response to the challenges early Christians encountered. Faced with pagans and Gnostics in one generation and Arians in another, early Christians had to address profound questions about God: What kind of "Father" did Christians believe in, and how far did his sovereignty extend? And was God *always* Father of his Son? It is to these questions we now turn.

Father of All That Exists

In a letter to one of his pagan friends, Saint Theophilus, the second-century bishop of Antioch, tries to show that "God is ineffable and indescribable, and cannot be seen by eyes of flesh."[17] God is incomprehensible, and any words we use for him are mere analogies. Theophilus picks up a dozen names from Scripture, including the term "Father," and explains what they mean: "If I call Him Word, I name but His sovereignty; if I call Him Mind, I speak but of His wisdom. . . . If I call Him Father, I speak of all things as being from Him."[18] And in the next paragraph, he explains that God is called "Father, because he is before all things."[19] Theophilus is concerned to

17. Theophilus of Antioch, *To Autolycus* 1.3 (*ANF* 2:89).
18. Theophilus, *To Autolycus* 1.3 (*ANF* 2:90).
19. Theophilus, *To Autolycus* 1.4 (*ANF* 2:90).

show his pagan friend how to think about God in a fitting way—that is, to distinguish him from the pagan gods. God is not one being among others, but the source of all beings. Theophilus is also concerned to show how the limited tool of human language operates when speaking about God. It always operates analogically. We cannot capture God's essence in words, so any term we use has to be properly modified to say something fitting about God. For Theophilus, the term "Father" is equivalent to "Creator" because God is prior to all created things and the initiator of their existence. Importantly, God is creator of "*all* things."

While in the early tradition the term "Creator" is appropriated to the Father, the Old Testament most often uses "Father" to refer to God's formation of Israel and his special relation to its leaders.[20] In one moving image, Isaiah pleads with God, "Yet, O LORD, you are our Father; we are the clay, and you are our potter; we are all the work of your hand" (Isa. 64:8 RSV-2CE). In Hosea, God is portrayed as a bereaved parent, lamenting the idolatry of his son: "When Israel was a child, I loved him, and out of Egypt I called my son. The more I called them, the more they went from me" (Hosea 11:1–2). God goes on to recall how, like a father, he loved and cared for his child even before they recognized him:

> Yet it was I who taught Ephraim to walk,
>   I took them up in my arms;
>   but they did not know that I healed them.
> I led them with cords of compassion,
>   with the bands of love,
> and I became to them as one
>   who raises an infant to his cheeks,
>   and I bent down to them and fed them. (Hosea 11:3–4 RSV-2CE)

God nurtures, feeds, heals, and shows tender affection for his child. But God's paternal love also includes discipline: "For the LORD reproves him whom he loves, as a father the son in whom he delights" (Prov. 3:12). God loves like a father who encourages, watches over, and corrects his children. These beautiful images show that God is not some distant deity or impersonal force, but a divine person who knows and loves his people as a father does his children.

---

20. Early Christians were unanimous that it is the whole Trinity that creates, but they also "appropriated" certain properties to distinct persons. By "appropriation," we mean that while God is one and his properties and activities are common to all three persons, there is a kind of fitting resemblance of a certain property or activity to a particular person. So it is fitting that the term "Creator" is appropriated to the Father, who is the source of all things.

The image of father in these and similar passages (e.g., Exod. 4:22; Isa. 1:2; Jer. 3:19) is not radically different from what we find in other ancient religions. Paternal imagery was common when treating the ruler of the city and the divine ruler of the cosmos. In the ancient world, fatherly rule was the primary model for rightly ordered monarchy, so it was natural to think of the chief god as father over the world. Zeus was considered the father of the gods and humans. (The name "Jupiter," the Roman version of Zeus, literally means "father in the sky.") Like the biblical God, Zeus was considered all-powerful, concerned with the peoples under his rule, and an enforcer of justice.

While there are important similarities between the biblical and the pagan use of the father image for God, there are even more important dissimilarities. And it is these that perhaps made the Israelites wary of adopting the title "father" for God without reservation. Zeus is "father" not just in the metaphorical sense, referring to his rule or solicitude, but he was considered, literally, the father of many since he had seduced or sexually coerced goddesses and mortal women to beget divine and semidivine offspring. Zeus has a genealogy, a beginning to his existence and, if his treatment (i.e., his overthrow and dismemberment) of his own father is any indication, a possible end to it. Moreover, while Zeus's rule extends over all of Olympus and earth, his power—at least according to pagan authorities like Homer and Hesiod—always seems limited. Other gods vie for power, he has to balance competing interests, and he often has to appease his jealous wife! So while Zeus's power is extensive, it is also hemmed in by rival powers.

For all the seeming similarities, Zeus's fatherhood is radically different from the fatherhood of God in the Bible. One really gets the sense that Zeus is a projection of human fatherhood onto the divine, in both its good and bad aspects. "Homer invented these tales," Cicero says, "ascribing human qualities to the gods."[21] In Scripture, we get the opposite motion: God gives us a share in his fatherhood. As Paul tells us, "the Father, from whom every family in heaven and on earth is named" (Eph. 3:14–15), sets the terms for fatherhood. We do not project human fatherhood onto God; rather, we model our own fatherhood on God's.

The Gnostic vision of the Father is more complex than the pagan vision, but it is equally problematic. On the one hand, Gnostics have a high view of the Father: he is beyond comprehension, invisible, and indescribable.[22] He

---

21. Cicero, *Tusculan Disputations* 1.26.65, quoted in Augustine, *Confessions* 1.16.25 (Williams, 15).
22. We follow Brakke's summary of the Gnostic stories in *The Gnostics*, 58–59.

is the one source of all things. In addition to Christian ideas, Gnostics also drew on Platonic ones, so their descriptions of the Father can, at times, sound similarly transcendent. Still, the differences are more telling.

The Gnostic Father emanated a divine realm of many other gods—divine beings or quasi-Platonic Forms—often paired male and female, who make up the heavenly realm called the Pleroma or the Entirety. The Father rules this heavenly realm and keeps it in harmony. Though accounts differ in detail, Gnostics agree that the material world was brought about not by the Father but by one of the emanated deities who went rogue. While there are multiple versions of who this minor deity is, the key point is that, for Gnostics, the Father is not the creator of the material world, which comes about against his will or without his knowledge.

While adherents of paganism and Gnosticism often made grand claims for their father-gods—claims seemingly similar at times to Christian ones—it became clear that their gods were radically different. Their father-gods were, in the end, limited deities. Christians distinguished their Father-God by emphasizing the biblical title "the Almighty." Irenaeus is typical when he says, "God is the Almighty and everything is from God."[23] God's fatherhood—his power, authority, knowledge, rule—is not circumscribed by other deities or circumstances. God's fatherhood knows no limits.

Irenaeus explains the logic of the Christian view:

> For it is necessary that things that have come into being have received the origin of their being . . . from some great cause; and the origin of all is God, for He Himself was not made by anyone, but everything was made by Him. And therefore it is proper, first of all, to believe that there is One God, the Father, who has created and fashioned all things, who made that which was not to be, who contains all and is alone uncontainable. Moreover, in this "all" is our world, and in the world, man; thus this world was also created by God.
>
> In this way, then, it is demonstrated [that there is] One God, [the] Father, uncreated, invisible, Creator of all, above whom there is no other God, and after whom there is no other God.[24]

For Irenaeus, all things that come to be cannot have their origin in themselves—they cannot be self-generated—but they must ultimately come from another cause who does not have a cause. There must be one without an origin who

---

23. Irenaeus, *Demonstration of the Apostolic Preaching* 3, in *On the Apostolic Preaching*, trans. John Behr, PPS 17 (Crestwood, NY: St. Vladimir's Seminary Press, 1997), 42.

24. Irenaeus, *Demonstration of the Apostolic Preaching* 4–5 (Behr, 42–43).

Why Is God Called "Father" and Not "Mother"?

Today, many people think that calling God "Father" is a leftover from a more sexist time. But it is Jesus primarily who teaches us to call God "Father," and if Jesus is sexist or capitulated to the sexism of his times, then Jesus would be limited by his era's prejudices, and if so, then the whole gospel falls apart. How, then, should we understand God's "fatherhood"?

God is Spirit and does not have a body. God, as the *Catechism* says, "is neither man nor woman: he is God. He also transcends human fatherhood and motherhood, although he is their origin and standard: no one is father as God is Father."[a] Scripture uses paternal analogies for God, though it also uses maternal similes to communicate truths about God:

> By calling God "Father," the language of faith indicates two main things: that God is the first origin of everything and transcendent authority; and that he is at the same time goodness and loving care for all his children. God's parental tenderness can also be expressed by the image of motherhood, which emphasizes God's immanence, the intimacy between Creator and creature.[b]

God created our bodies and gave them meaning. They function as signs that reveal supernatural truths. Men can generate life outside of themselves, while women receive and generate life within themselves. We see this in the common images of "Father Sky" and "Mother Earth." We also see it in the traditional designation of the soul as feminine, which signifies a receptivity to God's grace. "Father" more fittingly communicates the power of God, especially his power as source of all things.

While Scripture uses maternal similes to show God's closeness, they are not as fitting for revealing God as source and beginning. God is not "receptive"—that is, things are not done to him or in him. He is "pure act," the generator of life, prior to all things, and the source of all being. While God transcends the categories of male and female, God is revealed to us as "Father," a term that names his eternal relation to the Son and communicates more appropriately the truth that God is the source and creator of all things outside himself.

a. *CCC* 239.
b. *CCC* 239.

originates all. That one is God. If God had an origin, he would not be almighty; rather, he would be dependent on another more powerful than himself.

Note also how Irenaeus appropriates the term "Creator" to "Father" and shows him to be "almighty." There is one God who made all things, contains all things, and is not contained by them—that is, there is nothing that delimits his being. There is not one god who rules the heavenly realm and another the material, nor is there one god for the cosmos and one for human beings. There are no rivals to God's throne or things that happen outside his knowledge or will. No, there is one God for all, who rules all, knows all, and is the source of all. In a word, there is "one God, the Father almighty."

Finally, if there is one God for all creation who is "Father," then it follows that there must be some sense in which all humans are brothers and sisters.[25] We see God's universal fatherhood implied in the "image of God" texts (e.g., Gen. 1:26–28), which declare that all humans come from and reflect God in some way. We see it in texts like the Gospel of Luke, where in Christ's genealogy Adam is called "the son of God" (Luke 3:38). Since we all belong to Adam (see 1 Cor. 15:22), we all belong to one family under the universal fatherhood of God (cf. Acts 17:28). God's fatherhood of all humans, while important for recognizing the humanity and dignity of every person, should be distinguished from the more radical sense of God's fatherhood of those who are baptized into Christ (which we will discuss below).

Eternally Father of the Son

The early controversies with pagans and Gnostics clarified the kind of Father Christians worshiped—in a word, not a *kind* at all. As the one God who is "I AM," the Father is not one being among others, but the all-powerful source of being for all things. His divinity and his sovereignty know no limits. The one God, Father almighty, is "all-powerful" (*omnipotens*) and "ruler of all" (*pantokratōr*).

But this understanding of the Father still remains within the realm of analogy. Is there a sense of God's fatherhood that goes beyond analogy? In the Gospel of John, Jesus is called "the only-begotten Son from the Father" (John 1:14 RSV-2CE). Is this another analogical use of "Father"? Or is this a bolder

---

25. Saint Francis of Assisi brought the spirituality of God's universal fatherhood to its highest point. If God is Father and Creator of all things, then not just all human beings but *all created beings* are brothers and sisters. We all have one source, and so we all share a kinship bond with every creature God made. Thus, Saint Francis invokes Brother Sun and Sister Moon, Brother Wind and Sister Water, Brother Wolf and Sister Bodily Death, and so on.

ontological claim about the Son's relation to the Father? Certainly, some Jews thought Christ was making ontological claims, since some of them wanted to kill him because "he called God his Father, making himself equal with God" (5:18). While the Old Testament Scriptures certainly spoke of God as Father, Jesus seems to be doing something much more radical and offensive. He seems to be claiming that God is his own Father in a unique way.

We will discuss the divinity of Christ in the next chapter, but for now we must ponder what Christ reveals about God as Father. In the Old Testament, God's fatherhood was understood in relation to the things he had made. But can "Father" be God's name and not merely a title that describes an attribute? Or, put starkly, is God *always* a Father, or did he *become* a Father? Is God's fatherhood eternal, or is it something that comes about in relation to something he made? These questions about the meaning of God's fatherhood necessarily arise with the revelation of Christ. They were discussed in Scripture and the early Church, but they came into stark focus in the Arian controversy.

In his commentary on the Council of Nicaea, Athanasius lays out the Arian argument about God's fatherhood. Arians say,

> Not always Father, not always Son. The Son was not before his generation but he also came to be from non-being. Therefore God has not always been Father of the Son. But when the Son came to be and was created, then it was that God was called his Father. For the Word is a creature and a work and foreign and unlike . . . in essence to the Father.[26]

For the Arians, the Son is the first and the highest creature that God made. The Son is made directly by God, and all other things are made through the Son. In creating the Son, God endowed him with the grace of becoming a Son. In that endowing, God *became* a Father. For Arians, the relationship of Father and Son is only a superior version of the Father's relationship to the rest of creation. The Son is only one creation among others, albeit the highest and best.

Before we dismiss the Arian argument too quickly, we should note how paradoxical it is that we follow our profession of "one God" with a profession that he is "Father." The term "father" is inherently relational; it implies another, an offspring. Father implies Son, just as Son implies Father. Can we

---

26. Athanasius, *On the Council of Nicaea* 6, in Khaled Anatolios, *Athanasius*, The Early Church Fathers (London: Routledge, 2004), 183.

proclaim God as "Father" in the proper sense if we believe he is one? The answer lies in deepening our understanding of what it means that God is Father *almighty*.

Commenting on "Father almighty" (translated "omnipotent Father") in the Nicene Creed, Pope Leo the Great explains, "For, when there is belief in God and the omnipotent Father, then the Son is shown to be co-eternal with Him, in no way differing from the Father, because He was born God from God, the Omnipotent from the Omnipotent, the Co-eternal from the Eternal, not coming later in time or inferior in power, not of unequal glory, not separate in essence."[27] Leo argues that because God is Father and because God is almighty, he has the power to beget a Son who is equal to him. Therefore, God is *always* Father to his only-begotten Son.

We must be careful here not to think of God's fatherhood in the way we think of human fatherhood. That is, we should not think of sexual reproduction or the coupling with a female counterpart. God does not have a body; God is not male. God is not Zeus, who reproduces with divine and human females. In Christian theological terminology, to be "father" means "to pass on a nature" (this definition fits human as well as divine begetting). The Father is God; therefore, the Son is God ("God from God"). The Son is the same nature as the Father, which he receives not in time (that would make him a creation) but eternally. God is Father in the sense that he is always in relation with the Son.

This mystery is hard for us to imagine, and indeed, any imagining will ultimately reduce God to some image of the world. When we imagine fathers and sons, we always imagine a temporal sequence, a spatial relation, and a number of other differences. For humans, fatherhood *does* imply these things. On the one hand, human fathers pass on their human nature to their children, so that their children are equally human. But fathers are older than their children, have separate bodies, and have more power, authority, strength, knowledge, and so on than their children. This is because we live in time and space and have our being over time. This is constitutive of human nature. Human fathers pass on their temporal and spatial human nature to their human children, which means that children, like their fathers, at one time did not exist but received their being, live in time, have separate bodies, grow, and develop their powers over time. This is all implied in having and passing on a human nature.

27. Leo the Great, *Letter 28, Letter to Flavian*, also known as *Tome of Leo*, in *St. Leo the Great: Letters*, trans. Edmund Hunt, FOTC 34 (Washington, DC: Catholic University of America Press, 2004), 93.

But God is eternal and incorporeal. God does not live within time and space (he is their creator). The Father does not exist before the Son. The Father is eternal, so the Son, too, is eternal. Athanasius writes,

> But God, being without parts, is Father of the Son without partition or passibility, for neither outflow nor influx pertain to the Incorporeal as they do to human beings. Since his nature is simple, he is Father of the one and only Son. . . . God, who exists forever, is forever Father of the Son.[28]

The Father "passes on" his divine nature to the Son, which includes eternity and all the other divine attributes. The Father can do this because the Father is almighty. He has the power to "pass on" his divine nature to his Son from all eternity in such a way that his Son shares all the qualities of that divine nature.

The Father is always Father of the Son, who is of the same nature as the Father. As we say in the Creed (and will analyze more fully in the next chapter), the Son is "consubstantial with the Father." He is of the same divine substance (or nature) as the Father. Even if God never created, he would still be Father. Arians could not say this.

Jesus reveals that God is his own Father, not in some profound metaphorical sense but in a profound ontological sense. Jesus, while truly human, is also truly divine because he received his divine nature eternally from his divine Father. But Jesus also reveals that we, too, should call God "our Father." Jesus often makes a distinction between "my Father" and "your [plural] Father" (e.g., Matt. 6:9; 10:29–33; John 20:17), which suggests that we do not have exactly the same relationship to the Father. Christ is the only-begotten Son of the Father, "but to all who received him, who believed in his name, he gave power to become children of God; who were born, not of blood nor of the will of the flesh nor of the will of man, but of God" (John 1:12–13). In other words, we are born of our human parents, and so we are human beings, but Christ gives us the possibility to be "born again" or "born anew . . . of water and the Spirit" (3:3, 5). When we are born anew in baptism, we have a new Father and a new nature. We are born "of God," so the Spirit gives us a share in God's divine nature. We are now children of God who can call God "our Father." To live as a child of God is to "live the mystery" of God's fatherhood.

---

28. Athanasius, *On the Council of Nicaea* 11 (Anatolios, 188–89).

Living the Mystery

When we are baptized, we do not simply join a Christian club called the Church. In baptism, we receive God's Holy Spirit, who transforms us into Christ. We die and rise with Christ, so that we can cry out with Saint Paul, "It is no longer I who live, but Christ who lives in me" (Gal. 2:20). Augustine is so bold as to say of the baptized that "we have become not only Christians, but Christ himself."[29] If we *are* Christ, then God is our Father and we are his children.

We are so used to being called "children of God" that we have lost our sense of wonder at it. But it is wondrous! "See what love the Father has given us, that we should be called children of God," John the evangelist cries out, "and so we are" (1 John 3:1)! The Church, in her wisdom, reminds us every day at Mass how shocking this reality is: "At the Savior's command and formed by divine teaching," the priest says, "we *dare* to say: Our Father . . ."[30] We *dare* to call God "our Father" only because Christ told us to, but it is daring, bold, audacious, and perhaps even a bit crazy.

God is the all-powerful creator and ruler of the whole universe. He is not our Father in any obvious or natural sense. We are, naturally, children of our parents. We are not children of the one true and eternal God, except in the analogical sense that he created us. God has only one child: his *only*-begotten Son. Yet Jesus invites us to address God as an intimate, personal Father. We can do this because Christ invites us through baptism to enter into his own relationship with the Father.

We can live the mystery of God's Fatherhood by living into our vocation as sons and daughters of God. First, this means allowing ourselves to be loved by God. This is difficult for many people, especially those who feel unlovable or who have complicated relationships with their own fathers. But living into our vocation means accepting that God has an overwhelming paternal love for each and every one of us. He loves us infinitely, just as he loves his only-begotten Son. And his love transforms us.

Second, being a child of God means cultivating a childlike trust in God. Children instinctively turn to their fathers, run into their arms, want to be picked up, comforted, and caressed. We need to let our guard down, let go of our false self-sufficiency, and run to our Father with the full confidence of a child.

29. Augustine, *Tractates on John* 21.8 (our translation).
30. *Roman Missal*, 336.

Finally, trusting God means trusting his discipline and his pedagogy. Like a good father, God wants what is best for us, which often means that we need his chastisement. Often this comes in the form of the trials of life, which are meant to build us up in virtue and lead us closer to our Father. When times are tough, it is easy to think that God has abandoned us, but these times of suffering are precisely what we need to grow into true children of God. In fact, these are times when we are particularly close to God. God uses this suffering to unite us to his suffering Son and to transform us into his image.

Maker of Heaven and Earth

I believe in one God, the Father almighty, **maker of heaven and earth,** of all things visible and invisible.	Credo in unum Deum, Patrem omnipotentem, factorem caeli et terrae, visibilium omnium et invisibilium.	Πιστεύομεν εἰς ἕνα Θεόν, πατέρα παντοκράτορα, ποιητὴν οὐρανοῦ καὶ γῆς, ὁρατῶν τε πάντων καὶ ἀοράτων.

OT: Gen. 1–2; Ps. 19:1; Prov. 3:19; Wis. 11:17; 2 Macc. 7:28
NT: Matt. 18:10; John 1:1–18; Col. 1:15–17; Rev. 21–22
Catechism: creation and providence, 279–324; all things visible and invisible, 325–54

Theological Exposition

"In the beginning God created the heavens and the earth" (Gen. 1:1). From the very first words of the Bible, we learn that God is the "maker of heaven and earth." We learn that originally the earth was "without form and void" and that there was a deep darkness over the water (1:2). But we also learn that God's Spirit hovered over the abyss, an image that evokes a mother hen nourishing her unformed offspring and signifies God's superiority to the world. God speaks things into being—"Let there be light" (1:3)—and through the power of the word, God creates the universe. The mention of God, Spirit, and "word" in these opening lines was irresistibly interpreted by early Christians as an allusion to the Trinity.

Unlike other ancient creation stories, where the world is the result of violence or a fall, Genesis 1 tells the story of a good God who creates a good world through his creative reason. Through speech, God brings order out of chaos and light out of darkness. Written probably during the Babylonian exile, Genesis 1 is a kind of declaration of war on the Babylonian gods. The sun and the moon, deities of the surrounding culture, are mere creatures, formed a few days into the process (1:14–18). They are not to be worshiped but are God's cosmic clock and lamp to keep time and give light, especially for the purpose of remembering to worship the one God on the Sabbath. The sea monsters, traditionally thought to be the powerful divine rulers of chaos (symbolized by the deep waters), are not rivals to God but are his creations (1:21). If there is chaos, it is part of God's design and controlled by a mere word.

The rest of Scripture confirms and deepens what we learn in Genesis 1. "The LORD by wisdom founded the earth; by understanding he established the heavens" (Prov. 3:19). This wisdom, we learn in John's Gospel, is Christ, the eternal Son. The word God speaks in Genesis is not audible; rather, it is God's *Logos* through whom all things were made (John 1:1–3). Because God creates through the Word, all things bear the imprint of the Word. This means that the world is, at bottom, reasonable and that the things of the world are intelligible. They are not accidents or meaningless conglomerations of matter, but coherent realities, words, spoken by God. And the same God who made those things also made human beings in his image with minds that can understand those things. Indeed, since things bear the imprint of the Word, the things themselves speak. They speak a language we can understand rationally (and can investigate scientifically). They also speak the goodness of God: "The heavens are telling the glory of God; and the firmament proclaims his handiwork" (Ps. 19:1).

That God is the creator of all things would seem to be a rather unexceptionable teaching. Certainly, by the time of Nicaea, this doctrine was largely settled. The real issue at Nicaea was whether the Son was one of the "all things" that God had made. But like all the articles in the Creed, God as maker of all things was a hard-won truth. We have already seen how early Christians responded to Gnostic claims about creation. Here we will touch on two further key points relating to creation: first, the meaning of "heaven and earth" and "all things visible and invisible"; and second, the meaning of "maker" and whether it entails that God created from something or from nothing.

Heaven and Earth, Things Visible and Invisible

The Creed states that God is the "maker of heaven and earth, of all things visible and invisible," clearly drawing on Paul's phrasing in Colossians where he says that in Christ "all things were created, in heaven and on earth, visible and invisible, whether thrones or dominions or principalities or authorities" (Col. 1:16). At first it might seem redundant to include these two pairings, "heaven and earth" and "things visible and invisible," but due to challenges and misunderstandings (that Paul himself likely encountered), the Church has included both phrases in the Creed.

The phrase "heaven and earth" has a range of meanings in Scripture and the early Christian tradition. Naming the extremities of creation, "heaven and earth" often simply denotes "everything." It is meant to be an inclusive phrase that names the highest and the lowest and everything in between. Still, it sometimes refers more particularly to a contrast between the sky, with its heavenly bodies, and the earth, with all the things that dwell on the ground or below it. Other times, "heaven" denotes the heavenly realm, where angels and saints dwell in communion with God, whereas "earth" refers to our current life in the world.

CONTEMPORARY ISSUES

Creation and Evolution

The Catholic Church has always had a rather open stance toward the theory of evolution. Without committing ourselves to any particular iteration of this still-developing theory, we can say the following things with some confidence:

1. Creation and evolution address two different sets of questions. Creation deals with God's relationship to the world: God created all things, and he is always intimately present to them. Evolution describes the mechanisms by which species came to be over millions of years. There is no *necessary* tension between the idea of creation and the idea of evolution.

2. Genesis 1 does not necessarily commit Christians to a six-day (144-hour) creation event. Neither does it exclude the idea of evolution. In his *Literal Commentary on Genesis*, Augustine exegetes the Genesis stories to show how God created all things at once instantaneously, but also how God created some of those things fully developed (like the angels), while he gave power to the earth to bring forth others over time (like plants and humans). This is not the modern theory of evolution (which speaks of species transforming into other

It is this ambiguity that warranted the inclusion of the phrase "of all things visible and invisible." As we have seen already, Gnostics and others often said there were different makers for different realms. There was a Father of the heavenly realm, but also a malevolent Demiurge of the earthly realm. Or our souls came from a source of light, whereas our bodies came from a source of darkness. Alternatively, in a polytheistic culture, invisible spirits—whether God's rivals, equals, or subordinates—could be *ontologically* equal to God rather than his creatures. To preclude such heresies, the Creed states emphatically that God is the maker of "heaven and earth," which includes "all things visible and invisible."

God created all the visible things, from the life-giving sun to the blood-sucking mosquito. This claim would be quite offensive to those of a Gnostic

species), but it is an early and influential *literal* interpretation of Genesis with an evolutionary sensibility.[a]

3. Genesis teaches us the meaning of creation and human existence. Evolution tells us how creation and human existence developed over time. While evolution may describe how the human body came to be, it cannot account for the rational soul, which transcends material reality and comes directly from God. Evolution also cannot teach us our purpose or the meaning of life.

4. The *Catechism* makes rather modest claims about what Catholics should believe about the garden story and the historical Adam and Eve: "The account of the fall in Genesis 3 uses figurative language, but affirms a primeval event, a deed that took place at the beginning of the history of man."[b]

5. The *Catechism* reminds us what is ultimately important when working through these complex questions of faith and science: "Though faith is above reason, there can never be any real discrepancy between faith and reason. Since the same God who reveals mysteries and infuses faith has bestowed the light of reason on the human mind, God cannot deny himself, nor can truth ever contradict truth."[c]

a. Augustine, *Literal Interpretation of Genesis* 4–6.
b. CCC 390.
c. CCC 159.

LEX ORANDI

Worshiping with the Angels

The liturgy amply attests to the reality of angels and their part in worship. The prayers of the *Roman Missal* speak of "countless angels" whom we join in praising God:

> Through Christ the Angels praise your majesty,
> Dominions adore and Powers tremble before you.
> Heaven and the Virtues of heaven and the blessed Seraphim
> worship together with exultation.
> May our voices, we pray, join with theirs
> in humble praise, as we acclaim:
> Holy, Holy, Holy Lord God of hosts . . .[a]

An angel is also instrumental in making the Eucharist an acceptable sacrifice. In Eucharistic Prayer I, the priest prays,

> In humble prayer we ask you, almighty God:
> command that these gifts be borne
> by the hands of your holy Angel
> to your altar on high
> in the sight of your divine majesty,
> so that all of us, who through this participation at the altar
> receive the most holy Body and Blood of your Son,
> may be filled with every grace and heavenly blessing.[b]

a. *Roman Missal*, 552.
b. *Roman Missal*, 310.

bent, who would not want to attribute miserable things like mosquitoes to the good God. For orthodox Christians, though, while we find these creatures annoying or harmful and may wonder how they serve God's providence, we must affirm that God made them. And if God made them, then they are good.

The invisible things the Creed likely has in mind are angelic beings.[31] In the Christian tradition, some of these angels are good and some are not, but all of them were created by God. The evil ones are good by nature, because God

31. For a good survey of the biblical and patristic understanding of angels, see Jean Daniélou, *The Angels and Their Mission: According to the Fathers of the Church*, trans. David Heimann (1957; repr., Allen, TX: Christian Classics, 1982). For a more systematic account, see

created them, but bad by their choice. The Bible gives abundant testimony to the existence of angels and their providential role in God's plan. To name just a few examples, angels appear to the patriarchs at key moments (Gen. 22:11; 28:12), they lead the Israelites out of Egypt (Exod. 14:19), and they attend the prophets (1 Kings 19:5; Isa. 6:6). Angels appear at the annunciation of Christ's incarnation (Luke 1:26), his birth (2:13), his temptation in the desert (both bad and good angels, Mark 1:13), his agony in the garden (Luke 22:43), his resurrection (John 20:12–13), and his ascension (Acts 1:10–11). Jesus tells us that children have guardian angels who always behold the face of God (Matt. 18:10), and he also speaks about the role of angels in the final judgment (24:31; 25:31). The angels surround God's throne, singing "Holy, holy, holy" (Isa. 6:3), and we join their hymn of praise every time we worship. While angels did not create the universe, they are charged with governing it (cf. Rom. 8:38–39; Eph. 1:16–21). Early Christians believed that angels were involved in all aspects of creation and providence. The Creed enjoins upon us the belief not only that this invisible world exists (which few ancient persons would have doubted), but that God made it all.

The Logic of Creation from Nothing

By the time of the Nicene Creed, "maker of heaven and earth" was firmly understood to mean that God created all things, without exception, *from nothing*. But, surprising to many of us, *creatio ex nihilo* was not a doctrine held by the earliest Christians nor by the Jews who preceded them. Indeed, along with many of their pagan neighbors, they held that God created all things from preexistent matter. The question of the origin of matter—and its implications for God's being and power—did not arise in a clear way until the second century.[32] When Christians started arguing that God created all things *ex nihilo* (contrary to everyone else), it was a radical and bold move.

Scripture alone does not clearly resolve the question of the origin of matter. Genesis 1:2, which speaks of "the earth [being] without form and void" and the deep waters, was interpreted by ancient Jews and many early Christians to mean that God created the world from preexisting matter. This is also the

Serge-Thomas Bonino, *Angels and Demons: A Catholic Introduction*, trans. Michael J. Miller (Washington, DC: Catholic University of America Press, 2007).

32. See Gerhard May's excellent and accessible study of this question, *Creatio Ex Nihilo: The Doctrine of "Creation out of Nothing" in Early Christian Thought*, trans. A. S. Worrall (London: T&T Clark, 2004). For further study, see Paul Blowers, *Drama of the Divine Economy: Creator and Creation in Early Christian Theology and Piety* (Oxford: Oxford University Press, 2012).

consensus of modern biblical scholars. This reading of Genesis seems to be presupposed by the author of the Wisdom of Solomon, who refers to God's "all-powerful hand, which created the world out of formless matter" (Wis. 11:17). While these passages do not definitively rule out *creatio ex nihilo*, neither do they confirm it.

Other passages in Scripture sound more like what we today understand as creation from nothing. The most famous passage comes from 2 Maccabees, where the mother of the seven martyrs connects God's power to create with his power to resurrect her martyred sons. The mother exhorts her son,

> I beseech you, my child, to look at the heaven and the earth and see everything that is in them, and recognize that God did not make them out of things that existed. Thus also mankind comes into being. Do not fear this butcher, but prove worthy of your brothers. Accept death, so that in God's mercy I may get you back again with your brothers. (2 Macc. 7:28–29)

Paul is certainly echoing this sentiment when he says in Romans, "[God] gives life to the dead and calls into existence the things that do not exist" (Rom. 4:17; see also Heb. 11:3). The God who has the power to create all things from what did not exist certainly has the power to raise to life those who have ceased to live.

By the second and third centuries, these texts were taken as evidence of *creatio ex nihilo*.[33] Yet these passages were not decisive. The language used here is similar to the philosophical language of the Stoics and the Platonists. These philosophers held that matter always was there and that God gave form to matter, which, because it was formless, did not properly have the status of existing ("to ex-ist" means, literally, "to stand out"). But in light of the challenges of philosophy and Gnosticism, Christians in the second century asked more clearly about the extent of God's almighty power and the origin of matter. By working through these challenges, Christians drew out what was implicit in Scripture and their beliefs about God.

To see the logic of *creatio ex nihilo*, it will be helpful to think with Hermogenes, a little-known heretic of the second century who is featured in a polemical treatise by Tertullian. He was a teacher of Christianity and, like many educated Christians, was well-versed in Stoic and Platonist philosophy. Hermogenes believed, in accordance with Scripture, that God made all things. But, he wondered, *from what* did God make all things? Hermogenes offers

---

33. See, for example, Origen, *On First Principles* 2.1.5.

three possibilities: God made all things out of himself, out of something else, or out of nothing. Again, Scripture on its own does not decide this question. Hermogenes argues in favor of the second option, Tertullian the last. Let us consider the logic of all three.

The first option is that God creates out of himself. This would mean that God takes some part of his own substance and forms it into the world that we know.[34] If, in the beginning, God is all there is, then his own substance is the only material available to create from. Variations of this view can be found in pantheistic movements, as well as Gnostic ones, where the world is identified with the divine or understood as an attenuated form of it. Both Hermogenes and Tertullian reject this option. God is transcendent and one. God is unchangeable and indivisible. God is simple, and he cannot divide some of his substance to make the world. This conception of creation is unworthy of God.

The second option—the one favored by Hermogenes—is that God creates the world out of something already existing. This idea, as noted above, was the predominant idea in the ancient world, held by pagan philosophers, Jews, and early Christians alike. It is imaginable and even logical, considered on the analogy of human creating. A human artisan—a sculptor, for example—takes raw material that already exists (wood, stone, marble) and shapes it according to an idea in his mind. On this analogy, God is understood to be powerful enough to shape the whole universe from formless matter and even give it life, but the material is already there, available for him to work with. This view was given philosophical weight by Plato's famous dialogue *Timaeus*, which had a long reception in pagan, Jewish, and Christian thought. *Timaeus* offers a vision of three principles of creation: a creator God, preexisting matter, and the Ideas or Forms of things. Jews and early Christians saw *Timaeus* as compatible with certain readings of Genesis and other testimonies of Scripture.

Hermogenes adds two additional arguments rooted in his Christian faith to support his view that God created from something.[35] He argues that Christians must hold not only that God is always God but that God is always Lord. If God is always Lord, then he must be Lord over something. Hermogenes argues that God must be Lord over the eternal formless matter. Hermogenes's second argument pertains to the problem of evil. If there is only a good God who creates all things from no other source, then there would be no way to explain the origin of evil. All things, he thinks, would be good. Hermogenes

---

34. Tertullian, *Against Hermogenes* 2.
35. See Tertullian, *Against Hermogenes* 2–3.

The Problem of Evil

If God is a loving Father, why does he permit evil and suffering? If God is almighty, why doesn't he do something about them? If a good God created all things, where does evil come from? Christians and others have always asked some form of these questions, though they have been made particularly acute again after the horrors of the twentieth century.

Augustine famously wrestled with the problem of evil before his conversion. The turning point came when he finally asked, "What is evil?" Evil, he discovers, does not exist. It is nothing, no-thing. Evil does not have a nature. It is not a substance that God created; rather, evil is a perversion of something good God created.

Even the devil is good by nature. God created him as a blessed angel, so he, like everything else God made, is good. The devil is evil by choice, by turning away from God. The devil perverted his own goodness by wanting to be good by himself without God. So, by nature, the devil is still good because he is a creature of God; but by his continued rejection of God, he is evil.

The example of the devil tells us much about the origin of evil: the angelic and human will. Evil arises when a lesser good is chosen over a greater good or when we mistake something as good that is not. In the garden, humans are presented with a choice of whether to obey God or to eat fruit that will (seemingly) make them divine. Their decision has affected each and every one of us.

Should God have stopped them? Should God intervene every time something evil is about to happen? Or should he just remove

rejects *creatio ex nihilo* because there must be preexisting matter, independent of God, which can account for evil in the world.

Tertullian sees the weakness of Hermogenes's Christian rationalization of the common view of creation from preexisting matter. Tertullian draws out more coherently what is implicit in the biblical witness. How can God be almighty, as Scripture repeatedly says, if he does not have power to bring matter into existence?[36] Moreover, if matter exists independently of God, then

36. Tertullian, *Against Hermogenes* 8.

or alter the part of us that thinks or chooses evil? Most of us would, rightly, not want that kind of world. So we must accept a certain amount of evil and suffering as the price of freedom. God does. For, ultimately, God wants us to love him, and love cannot be forced; it must be freely given.

Suffering, too, is a mystery, especially when we are in the midst of it. But we can make some sense of it. Often, in retrospect, we find suffering beneficial: a coach drives us hard and we become a better athlete; we experience a serious emotional pain as a youth and realize later that we have become wiser; we struggle through hard readings and rage against a blank screen only to produce a fine essay in the end. Good comes from suffering. Paul even says we should "rejoice in our sufferings, knowing that suffering produces endurance, and endurance produces character, and character produces hope, and hope does not disappoint us" (Rom. 5:3–5). If this is true of our daily life struggles, can it also be true of more tragic human events like mass genocide or the loss of a child?

God is almighty, which means that he can draw good even out of the nothingness of evil. When we experience profound suffering or evil, it is difficult, maybe even impossible, to see this. But reflection on our experience teaches us that this can be true. And our faith teaches us this even more clearly. "For God so loved the world that he gave his only-begotten Son, that whoever believes in him should not perish but have eternal life" (John 3:16 RSV-2CE). Out of love, God came to us in the flesh, and we killed him. This is the greatest evil ever committed. Yet from the greatest evil, God brought the greatest good: the salvation of the whole world.

God is ruler by force and not by creative power. That is, he must impose his will on something other, rather than bringing into existence what properly belongs to him. Matter would not belong to God; it would belong to itself. Even if God could do as he pleased with it, preexisting matter would always be an ontological limit on God's sovereignty. And God would either have to borrow or take it for his own purposes. Tertullian argues that preexistent matter would mean that God lacks something that matter supplies. Imagine, on this account, what would happen to God or creation if matter did not always exist: God would be idle forever! Finally, Tertullian argues, if matter exists eternally, then it must have some kind of divine quality. This, in effect, gives us two gods.[37] Indeed, Tertullian argues that on Hermogenes's account, matter is the helper of God, and so it is in some sense superior!

The affirmation of *creatio ex nihilo* means that creation is not divine and that God did not need any other principle to help him create. Rather, God is so powerful that he can bring into existence the matter as well as the forms of things. Early Christians had to develop the biblical and philosophical traditions they inherited. The principles of "one God" and "Father almighty" and "maker of heaven and earth" were present, but their meaning was not fully appreciated until the question of the origin of matter was made explicit. If there is one God who is utterly simple, unchangeable, and lacking in nothing, then he must be the source of all that exists. If God is "the Father almighty," then he has the power to do what he wills. Because these things are true about God, it *necessarily* follows that he is the maker of all things from nothing.

The Radical Meaning of the Christian Understanding of Creation

The ancient errors about God and creation are rooted in a tendency to reduce God to another being in the world. This is understandable and common. The world provides the setting in which we understand things. It is natural to think of God as the highest thing in the world, a superior being within the cosmos. This tendency arises not just in philosophical speculations of ancient pagans, Jews, and Christians, but even in our everyday thinking about these questions.[38]

Children (and, let's be honest, adults) often wonder what God was doing before he created the world. And we imagine God (as an old man or as a light-filled cloudy mass) creating the universe by looking out into blank space and making things within it. These imaginative efforts make God subject to time and space. They put God on the timeline of creation and contain him within the space of the universe.

It was a radical and bold move in second-century Christianity to say that God is not the highest thing in the world but rather the radically transcendent creator of it. He is not subject to time or space but is the creator of time and space. Creation is not ultimate, so that God finds a place within it. God is not

---

37. Tertullian, *Against Hermogenes* 4.
38. The following is indebted to Msgr. Robert Sokolowski's brilliant discussion in *The God of Faith and Reason: Foundations of Christian Theology* (Washington, DC: Catholic University of America Press, 1995).

a being that is situated within creation; rather, he is the source of all creation and all the beings found within it.

God is always God and does not need to create. God could be God without creation. Indeed, creation adds nothing to God's goodness or happiness or being. But God does create the world, and, since it did not have to be, we must believe that God *chose* it to exist. Creation is radically contingent. God does not create out of need or loneliness or a desire for fulfillment. The God Christians believe in does not lack anything. This means that God chooses to create only out of his own goodness in order to share his goodness with others.

The Christian understanding of creation makes possible the doctrines of the Trinity and the incarnation. It is only by radicalizing God's transcendence and showing the contingency of creation that the conceptual space opens up for a three-in-one God and a Savior who is true God and true man at the same time. Only because God is not a part of the whole, but the transcendent creator of the whole, is it possible to say that one God can also be three. In the world, each thing is its own thing. Each person is a countable individual. But God is not a part of the world, so it is not a contradiction to say that each person of the Trinity is fully God and yet there is only one God. It is also not a contradiction to say that Christ is God who became man and that he became man without any diminution of his divinity and without any compromise to his humanity. Only if God is not a part of the world and therefore not in competition with it can he unite himself to it in such a perfect union.

Living the Mystery

"You made us for yourself," Augustine famously says, "and our heart is restless until it comes to rest in you."[39] Augustine's Latin is quite striking here: God makes us *ad te*, which can mean "for yourself" or "toward yourself." God made us with a dynamic orientation *toward* himself. He made us with a "God torque" or with a kind of magnetism that makes us naturally drawn to him. He also made us *for* himself. That is, God is our final end, our highest good, our destination. God is where we find our fulfillment in life. This is how God made each and every human being.

Yet we are restless. Why? For Augustine, we are restless because we are not fully in communion with God. Everything in creation has its place: birds have nests, foxes have dens, and sea monsters have the deep. Everything seeks its

---

39. Augustine, *Confessions* 1.1.1 (Williams, 1).

natural place: fire goes up, rocks go down. When something is not in its place, it is restless. The fish out of water flails until it returns to its place; the caged bird longs to fly. But what is the place of the human being? Physically, our place is the land, but where is our place spiritually? We belong with God. But we have been exiled from our place. We are strangers in a strange land who long for home. The more we sin, the further we wander. So we are restless. We pine for God, "as in a dry and weary land where no water is" (Ps. 63:1). We find no rest until we find God, the "place" where God created our heart to rest.

But how do we make progress toward our destination? Augustine's famous quote gives us the clue: he uses the phrase "our heart," which is a subtle reference to the eucharistic liturgy. In Augustine's time, as well as ours, the priest says, "Lift up your heart," and the people respond, "We lift it up to the Lord." In the Eucharist, we lift up our one ecclesial heart so that it can be in heaven where it belongs and we get a foretaste of the rest we so desire. On the Feast of Corpus Christi, we hear a prayer that captures this beautifully: "Grant, O Lord, that we may delight for all eternity in that share in your divine life, which is foreshadowed in the present age by our reception of your precious Body and Blood."[40]

The eucharistic liturgy is a profound reminder of the meaning of creation. Because God did not have to create, creation itself—and our existence as created beings—must be understood as a completely unmerited gift. The nature of reality is gift. And the proper response to a gift is gratitude. God has given us all and asks that we return all in gratitude. For "it is truly right and just, our duty and our salvation, always and everywhere to give you thanks, Lord, holy Father, almighty and eternal God."[41] That is why we celebrate the Eucharist, a word and action that means "thanksgiving."

In the eucharistic liturgy, we are taught and enabled to offer back to God what he has given us:

> Blessed are you, Lord God of all creation,
> for through your goodness we have received
> the bread we offer you:
> fruit of the earth and work of human hands,
> it will become for us the bread of life.[42]

God gives us the gifts that we give back to him. We add our work and ingenuity (also God's gifts) to the gifts of bread and wine, which God, in turn, receives

---

40. *Roman Missal*, 501.
41. *Roman Missal*, 205.
42. *Roman Missal*, 528. A similar prayer is said over the wine.

and transforms again into himself. We, too, like the bread and wine, are invited to be transformed. By uniting ourselves to the Eucharist, we become what we receive. As another prayer from the *Roman Missal* beautifully says, "Grant that *we ourselves* may become a sacrifice acceptable to you for the salvation of all the world."[43]

We will rest in God when we are in our place—that is, in full communion with God. We will be at rest when God is "everything to everyone" or, as older translations put it, "all in all" (1 Cor. 15:28). The God who made us wants to remake us, and our re-creation will mean a more perfect union with God.

> O God, who wonderfully created the dignity of human nature
> and still more wonderfully restored it,
> grant, we pray,
> that we may share in the divinity of Christ,
> who humbled himself to share in our humanity.[44]

Our destiny, as well as the destiny of all creation, is to be transformed in Christ. God wants to create a new heaven and a new earth where our transformed hearts can find true rest. We get a foretaste of that destiny every time we lift up our hearts and offer them to God in the Eucharist.

43. *Roman Missal*, 952.
44. *Roman Missal*, 175.

CHAPTER 3

GOD *the* SON DIVINE

Introduction

We now embark on the second main section of the Creed, centered on the identity of Jesus the Son. The Creed seeks to answer the same question that people were asking in Jesus's own day: "Who is Jesus?" When Jesus enters Jerusalem on Palm Sunday, the whole city is asking, "Who is this?" (Matt. 21:10). The Jewish leaders challenge Jesus, asking him directly, "Who are you?" (John 8:25). Jesus himself questions his disciples, "Who do people say that the Son of Man is?" (Matt. 16:13 NRSV). The disciples give the range of opinions they are hearing—John the Baptist, Elijah, Jeremiah, or one of the prophets. Jesus then puts the question to them: "But who do you say that I am?" Peter answers, "You are the Christ, the Son of the living God" (Matt. 16:15–16). Peter gets it right.

The opening lines of the creedal statement on the Son basically sum up Peter's answer. It is crucial to see that the confession of the Creed begins with the *scriptural revelation* of Jesus the Son, using biblical titles to display the true identity of Jesus. Only then does the Creed employ a nonbiblical expression to sharpen and clarify our understanding of who Jesus is.

In this chapter we are exploring the first half of the section on the Son. It centers on who Jesus is in relation to God his Father—that is, on his *divine* identity. In the next chapter, we will examine the testimony of the Creed about Jesus's earthly ministry from his incarnation through his ascension and the promise of his glorious return.

I Believe in One Lord Jesus Christ

I believe in one Lord Jesus Christ, the Only Begotten Son of God,	Et in unum Dominum Iesum Christum, Filium Dei Unigenitum,	καὶ εἰς ἕνα κύριον Ἰησοῦν Χριστόν, τὸν υἱὸν τοῦ Θεοῦ τὸν μονογενῆ,

OT: Exod. 3:13–15; 1 Chron. 17:13; Ps. 2:7; Isa. 45:22–23

NT: John 1:14, 18; 3:16, 18; 20:28; 1 Cor. 2:8; 8:6; 12:3; Phil. 2:11

Catechism: God sends the Son, 422–29; Jesus, 430–35; Christ, 436–40; Son of God, 441–45; Lord, 446–51

Theological Exposition

One Lord Jesus Christ

In our recitation of the Nicene Creed today, we begin this section by repeating "I believe," but in both the Latin and the Greek versions, the statement "I/we believe" is assumed, and the text just begins, "And in one Lord Jesus Christ." These three biblical names/titles provide the core understanding of who Jesus is.

"Jesus," of course, is the proper name of this person, the name he received at birth and the name by which he was called during his entire life. The name, however, was not chosen by his parents but given to Joseph by the angel: "Do not fear to take Mary your wife, for that which is conceived in her is of the Holy Spirit; she will bear a son, and you shall call his name Jesus, for he will save his people from their sins" (Matt. 1:20–21). This name in Hebrew is *Yeshua* (Joshua), and it means "YHWH saves." These four Hebrew letters, YHWH, stand for the divine name, commonly vocalized as "Yahweh" (see Exod. 3:13–16). The name "Jesus," then, is perfectly suited to the identity and call of this human child, because in him the God of Israel himself has come to save his people from their sins.

The title "Christ" translates a Greek word (*Christos*) that means "anointed one" (in Hebrew, *mashiakh*). In the Old Testament, this title could refer to several different figures,[1] but by the time of Jesus it was applied predominantly to the longed-for son of David—the "Messiah"—who would reign as king over

---

1. For example, the title "messiah" can refer to the high priest (Lev. 6:22), to the royal son of David (Ps. 18:50), and even to a pagan king such as Cyrus (Isa. 45:1).

his people in righteousness. When Jesus is identified as "the son of David" in the Gospels, this is another way of calling him "the Messiah."[2] The opening line of Matthew's Gospel makes this connection explicit: "The book of the genealogy of Jesus Christ, the son of David" (Matt. 1:1). And this is just what Peter confessed—"You are the Christ"—when Jesus asked, "Who do you say that I am?" (16:15–16). And while Jesus received the title "Messiah" as belonging to him (see John 4:25–26) and confessed it solemnly before the high priest and the Sanhedrin (see Mark 14:61–62), he had to work hard to communicate the true mission of the Messiah. The people were expecting an earthly king who would overthrow their despised enemies; Jesus came to bring God's kingdom on earth not by reigning as an earthly king but by bringing God's full redemption from sin and coming to reign as the heavenly king.

This brings us to the significance of the title "Lord" in the creedal phrase "one *Lord* Jesus Christ." What does this add? The term "lord" in the Bible can indicate simply a title of respect and honor—Jesus is called "lord" in just this way (e.g., Matt. 8:2; John 4:11).[3] But the word "LORD" (printed with small capital letters) was also used in the Old Testament to name the God of Israel himself. When the divine name (YHWH) appears in the Old Testament Scriptures, Jewish readers, out of reverence, substitute the word "Lord" (Adonai) instead of vocalizing this name.[4] One noteworthy instance appears in the prophet Isaiah: "I am the LORD, and there is no other. . . . 'To me every knee shall bow, every tongue shall swear'" (Isa. 45:18, 23). When Paul proclaims "that at the name of Jesus every knee should bow, in heaven and on earth and under the earth, and every tongue confess that *Jesus Christ is Lord*, to the glory of God the Father" (Phil. 2:10–11), he is alluding to this passage in Isaiah and pointing directly to the divine identity of Jesus. The title "Lord" belongs to God alone, but now to *Jesus* every knee will bow and every tongue will confess that he is Lord. The apostle Thomas, when confronted with the risen Jesus, also uses the title "Lord" as an acknowledgment of Jesus's divinity: "My Lord and my God!" (John 20:28).

The phrases "Jesus Christ," "Christ Jesus," and "Lord Jesus Christ" appear numerous times in nearly all the books of the New Testament.[5] But the

2. For Jesus as the "son of David" in the Gospels, see, for example, Matt. 1:1; 9:27; 15:22; 20:30; 21:9; Mark 10:47–48; Luke 1:32.

3. To capture this sense of respect, *kyrie* is translated "Sir" in John 4:11 by the RSV and RSV-2CE.

4. In many contemporary translations of the Bible, the word "Lord" is written with small capital letters (LORD) to indicate the presence of the divine name YHWH.

5. The phrases "Jesus Christ" and "Christ Jesus" occur more than 250 times in the New Testament; the combined phrase "Lord Jesus Christ" occurs more than 60 times.

LEX ORANDI

"All Hail the Power of Jesus' Name"

The hymn "All Hail the Power of Jesus' Name" powerfully expresses in praise and worship what we confess in faith about the lordship and divinity of Jesus:

> All hail the power of Jesus' name!
> Let angels prostrate fall.
> Bring forth the royal diadem,
> and crown him Lord of all.
> Bring forth the royal diadem,
> and crown him Lord of all!
>
> Oh, that with all the sacred throng
> we at his feet may fall!
> We'll join the everlasting song
> and crown him Lord of all.
> We'll join the everlasting song
> and crown him Lord of all.[a]

a. Edward Perronet, "All Hail the Power of Jesus' Name," Hymnary.org, accessed January 20, 2023, https://hymnary.org/text/all_hail_the_power_of_jesus_name_let.

precise phrase in the Creed, "one Lord Jesus Christ," appears just once in the New Testament: "Yet for us there is one God, the Father, from whom are all things and for whom we exist, and *one Lord, Jesus Christ*, through whom are all things and through whom we exist" (1 Cor. 8:6).[6] Many scholars believe that Paul here refers to the great confession of the oneness of God found in Deuteronomy 6:4 (known as the Shema): "Hear, O Israel: The LORD our God is one LORD." By expanding this confession and naming Jesus as the "one Lord" who sustains all things, Paul locates the Son within the Godhead as fully divine and worthy of divine honor. And so when we confess the phrase "I believe in one Lord Jesus Christ," all of this biblical revelation resides within this phrase. Jesus is "the God who saves," born as a child on the earth; he is the Christ, the son of David, who has come to bring the fullness of the kingdom of God; and he is truly Lord, the divine Son who is worthy of our adoration.

6. The main difference between the text from Paul and the creedal statement is that the former is in the nominative case (i.e., it is the subject of the sentence) and the latter is in the accusative case (i.e., it is the direct object of the sentence).

WITNESS TO THE TRADITION

Irenaeus on the Oneness of Jesus Christ

Writing at the end of the second century, Saint Irenaeus rejects the view that "Jesus" and "the Christ" are two distinct entities. He insists that there is just one Lord Jesus Christ who is both divine and human. Jesus simply *is* the Word of God made flesh. Referring to the baptism of Jesus, Irenaeus writes the following:

> For Christ did not at that time descend upon Jesus, neither was Christ one and Jesus another: but the Word of God—who is the Saviour of all, and the ruler of heaven and earth, who is Jesus, as I have already pointed out, who did also take upon Him flesh, and was anointed by the Spirit from the Father—was made Jesus Christ. . . . For inasmuch as the Word of God was man from the root of Jesse, and son of Abraham, in this respect did the Spirit of God rest upon Him, and anoint Him to preach the Gospel to the lowly. But inasmuch as He was God, He did not judge according to glory, nor reprove after the manner of speech.[a]

a. Irenaeus, *Against Heresies* 3.9.3 (ANF 1:493).

The inclusion of the word "one" ("*one* Lord Jesus Christ") also reflects a doctrinal concern to ensure that we do not divide Jesus Christ into two figures or persons. In the second century, the Church had to contend with Gnostic teaching that distinguished between "the Christ," who came from above, and the man "Jesus," who came from the earth. A similar tendency emerged in the third and fourth centuries when some Christian leaders taught that Jesus was a mere man who was adopted and filled by the Word of God but who remained a distinct human person, separate from the divine Word. This brought about a disjunction between the eternal Word, on the one hand, and the man Jesus, on the other. This view of Jesus, known as †adoptionism, was decisively rejected by the Church.[7] And to counter any such notion, the Creed

7. Adoptionism was attributed principally to Paul of Samosata, whose teaching was condemned in 268 at the Council of Antioch: "The basic criticism of Paul . . . is that he differentiated between the one who is Jesus Christ and the other who is the Word" (John Behr, *The Formation of Christian Theology*, vol. 1, *The Way to Nicaea* [Crestwood, NY: St. Vladimir's Seminary Press, 2001], 227). The specter of adoptionism, of separating Jesus from the Word, was also charged (fairly or not) against the bishop Marcellus of Ancyra in the mid-fourth century, contributing to the concern to ensure a confession of "*one* Lord Jesus Christ."

confesses that our Lord Jesus Christ is "one" and undivided. Jesus is not a man who was at some point adopted by the Word of God; he *is* the Word who has become a man: "And the Word became flesh" (John 1:14).

The Only-Begotten Son of God

The second phrase of the creedal statement on the Son fills out the identity of the one recognized as "one Lord Jesus Christ." The designation "Son of God" is one of the most commonly used titles for Jesus in the New Testament.[8] When we hear this title, we tend to think immediately of Jesus's *divine* identity, but in fact it designates his *human* identity as well. As the *Catechism* observes, "In the Old Testament, '*son of God*' is a title given to the angels, the Chosen People, the children of Israel, and their kings."[9] In the prophet Hosea, the people of Israel are designated as God's "son": "When Israel was a child, I loved him, and out of Egypt I called my son" (Hosea 11:1). It is no coincidence that Matthew quotes this passage when relaying the story of Jesus and the Holy Family fleeing to Egypt (Matt. 2:15). Jesus is the new Israel who also comes out of Egypt.

But in a special way, the title "son" was bestowed on the son of David (i.e., the Messiah). We see this clearly expressed in Psalm 2:7: "He said to me, 'You are my son, today I have begotten you.'"[10] The Magnificat also expresses this link between the Son of God and the heir of David: "He will be great, and will be called the Son of the Most High; and the Lord God will give to him the throne of his father David" (Luke 1:32). And so, according to his *humanity*, as the true Israel and the anointed son of David, Jesus is uniquely "the Son of God."

Jesus, though, is also "the Son of God" according to his *divinity*. We see this in the event of the transfiguration, in which Jesus appears in the radiance of divine glory and the Father says, "This is my beloved Son, with whom I am well pleased" (Matt. 17:5). And when the Roman centurion confesses at the cross, "Truly this was the Son of God" (27:54), he almost certainly has in mind a divine-like sonship. This divine sonship of Jesus is especially underlined in the Fourth Gospel. For John, the *Logos*, who *is* God and who was *with* God at the beginning (John 1:1), is the "only-begotten" (Greek *monogenēs*) Son:

8. The title "Son of God" as applied to Jesus occurs more than forty times in the New Testament.

9. CCC 441.

10. Psalm 2 is recognized as a "messianic psalm"—that is, a psalm about David's kingly heirs. The New Testament applies Ps. 2:7 to Jesus on several occasions (see, e.g., Acts 13:33; Heb. 1:5; 5:5).

Through the Son

In the collect for the Tuesday of the third week of Advent, the Church acknowledges that the Father has made us a new creation through his "Only Begotten Son," and it prays that at his coming we might be cleansed from every stain of our old way of life. This prayer is made "through our Lord Jesus Christ." The Church prays as it believes, and it believes and confesses as it prays.

> O God, who through your Only Begotten Son
> have made us a new creation,
> look kindly, we pray,
> on the handiwork of your mercy,
> and at your Son's coming
> cleanse us from every stain of the old way of life.
> Through our Lord Jesus Christ, your Son,
> who lives and reigns with you in the unity of the Holy Spirit,
> God, for ever and ever.[a]

a. *Roman Missal*, 155 (modified).

"We have beheld his glory, glory as of the only Son [*monogenēs*] from the Father" (1:14).[11] Later, when describing the Father sending the Son into the world, John again employs this key word to describe the unique divine identity of the Son: "For God so loved the world that he gave his only-begotten [*monogenēs*] Son, that whoever believes in him should not perish but have eternal life" (John 3:16 RSV-2CE; see also 3:18). According to Bishop Robert Barron, "When the Creed, reflecting this biblical consensus, refers to Jesus as the 'Only Begotten Son of God,' . . . it is insisting that Jesus the Son shares divinity with the Father who sent him, 'Son' and 'sent' in no way implying ontological inferiority to the Father and Sender."[12]

---

11. The term *monogenēs* can be translated "only-begotten" (RSV-2CE) or "only" (ESV, NRSV, NABRE), meaning "unique." Many contemporary scholars argue that "only" is the best translation, giving the sense of Jesus as the unique and only Son, which is certainly true. But the Creed, confessing that Jesus is "begotten, not made," underlines Jesus's unique and eternal divine sonship as the "only-begotten" Son of the Father.

12. Robert Barron, *Light from Light: A Theological Reflection on the Nicene Creed* (Park Ridge, IL: Word on Fire Academic, 2021), 50.

So when the Creed identifies Jesus as "the Only Begotten Son of God," it is using this common scriptural title to point to Jesus's human and divine identity at the same time. In Jesus "the Son of God," the human son descended from Abraham and David (see Matt. 1:2–17) is at one and the same time the divine Son who has come down from the Father (see John 6:38). He is "one" Son of God, who, in his single personal identity, unites and embodies both the human and the divine.

Living the Mystery

When we confess the words of the Creed—"I believe in one Lord Jesus Christ"—we are doing much more than just making a statement that we happen to believe is true. We are making a *declaration* of commitment made possible by the Holy Spirit acting within us, renouncing all other claimants and announcing the lordship and reign of Jesus Christ.

The phrase "Jesus is Lord" is the gospel message proclaimed in miniature. Paul recognizes this when he says, "For what we preach is not ourselves, but *Jesus Christ as Lord*" (2 Cor. 4:5). That message is also found on the lips of the faithful: "If you confess with your lips that *Jesus is Lord* and believe in your heart that God raised him from the dead, you will be saved" (Rom. 10:9). This announcement of Jesus's lordship is only possible because the Holy Spirit that we have received leads us to say this: "Therefore I want you to understand that no one speaking by the Spirit of God ever says 'Jesus be cursed!' and no one can say '*Jesus is Lord*' except by the Holy Spirit" (1 Cor. 12:3). Anyone, of course, can say the words "Jesus is Lord," but only those who have the Holy Spirit can proclaim this in faith as heralds of the gospel.

When we acknowledge that Jesus is Lord, we are also joining the entire creation in an act of profound worship. At the present time, only a small proportion of people proclaim this, but there will come a day when all people, even all of creation, will confess Jesus as Lord of all: "Therefore God has highly exalted him and bestowed on him the name which is above every name, that at the name of Jesus every knee should bow, in heaven and on earth and under the earth, and every tongue confess that *Jesus Christ is Lord*, to the glory of God the Father" (Phil. 2:9–11).

To acknowledge that Jesus is Lord is also to take a stand against other claimants to sovereignty. It is, in a sense, an act of war against all other human and spiritual powers that would place themselves in the position of "Lord." When Satan tempts Jesus in the wilderness, he offers him all the kingdoms of the world if he will only bow down and worship Satan himself: "All these I will give you, if you will fall down and worship me" (Matt. 4:9). Jesus refuses and banishes the devil; we do the same when we bow down and worship Jesus as Lord. Human authorities too often seek a kind of lordship over their citizens. Both Paul and Peter teach the faithful to "honor" the emperor (Rom. 13:7; 1 Pet. 2:17), but only God is to be feared and worshiped. Many Christians in the first centuries of the Church died as martyrs because of their refusal to acknowledge Caesar as Lord. We are called to imitate their faithful confession and to thereby prepare ourselves for martyrdom—that is, for the witness before the world that Jesus is Lord.

When we confess and proclaim that Jesus Christ is Lord, we are also calling upon his lordship to be active in our lives individually and corporately as the Church. There is a power unleashed when we call upon the name of Jesus and acclaim him as Lord: "And whatever you do, in word or deed, do everything in the name of the Lord Jesus, giving thanks to God the Father through him" (Col. 3:17).

Born of the Father before All Ages

Born of the Father before all ages, God from God, Light from Light, true God from true God, begotten, not made.	et ex Patre natum ante omnia saecula, Deum de Deo, lumen de lumine, Deum verum de Deo vero, genitum, non factum.	τὸν ἐκ τοῦ πατρὸς γεννηθέντα πρὸ πάντων τῶν αἰώνων, φῶς ἐκ φωτός, Θεὸν ἀληθινὸν ἐκ Θεοῦ ἀληθινοῦ, γεννηθέντα οὐ ποιηθέντα.

OT: Pss. 2:7; 27:1; Prov. 8:25
NT: John 1:1, 9; 12:46; 20:28; Acts 13:33; Heb. 1:3, 5, 9; Jude 25; Rev. 5:12–14; 21:23
Catechism: the Son begotten of the Father, 242, 465, 467, 663

Theological Exposition

Born of the Father before All Ages; Begotten, Not Made

This section of the Creed is bracketed in its opening and closing lines by the words "born" and "begotten," so we will treat these two statements together. In our English translation we say "born of the Father" and "begotten, not made," but in the original Greek text of the Creed the same word is used in both expressions (*gennaō*, "to beget").[13] This Greek term was chosen carefully to designate the origin of the Son from the Father: the Son was *born* or *begotten* of the Father, not *made* (that is, not *created from nothing*). To be born or begotten communicates a sharing in the same nature. Fathers beget sons of the same nature—this is the key truth being communicated here.

The Council Fathers who composed the Creed drew on a rich vein of scriptural testimony to indicate the *kind* of origin that the Son had from the Father: he was a son "born" or "begotten" of God the Father. This term "born/begotten" is used in the major genealogies of both the Old and New Testaments (Gen. 5; 11; 1 Chron. 2–9; Matt. 1:5–20) and designates the birth of the Messiah in prophecy (Isa. 9:6). Strikingly, it is also used to describe *God's* begetting of the people of Israel (Deut. 32:18; Isa. 1:2): God himself is a father to his people. In the New Testament, the term "born/begotten" describes the birth of Jesus from Mary (Matt. 2:1; Luke 1:35) and is used especially in the Johannine literature to speak of our spiritual birth from God (John 3:3–8; 1 John 2:29; 3:9; 4:7; 5:1, 4).

The most significant scriptural background for the creedal statement, however, comes from two passages in the Old Testament. The first occurs in the Greek text of Proverbs 8:25, where divine Wisdom, by which God created the world, speaks and says, "Before the mountains were established, and before all the hills, *he begot me*."[14] This is the same verb, "to beget," that is found in the Creed, and it points to the "begetting" of divine Wisdom by the Lord God. The Fathers of the Church recognized in this divine Wisdom a reference to the eternal Wisdom of God, who became incarnate as Jesus Christ, as the apostle Paul describes him: "Christ the power of God and the wisdom of God" (1 Cor. 1:24). A problem arises, however, because only a few verses earlier, the Greek text of Proverbs 8:22 makes use of the verb "create" to describe the origin of this divine Wisdom: "The Lord *created* me, the beginning of his ways."[15] Those who believed the Son was not God but rather a creature claimed *this* verse in support of their position. And so there arose an exegetical contest in the fourth century over this famous passage from Proverbs 8. Is the divine Wisdom *created* by God or *begotten* from God? Athanasius of Alexandria devoted pages of commentary to argue

13. The Latin text of the Creed also uses two distinct words, *natum* (born) and *genitum* (begotten).

14. Our translation from the Septuagint.

15. Our translation from the Septuagint. The Hebrew verb in Prov. 8:22 (*qanah*) sometimes describes creation from nothing but is also used for the act of begetting a son (e.g., Gen. 4:1). The NAB translates Prov. 8:22, "The Lord begot me."

that Proverbs 8, rightly understood, supports the eternal, divine begetting of the Son.[16]

The second Old Testament text is Psalm 2:7: "He said to me, 'You are my Son, today I have begotten you.'" This passage is explicitly applied to Christ in Acts 13:33, but even more significantly, it is applied to the Son's eternal begetting in Hebrews 1:5 (RSV-2CE): "For to what angel did God ever say, 'You are my Son, today I have begotten you'?" Hebrews is making the claim that Jesus is God's unique Son, who is "the radiance of the glory of God and the exact imprint of his nature" (Heb. 1:3 ESV).

By using the term "born/begotten," the Creed identifies Jesus as the uniquely begotten Son of God according to the Scriptures. Jesus is not just *any* son, but the unique Son, the radiance of the Father. When we confess Jesus as "born of the Father," we are identifying and confessing the divine Son, the unique offspring, of God the Father.

The creedal phrase "before all ages" defines the occasion of this divine begetting. It did not happen *in time*, in the period of the ages of the world, but *before* all times. The word "age" (Greek *aiōn*) can refer to "the world" in general but normally carries the sense of "a period of time."[17] In biblical terms, "the ages" are the periods of time in the created order in which God is working out his plan of redemption, and "the age to come" is the period when God will re-create the world and dwell with his people forever.[18]

By stating that Jesus was begotten "before all ages," the Creed is underlining the truth that Jesus existed before the entire created order came into existence. Paul confirms this when he tells Timothy that God saved us "because of his own purpose and grace, which he gave us in Christ Jesus before the ages began" (2 Tim. 1:9 ESV). Paul assumes here that God determined to act *before all ages* in Christ Jesus, pointing to the preexistence of Christ. In the same way, the Letter to the Hebrews identifies Jesus as the Son through whom God "created the world" (literally, "created the ages") (Heb. 1:2). The Son is not created; rather, he is the one through whom all the ages were created in time.[19]

Yet it is in the brief and often-overlooked Letter of Jude that we find the closest parallel to the language of the Creed. In the final verse of the letter, Jude closes with a prayer to the Father and the Son: "To the only God, our

16. See Athanasius, *Second Discourse against the Arians* 16–22.

17. The Latin term *saeculum* can simply mean "world" but also conveys the sense of a period of time.

18. We see this illustrated in Jesus's saying about the Holy Spirit: "Whoever speaks against the Holy Spirit will not be forgiven, either in this age or in the age to come" (Matt. 12:32).

19. For God deciding or acting "before the ages," see also 1 Cor. 2:7 and Titus 1:2.

"O Come, All Ye Faithful"

The renowned traditional hymn "O Come, All Ye Faithful," echoing the Nicene Creed, beautifully captures the truth of Jesus as the only-begotten Son, who is truly God and who took flesh from the Virgin Mary and became man for our salvation.

> O come, all ye faithful, joyful and triumphant,
> O come ye, O come ye to Bethlehem;
> Come and behold him, born the King of angels. . . .
>
> God of God, Light of Light,
> Lo! He comes forth from the Virgin's womb.
> Our very God, begotten not created. . . .
>
> Sing, choirs of angels, sing in exultation,
> Sing, all ye citizens of heav'n above!
> Glory to God, all glory in the highest. . . .
>
> Yea, Lord, we greet thee, born this happy morning,
> Jesus, to thee be all glory giv'n;
> Word of the Father, now in flesh appearing.
>
> O come, let us adore him,
> O come, let us adore him,
> O come, let us adore him, Christ, the Lord![a]

a. Robert J. Batastini, ed., *Gather Comprehensive*, 2nd ed. (Chicago: GIA, 2004), no. 357, https://hymnary.org/hymn/GC2/357.

Savior through Jesus Christ our Lord, be glory, majesty, dominion, and authority, before all time and now and for ever" (Jude 25). The phrase "before all time" is literally "before every age," and "for ever" is literally "unto all the ages." Jude is offering worship to both the Father and the Son, declaring that this worship was fittingly given before time began, is rightly offered in the present time, and will be given in the age to come. The clear implication is that *before every age*—in eternity—the Son is honored with divine worship along with the Father.

Why, then, did the Council Fathers think it necessary to add the phrase "begotten, not made"? Because Arius was prepared both to confess that the Son was brought into being "before the ages" and to deny that the Son was God. For Arius, the Father, before all times and ages, caused the Son, a perfect

WITNESS TO THE TRADITION

Gregory of Nazianzus on the Incomprehensibility of the Begetting of the Son

Saint Gregory of Nazianzus delivered his renowned theological orations in the city of Constantinople in 379–80, rebutting claims made by teachers who denied that the Son was God or eternal, like the Father. In the following selection from the third theological oration, Gregory underlines the fact that though we believe in the eternal begetting of the Son, we cannot know or comprehend the nature of this eternal begetting of the Son by the Father.

> How, then, has he been begotten? . . . The heavenly begetting is more incomprehensible than your own, to the same extent that God is harder to trace out than Man. . . . Drop your ideas of flux, division and cleavage, drop the habit of treating the incorporeal nature as if it were a body and you might well get a worthy notion of God's begetting. How has he been begotten?—I re-utter the question with loathing. God's begetting ought to have the tribute of our reverent silence. The important point is for you to learn that he has been begotten. As to the way it happens, we shall not concede that even angels, much less you, know that. Shall I tell you the way? It is a way known only to the begetting Father and the begotten Son. Anything beyond this fact is hidden by a cloud and escapes your dull vision.[a]

a. Gregory of Nazianzus, *Oration* 29.8, in *On God and Christ: The Five Theological Orations and Two Letters to Cledonius*, trans. Lionel Wickham, PPS 23 (Crestwood, NY: St. Vladimir's Seminary Press, 2002), 75–76.

creature, to exist. And so to rule out this position, the Creed adds that the Son is "begotten, not made," thus closing the door on every attempt to make the Son to be a creature. "What is clearly acknowledged here is that what is originated/made is always of a different nature, a different kind of being, than the originator/maker. However, what is begotten is always the same kind of being as the begetter."[20] The Creed, in fact, draws a clear distinction—a sharp line—between God the Creator and all other things that are "created"

20. Thomas G. Weinandy, *Athanasius: A Theological Introduction* (Burlington, VT: Ashgate, 2007), 62.

or "made." There are only two options. Either the Son is truly God—and therefore eternally begotten of the Father, of the same divine nature—or else he is a creature, made from nothing. There is no possible intermediate position or rank. On the one side is God, the "maker of heaven and earth, of all things visible and invisible." And on the other side is the created order, including angels, human beings, and all other material beings. Jesus the Son, "begotten, not made," is definitively on the "maker" side of this line.

So when we confess in the Creed that the Son is "born of the Father before all ages" and is "begotten, not made," we are recognizing and confessing the divine status of the Son, who has existed from eternity and is worthy to receive praise and worship along with the Father.

God from God, Light from Light, True God from True God

The phrases "God from God," "Light from Light," and "true God from true God" come originally from the Creed of Nicaea (325),[21] and together they communicate several truths about the Son: (1) the nature of the Son (what the Son is); (2) the origin of the Son (from whom the Son comes); and (3) the distinctiveness of the Son (that he is distinct from the Father). First, the Son is confessed as "God," and if there is any doubt on the matter, he is proclaimed as "true God from true God." This expanded statement "specifically excludes any attempt to speak of the Son as being a 'lesser' God than the Father, a second divinity or some kind of intermediary Demiurge. Rather, in whatever way the Father is thought of as God, this is to be held also of the Son."[22] The Son is neither a creature nor a lesser divinity. He is fully and truly God.

Second, the Son comes *from* the Father. The Son is not the source of his own origin; he is not a freestanding divine being. He comes from the Father as light comes from light. The terms of origin are not reversible: we do not say that the Father is from the Son. This revelation of the Son's origin reflects the constant testimony of Jesus himself in the Gospels—that he comes from the Father and only does what the Father does (John 5:26, 30; 16:27–28).

Third, the first and last of these expressions point to the distinction of the Son from the Father—what the tradition calls the "subsistence" of the

---

21. In the Greek text of the Nicene Creed (381), the first phrase, "God from God," is omitted, probably because the final phrase, "true God from true God," was recognized as more than adequate to make the point. In the Latin version of the Creed, the phrase "God from God" is reincluded, and thus we use all three phrases in our recitation of the Creed.

22. John Behr, *The Formation of Christian Theology*, vol. 2, *The Nicene Faith, Part One* (Crestwood, NY: St. Vladimir's Seminary Press, 2004), 156.

Son. Now the middle expression, "Light from Light," does not *as an image* communicate that the Son has his own distinct subsistence. It could be interpreted as implying that the Son is just a radiance or power emanating from the Father, not a distinct person. But the surrounding expressions—"God from God," "true God from true God"—indicate that Jesus is the unique and only-begotten Son who comes from the Father and has his own existence as a person. As we shall see when considering the meaning of the term "consubstantial," the controversies of the fourth century were strongly marked by a concern to preserve the distinct subsistence of the Son. It was a question that needed clarification if consensus was to be reached regarding the person of the Son, Jesus.

The historical context of the early Arian controversy (318–25) explains why these expressions were originally chosen to ensure a right understanding of the Son. Arius, a priest from the city of Alexandria, began to teach that Jesus, the Son, was a *creature* made by the Father through an act of the will. For Arius, the Son—the Word of God—was brought into being by the Father as a kind of semidivine creature, and it was through this creaturely Word that the Father then made and redeemed the world. But Arius was insistent that only the Father was "true God." For him, there could be only one true God—and this was the Father. For Arius, the Father existed before the Son came into being, and consequently he believed that "there was when he was not."[23]

Some of Arius's initial supporters among the bishops, though not as radical as Arius, nonetheless believed that only the Father was "true God," whereas the Son represented a kind of derived and lesser divinity. Following this line of thinking, they also placed the Spirit below the Son. Simply put, they considered the Father to be "God in himself" and viewed the Son and the Spirit as having a subordinate divinity, sharing in the Father's divinity but in a lesser way. To rule out this way of thinking (that the Son was either a creature or of a lesser grade of divinity), the Fathers at the Council of Nicaea chose these three expressions to emphasize that the Son is fully and truly God. They wanted to leave no ambiguity—no wiggle room—concerning the full divinity of the Son.

The Fathers at Nicaea in 325 were confident in stating these truths boldly because they saw them plainly revealed in the Scriptures. The clearest scriptural testimony that Jesus is truly God comes at the beginning and the end

---

23. See appendix 1 for our translation of the condemnations of Arian statements in the Creed of Nicaea.

of John's Gospel. In the opening verse, we are told that "the Word was with God, *and the Word was God*" (John 1:1). Then, in a closing scene, the apostle Thomas acknowledges Jesus's full divine identity when he cries out, "My Lord and my God!" (John 20:28). For its part, the Letter to the Hebrews unequivocally describes the Son as God: "He is the radiance of the glory of God and the exact imprint of his nature" (Heb. 1:3 ESV). If we are in any doubt, the letter then goes on to address the Son directly as "God": "But of the Son he says, 'Your throne, O God, is for ever and ever'" (1:8). In confirmation of this, the book of Revelation portrays in visionary description the full and equal divinity of the Father and the Son as they together receive worship from the heavenly chorus:

> "Worthy is the Lamb who was slain, to receive power and wealth and wisdom and might and honor and glory and blessing!" And I heard every creature in heaven and on earth and under the earth and in the sea, and all therein, saying, "To him who sits upon the throne and to the Lamb be blessing and honor and glory and might for ever and ever!" And the four living creatures said, "Amen!" and the elders fell down and worshiped. (Rev. 5:12–14)

The explicit confession of the Son as "God" in the pages of the New Testament, as well as the testimony that the Father and the Son receive joint worship, gave boldness to the Council Fathers to declare that the Son is "God from God" and "true God from true God."[24]

In a similar way, the notion that God is light appears in both the Old and New Testaments: "The LORD is my light and my salvation" (Ps. 27:1); "This is the message we have heard from him and proclaim to you, that God is light and in him is no darkness at all" (1 John 1:5). But the Son, too, is identified as the light. Jesus says of himself, "I am the light of the world" (John 8:12), and "I have come as light into the world" (12:46). The prologue to the Fourth Gospel even names the Son as "the true light": "The true light that enlightens every man was coming into the world" (1:9). The final vision in the book of Revelation communicates in picture language that the Father and the Son together are the "light" in the new creation: "And the city has no need of sun or moon to shine upon it, for the glory of God is its light, and its lamp is the Lamb" (Rev. 21:23). This revelation of Scripture anchored the creedal confession that the Son is truly "Light from Light."

---

24. For the witness of Scripture that the Son is God, see also Rom. 9:5; Titus 2:13; 2 Pet. 1:1; 1 John 5:20.

LEX ORANDI

Christ as Light from Light

The solemn closing blessing for the Feast of Epiphany offers this inspiring prayer, that Christ who is "Light from Light" may illuminate our lives to the end of our pilgrimage on earth:

> May God, who has called you
> Out of darkness into his wonderful light,
> Pour out in kindness his blessing upon you
> And make your hearts firm in faith, hope and charity.
>
> And so when your pilgrimage is ended,
> May you come to him whom the Magi sought
> As they followed the star and whom they found with great joy,
> The Light from Light, who is Christ the Lord.[a]

a. *Roman Missal*, 676.

Living the Mystery

Does it really make any difference whether we believe Jesus Christ is the only-begotten Son of God and that he is truly "Light from Light" and "true God from true God"? How does this play out in the living of our faith? First, it means that when we have contact with Jesus (for example, through faith, through the gift of the Spirit, through the Eucharist), we are in genuine contact with God himself. We are touching God in a real way. If we wanted to have real, living contact with a certain famous person (e.g., a politician, athlete, or entertainer), but that person, instead of coming in person, sent a messenger—a delegate—to represent him or her, we would be hugely disappointed. In Jesus, we are in touch not just with a messenger or delegate of God but with God himself—with God the Son. Jesus is not a semidivine creature on mission from God, as Arius thought, nor is he just an anointed man, as adoptionism claimed. He is God the Son appearing in flesh as a full human being. When we see Jesus, we see God the Father. The short dialogue between Jesus and the apostle Philip shows this: "Philip said to him, 'Lord, show us the Father, and we shall be satisfied.' Jesus said to him, 'Have I been with you so long, and yet you do not know me, Philip? He who has seen me has seen the Father; how can you say, "Show us the Father"?'" (John 14:8–9).

The human race—you and us and everyone else—needed more than a "message" from God or even a "messenger" from God. We needed God himself to come and redeem us and make us his own sons and daughters. In Jesus Christ, God has truly come to save us.

Second, the fact that Jesus is "true God from true God" means that he is unique and one of a kind. There are many religions and many religious founders and teachers, and we want to recognize and be open to whatever truth we can discover in them. But there is only one unique Son of God, who has taken human form, who walked among us, who taught us what is true, and who redeemed us from our slavery. To confess Jesus as Lord, as the only-begotten of the Father, as true God from true God, means that we look to him as the only fully reliable teacher and guide. "In him the whole fulness of deity dwells bodily" (Col. 2:9), and "there is salvation in no one else, for there is no other name under heaven given among men by which we must be saved" (Acts 4:12). As Archbishop Fulton Sheen writes,

> Our Blessed Lord left the world without leaving any written message. . . . The truth that all other ethical teachers proclaimed, and the light that they gave to the world, was not *in* them, but *outside* them. Our Divine Lord, however, identified Divine Wisdom with Himself. It was the first time in history that it was ever done, and it has never been done since.[25]

When Jesus speaks, it is God speaking directly to us. When Jesus acts to redeem us, it is God himself acting for our sake. Because Jesus is the unique and only Son of God—light from light and true God from true God—we can trust his words and rely entirely upon him for our life and happiness.

Consubstantial with the Father

Consubstantial with the Father; through him all things were made.	Consubstantialem Patri: per quem omnia facta sunt.	ὁμοούσιον τῷ πατρί, δι' οὗ τὰ πάντα ἐγένετο.

OT: Gen. 1:1–3; Pss. 33:6, 9; 104:24; Wis. 9:1–2
NT: John 1:2, 10; 1 Cor. 8:6; Col. 1:16–17; Heb. 1:2
Catechism: the Son consubstantial with the Father, 242, 248; the consubstantial Trinity, 253, 291, 685, 689

25. Fulton J. Sheen, *The Life of Christ* (New York: Doubleday, 2008), 156.

Theological Exposition

Consubstantial with the Father

The term "consubstantial" (Greek *homoousios*, Latin *consubstantialis*) was inserted by the Council Fathers into the Creed of Nicaea in 325 and retained in the Nicene Creed of 381. It means literally "one in being" or "the same in being." It became the most contested part of the Creed in the debates that ran the length of the fourth century. Notably, this term is not found in the Scriptures, and this raised difficulties in the minds of many bishops. Why make use of a nonscriptural term to define the faith? Here we will explore where this nonscriptural term came from, why it was used in the creed of 325, and what meaning it conveyed for the Council Fathers.

We have only a piecemeal knowledge about the use of the term *homoousios* (consubstantial) before 325. It first appears in Gnostic writings of the second century, where it communicates a kind of emanation of one divine being from another, with the derived deity possessing *part* of the divinity from which it emanated. This reflects a conception of God foreign to Christian faith and plainly was not acceptable to describe the relationship between the Father and the Son as found in the Scriptures. In the third century, *homoousios* was used positively on occasion to describe the relationship between the Father and the Son—that the Son was *homoousios* with the Father. In general, when used positively, *homoousios* tended to communicate the sense of "the same order of being." But at the same time, the term was condemned at the Council of Antioch in 268. The exact reason for this condemnation is unclear, but it was probably condemned as communicating a kind of materialistic emanation of the Son from the Father—the idea that the Son possessed *part* of the Father's being. Thus, before 325 the term *homoousios* itself had a mixed heritage in the Christian tradition.

Why, then, did the Council Fathers decide to include this potentially controversial term in the confession of faith in the Son? According to the testimony of the Church Fathers themselves (e.g., Athanasius and Ambrose), the term was chosen principally because Arius and his party could not agree to its use.[26] It was used to strengthen what the Creed already confessed—namely, that the Son is "God from God" and "true God from true God"—and to decisively

---

26. See Athanasius, *On the Council of Nicaea* 20; Ambrose, *Exposition of the Faith* 3.15. According to Lewis Ayres, "the choice of the term *homoousios* seems to have been motivated in large part because Arius was known to reject it" (*Nicaea and Its Legacy: An Approach to Fourth-Century Trinitarian Theology* [Oxford: Oxford University Press, 2004], 90).

refute Arius's teaching that the Son was a creature. This nonscriptural word secured the belief that the Son was not made—like a creature—but was of the same "being" as the Father. In short, the confession that the Son was *homoousios* with the Father was intended to seal the fundamental affirmation of the Creed, that the Son was God and in no sense a creature.

At the same time, *homoousios* was not given a precise meaning at Nicaea. Its purpose was to uphold the full divinity of the Son, not to express a particular view of the inner relationship between the Father and the Son. As a result, it became the focus of intense debate in the period following Nicaea, from the 340s through the 370s.[27] Why did *homoousios* create such a stir? For many bishops, the term had unwelcome overtones. It seemed to imply that the Father and the Son were the very same *being*—that is, the very same *person*. They were worried that it did not adequately uphold the real distinction between the Father and the Son. Their concern was fueled by the teaching of Marcellus, bishop of Ancyra, who ardently defended the Creed of Nicaea and the use of *homoousios* to describe the Son's relationship to the Father, but who also believed that the Son's individual identity was only temporary. For Marcellus, when the new creation is completed, the Son will in some sense merge back into the Father. He appears to have taught a version of what we call "modalism."

As we have already seen, modalism claims that there is no *real* or *eternal* distinction between the Father and the Son (and the Spirit) but that these identities are temporary arrangements that manifest the one God in different modes.[28] Attributed to the figure Sabellius, modalism was known in the ancient Church as "Sabellianism." And so some bishops, seeing what Marcellus was teaching, objected to the implications of the nonscriptural term *homoousios*, believing that it led toward the false teaching of modalism. Their primary concern was to ensure that the Father and the Son were believed and confessed as eternally distinct, not as different modes or faces of the one God.

So in place of *homoousios*, other terms were proposed. The most popular was a slight variation that confessed that the Son was †*homoiousios* with the Father. The addition of one letter (the Greek letter *iōta*) changed the meaning to "like in being." The goal in using this term was to confess that Christ is truly divine and that his divinity is "like" that of the Father, while also

---

27. The debate over the meaning and legitimacy of the term *homoousios* did not occur directly after the Council of Nicaea but arose approximately twenty years later, probably because of concerns with the modalist-leaning teaching of Marcellus of Ancyra.

28. See "False Oneness: Modalism and Subordinationism" in chap. 2.

ensuring that he is recognized as a distinct person in no way merged with the Father. But this gave rise to the question, How can the Son be only "like in being" to the Father if he is truly God? Would there not, then, be two distinct Gods who are alike in nature but by no means "one God"? The revised term,

WITNESS TO THE TRADITION

Athanasius on the Term *Homoousios*

In several works, Athanasius defended the importance and legitimacy of the term *homoousios* and sought to clarify its meaning. The key for Athanasius was the eternal relationship between the Father and the Son. The Father was never not a father; he is always and eternally *the Father of the Son*. Therefore, the one God is not the Father who chose at some point to have a Son, but is rather the Father eternally begetting the Son. The Son, then, possesses the full "being" of the Father from all eternity and yet is distinct from the Father as being the Son. In the treatise *On the Council of Nicaea*, written in the mid-350s, Athanasius offers this explanation of the meaning of *homoousios*:

> Since this explanation is thus shown to be pious, the enemies of Christ should not be shocked by the *homoousios* either, since this term also has a sound sense and rationale. For if we say that the Word is from the essence of God . . . , what is that except to say that he is truly and eternally of the essence from which he is begotten? For he is not different in kind, as if he were something foreign and dissimilar . . . that is mixed in with the essence of the Father. Nor is his likeness merely extrinsic, as if he were in some other respect or completely of a different essence. . . . But if the Son is Word, Wisdom, Image of the Father, and Radiance, then it follows reasonably that he is "one in essence." . . . When we hear the term, "*homoousios*," let us not fall back on our human senses and think of parts and divisions of divinity. Rather, let us bring to mind incorporeal realities and not tear asunder the unity of nature and the identity of light, for such is the proper . . . relation of the Son to the Father, showing God to be truly Father of the Word.[a]

a. Athanasius, *On the Council of Nicaea* 23–24, in Khaled Anatolios, *Athanasius*, The Early Church Fathers (London: Routledge, 2004), 200–201 (translation modified).

homoiousios, seemed to imply a division within the single divine nature. Another proposal recommended saying simply that the Son was "like" the Father with no reference to the language of "being."

In the end, these alternatives were recognized as insufficient for capturing and expressing the mystery of the Trinity. It was preeminently Athanasius who patiently contended for the use of the original term, *homoousios*, by showing that it preserved and expressed both aspects of the mystery: the Son was of the same "being" or "nature" as the Father but was a distinct subject, because he was "the Son" and not "the Father."

What, then, does the term "consubstantial" (*homoousios*) in the Creed mean? It means that the Father and the Son possess the same, identical divine nature. They do not each have half of it (it is not divided between them), but they each possess it fully. And yet the Father and the Son are distinct from one another—one is the Father and the other is the Son. If a Father, then a Son, and the two are not to be confused or blended together. This same understanding was then applied to the Spirit as well: "The persons of the Trinity are one in being, and therefore are the one God, such that each person is truly and completely God."[29] And yet the Father, the Son, and the Spirit are not like three human beings who have a close unity. As humans, we possess the same nature, but each of us possesses that nature differently and uniquely. The persons of the Trinity simply *are* the one divine nature, the difference being only relational—the Father is the Father, the Son is the Son, and the Spirit is the Spirit. Saint Ambrose expresses this truth with great clarity: "Rightly, then, do we call the Son [*homoousios*] (of the same substance), with the Father, forasmuch as that term expresses both the distinction of Persons and the unity of nature."[30]

Three Persons in One God

Controversy over the word *homoousios* alerts us to the wider question of how the Church decided what terms would be most appropriate to signify the reality of God revealed in the Scriptures. The Church confessed that there is one God but also recognized that the Father, the Son, and the Holy Spirit are

29. Thomas Joseph White, *The Trinity: On the Nature and Mystery of the One God* (Washington, DC: Catholic University of America Press, 2022), 2.

30. Ambrose, *Exposition of the Faith* 3.15 (NPNF[2] 10:260). The *Catechism* expresses this same truth: "The divine persons do not share the one divinity among themselves but each of them is God whole and entire. . . . 'Father,' 'Son,' 'Holy Spirit' are not simply names designating modalities of the divine being, for they are really distinct from one another" (CCC 253, 254).

fully and entirely God and yet distinct from one another. What terminology would be adequate to represent this great revelation? The word "Trinity" (Greek *Trias*, Latin *Trinitas*) was coined in the second century to signify this revelation of God as One in Three and Three in One.[31]

In the Latin-speaking tradition in the West, the words "substance" (*substantia*), "essence" (*essentia*), and "nature" (*natura*) were used to denote the oneness of God (what all three persons are and share), and the word "person" (*persona*) was employed to denote each of the three: Father, Son, and Holy Spirit. So in the Latin tradition, the triune God is typically identified as one substance, essence, or nature in three persons. In the Greek-speaking tradition in the East, the terms most typically used to describe the oneness of God were *ousia* (being or essence) and *physis* (nature), while the commonly used word to designate each of the three persons was *prosōpon* (person). The term *hypostasis* was used by some writers to denote God's oneness, but it was confusingly used by other writers to denote each of the three persons. Thus, at the beginning of the fourth century, for some there was one *hypostasis* in God (referring to the common nature), whereas for others there were three *hypostases* in God (referring to the three persons).

This difference in terminology frequently led the bishops to misunderstand one another. The term *hypostasis*, which translates literally as "substance," is a metaphysically weighty word. It is formed from two words, "under" and "stand," and conveys "the reality that stands under" or the "rock-bottom reality" of a thing. The claim that there were three *hypostases* sounded to some ears as if there were three distinct gods. Conversely, the word *prosōpon*, which literally means "face," seemed to others to underrepresent the real distinction between Father, Son, and Spirit. This term appeared to lean into modalism by identifying Father, Son, and Spirit as only "faces" without any underlying reality.

The Council of Constantinople in 381 clarified one major issue in terminology. Though the terms do not appear in the Nicene Creed itself, it was at the time of the council that the Church settled on the terminology "one *ousia* and three *hypostases*" to designate the trinitarian God revealed in the Scriptures, though other equivalent terms, such as "one nature" and "three modes of being," also continued to be employed. And it was at the Council of Chalcedon in 451 that the Church received the terms *hypostasis* and

---

31. The first Christian writer to use the term "Triad" or "Trinity" (Greek *Trias*) was Theophilus, bishop of Antioch, in about the year 180 (see *To Autolycus* 2.15). The first occurrence of the Latin term *Trinitas* appears in Tertullian in the early third century (see *Against Praxeas* 3).

LEX ORANDI

A Trinity of One Substance

In the preface for the Mass of the Feast of the Most Holy Trinity, the Church confesses her belief that the Father, the Son, and the Spirit are a Trinity of one substance—one being—eminently worthy of our worship and praise.

> For with your Only Begotten Son and the Holy Spirit
> You are one God, one Lord:
> Not in the unity of a single person,
> But in a Trinity of one substance.

> For what you have revealed to us of your glory
> We believe equally of your Son and of the Holy Spirit,
> So that, in the confessing of the true and eternal Godhead,
> You might be adored in what is proper to each Person,
> Their unity in substance, and their equality in majesty.[a]

a. *Roman Missal*, 1328.

prosōpon as synonyms to designate the three persons. This terminological clarification is neatly summed up in the *Catechism*: "We do not confess three Gods, but one God in three persons, the 'consubstantial Trinity.' . . . 'Each of the three persons is that supreme reality, viz., the divine substance, essence or nature.'"[32]

Through Him All Things Were Made

The final phrase of this section stands as a counterpoint to an earlier confession: Jesus the Son is *not made*; rather, it is *through him* that *all things were made*. He is not a creature but rather the one through whom all things were created. This is one of the strongest testimonies to the Son's divine nature, for only God can truly create from nothing.

The Son's role in creation appears multiple times in the New Testament. The formula of the creedal statement, "through him all things were made," closely follows the prologue to the Gospel of John: "All things were made through him, and without him was not anything made that was made" (John

32. CCC 253.

LEX ORANDI

The Colossians Hymn

Many scholars believe that Paul's great "hymn" to Christ in his Letter to the Colossians was originally a hymn taken from the early Church. This hymn confesses Jesus as God and declares him to be the one through whom all things, whether on earth or in heaven, came into being:

> He is the image of the invisible God,
> the first-born of all creation;
> for in him all things were created,
> in heaven and on earth, visible and invisible,
> whether thrones or dominions or principalities or authorities—
> all things were created through him and for him. . . .
> For in him all the fulness of God was pleased to dwell. (Col. 1:15–16, 19)[a]

a. Col. 1:15–16, 19 has been reformatted here to show the hymnlike quality of the text.

1:3).[33] The Word (the *Logos*), who is Jesus, the only-begotten Son, is the person through whom all created things came into being: "The world was made through him" (1:10). The creedal statement also closely follows Paul when he speaks of our "one Lord, Jesus Christ, *through whom are all things* and through whom we exist" (1 Cor. 8:6). In another place, Paul expands on this truth concerning the Son's role in creation: "In him all things were created, in heaven and on earth, visible and invisible, whether thrones or dominions or principalities or authorities—all things were created through him and for him" (Col. 1:16). Here the verb "create" is used, but the meaning is the same. Paul is at pains to underline that every created thing, visible or invisible (material or immaterial)—even the great angels of heaven—was created through the Son. The Letter to the Hebrews, too, confesses that all things were created through Jesus the Son: "In these last days he has spoken to us by a Son, whom he appointed the heir of all things, through whom also he created the ages" (Heb. 1:2 RSV-2CE).

33. The verb translated "make" in both the Creed and the Gospel of John is *ginomai*, meaning "come to be." The Gospel phrase could also be translated "Through him all things came to be" or "came into being."

This creative role of God's word has its foundation in the Old Testament. In the opening verses of the Bible, we hear that "in the beginning" God created the world by his word; he spoke, and it came into being (Gen. 1:1–3). The *word of God* is the primary cause and agent of creation (2 Pet. 3:5). Creation by God's word and wisdom appears in the Psalms: "By the word of the LORD the heavens were made, and all their host by the breath of his mouth. . . . For he spoke, and it came to be; he commanded, and it stood forth" (Ps. 33:6, 9). The book of Wisdom offers the same testimony: "O God of my fathers and Lord of mercy, who have made all things by your word, and by your wisdom have formed man . . ." (Wis. 9:1–2 RSV-2CE). Jesus the Son is none other than the Word and Wisdom of God, through whom the whole world and everything in it was made.

There is an apologetic edge to this confession. The first great doctrinal controversy in the Church concerned creation: Is the God who made the world (Gen. 1) the Father of Jesus Christ, or is he a wicked god who brought the evil of materiality into being? For many Gnostic groups—and also for the followers of Marcion and Mani—the world, the material creation, was a bad thing, something to be left behind when we are truly enlightened and redeemed. By confessing that through Jesus all things were made, we are rejecting all such claims. We are saying that the created order—and all things within it—is intrinsically good. Not only is the creation from God the Father, the "maker of heaven and earth," but he made all things through his Son, his Word. By linking Jesus to the original creation—by making him the cause and agent of creation—the New Testament and the Creed explicitly tie themselves to a reverence for the created, material world. The "world" into which the Son came in his incarnation is not a world bound for abandonment or destruction but a world that he seeks to save and remake.

When we confess in the Creed that Jesus is the one through whom all things were made, we are singing the praises of our creator Lord and acknowledging with the psalmist, "O LORD, how manifold are your works! In wisdom you have made them all; the earth is full of your creatures" (Ps. 104:24 RSV-2CE).

Living the Mystery

Knowing that *all things were made through the Son* can have a powerful impact on how we think of ourselves and how we engage life in the world. We come to know that everything created—everything in the world—is "good" because it comes from God: "And God saw that it was good" (Gen. 1:12, 18,

21, 25). By this knowledge we unmask two deadly untruths (lies) about the world. The first untruth is the view that the world—or at least part of the world—is intrinsically evil. But by our confession of God as creator, we know that all created things are intrinsically good. We are not seeking to escape from an evil world but to live at peace within the good world God has given. The second is the view of the world as somehow self-created or even random. The person who believes that there is nothing outside of matter and energy and that the world as we know it is just a great accident can never find *meaning* or *purpose* in the world. That world is intrinsically meaningless. But because we know that the world was made in wisdom through the Son (who is the Wisdom of God), we can see that the world is both good and meaningful. It has a purpose, and we have a purpose within it.

CONTEMPORARY ISSUES

Stewardship of the Natural World

Concern for the natural world—for the care and protection of the environment—is a burning issue in the modern world. And rightly so. If indeed God is the "maker of heaven and earth" and "all things were made" through the Son, as the Creed confesses, then we have a profound responsibility toward the natural world as its stewards. Two recent popes have given considerable attention to this question and provide wisdom and balance for the right exercise of our stewardship.

Benedict XVI proposes that "we need to care for the environment: it has been entrusted to men and women to be protected and cultivated with responsible freedom, with the good of all as a constant guiding criterion."[a] He identifies two extreme positions that fail to capture our true relationship to the creation. The first is a "position, which aims at total technical dominion over nature."[b] Pope Francis also draws attention to this approach, which he calls "a Promethean vision of mastery over the world" instead of a proper "sense of responsible stewardship."[c] The second extreme is a position that views "nature as something more important than the human person. This position leads to attitudes of neo-paganism or a new pantheism."[d] Francis, too, insists that "our relationship with the environment can never be isolated from our relationship with others and with God. Otherwise, it would be nothing more

Even more so, we come to recognize that our bodies are fundamentally good and given by God for a good purpose. Our bodies are neither evil nor meaningless. The body is neither a prison for the soul nor a meaningless product of a blind and purposeless evolutionary process. Our bodies are good in themselves and ordered to God's purpose for life in this world and for marriage and family. We also know through divine revelation that we are "fallen" in both body and soul; our lives are marked by sin and death in a way never originally intended by God. Even the created order, in some mysterious way, suffers from a futility that awaits its full redemption (Rom. 8:19–23). But we also know that we have been redeemed by Christ and that our bodies have been sanctified by the Spirit of God. Pope John Paul II recalls this bodily sanctification, which gives new meaning and purpose to our life:

than romantic individualism dressed up in ecological garb, locking us into a stifling immanence."[e] More positively, Pope Francis calls us to embrace and care for the natural world with the reverence and awe that arises when we recognize God as its creator: "If we approach nature and the environment without this openness to awe and wonder, if we no longer speak the language of fraternity and beauty in our relationship with the world, our attitude will be that of masters, consumers, ruthless exploiters, unable to set limits on their immediate needs."[f] The creedal confession that "all things were made" through the Son requires that we take seriously our vocation as stewards to care for the good world that is our home. Just as the Son of God is the true and perfect steward of the entire created order, so we are called to be good stewards of our world in imitation of him.

a. Pope Benedict XVI, "The Human Family, a Community of Peace," para. 7, January 1, 2008, https://www.vatican.va/content/benedict-xvi/en/messages/peace/documents/hf_ben-xvi_mes_20071208_xli-world-day-peace.html.

b. Pope Benedict XVI, Caritas in Veritate, para. 48, June 29, 2009, https://www.vatican.va/content/benedict-xvi/en/encyclicals/documents/hf_ben-xvi_enc_20090629_caritas-in-veritate.html.

c. Pope Francis, Laudato Si', para. 116, May 24, 2015, https://www.vatican.va/content/francesco/en/encyclicals/documents/papa-francesco_20150524_enciclica-laudato-si.html.

d. Pope Benedict XVI, Caritas in Veritate, para. 48.

e. Pope Francis, Laudato Si', para. 119.

f. Pope Francis, Laudato Si', para. 11.

Through redemption, every man has received from God again, as it were, himself and his own body. Christ has imprinted new dignity on the human body—on the body of every man and every woman, since in Christ the human body has been admitted, together with the soul, to union with the Person of the Son-Word. . . . The fruit of redemption is the Holy Spirit, who dwells in man and in his body as in a temple. In this gift, which sanctifies every man, the Christian receives himself again as a gift from God.[34]

Especially during a time of profound confusion about the gift of the body and the goodness of being male and female, we need to recapture the created and redeemed goodness of our embodied identity, as underlined by Pope Francis:

The acceptance of our bodies as God's gift is vital for welcoming and accepting the entire world as a gift from the Father and our common home, whereas thinking that we enjoy absolute power over our own bodies turns, often subtly, into thinking that we enjoy absolute power over creation. Learning to accept our body, to care for it and to respect its fullest meaning, is an essential element of any genuine human ecology. Also, valuing one's own body in its femininity or masculinity is necessary if I am going to be able to recognize myself in an encounter with someone who is different. In this way we can joyfully accept the specific gifts of another man or woman, the work of God the Creator, and find mutual enrichment.[35]

---

34. Pope John Paul II, *The Theology of the Body: Human Love in the Divine Plan* (Boston: Daughters of St. Paul, 1997), 206–7.

35. Pope Francis, *Laudato Si'*, para. 155.

CHAPTER 4

GOD *the* SON INCARNATE

Introduction

We just completed our study of the first half of the section on the Son in the Nicene Creed, centered on the *divine* identity of Jesus. In this chapter we will examine the testimony of the Creed concerning the saving work of Jesus, the Word made flesh, in his *earthly* life.

This section of the Creed deals with what we call the "economy of salvation." The word "economy" comes from a Greek term (*oikonomia*) that means "plan" or "purpose." The Creed names the main events in the life of Jesus through which the Father brought about his purpose and plan for the human race. They include

- the incarnation of the Word
- the saving passion and death of Jesus on the cross
- his glorious resurrection from the dead and ascension to the right hand of the Father
- the promise of his second coming

These are the "peaks" of Christ's saving work. They represent, of course, just a summary of the whole life of Christ as recorded in the Gospels, and surrounding Christ's life is the entire divine plan outlined in sacred Scripture, beginning with the creation of the world and including the long story of the people of Israel. When we confess these peak events in the Creed, we are also implicitly including the entire scriptural narrative of salvation.

This section of the Nicene Creed (381) builds upon—and expands—a similar section found in the Creed of Nicaea (325).[1] Not one word from that first creed was removed, but several explanatory phrases were added to the second creed to describe more fully what Christ did for our salvation. These additions concern three areas: "the role of the Holy Spirit and Mary in the incarnation, the reality and historicity of the suffering and death of Christ, and his †eschatological function as ruler and judge."[2]

We should note that for this section of the Creed, historical context from the fourth century plays a reduced role overall. Scholars typically conclude that the inclusion of these saving events in the Creed was driven not so much by special issues or controversies of the day but rather by a desire to follow the example of the baptismal creeds of that time, which offered a fitting summary of the main events of Christ's saving actions.

Still, by confessing these saving events—and by naming the Roman procurator Pontius Pilate—the Creed is underlining the true humanity of Jesus and the historical nature of Christian belief. The Word of God, by becoming man, enters into the history of the world and genuinely submits to the conditions of time and space. In a profound sense, the author becomes a character in his own story. Our Christian faith is not a set of timeless myths but a story of God making a real world, truly interacting with that world, and finally entering that world through the incarnation in order to bring it to perfection.

He Came Down from Heaven

For us men and for our salvation he came down from heaven,	Qui propter nos homines et propter nostram salutem descendit de caelis,	τὸν δι' ἡμᾶς τοὺς ἀνθρώπους καὶ διὰ τὴν ἡμετέραν σωτηρίαν κατελθόντα ἐκ τῶν οὐρανῶν,
and by the Holy Spirit was incarnate of the Virgin Mary, and became man.	et incarnatus est de Spiritu Sancto ex Maria virgine, et homo factus est.	καὶ σαρκωθέντα ἐκ πνεύματος ἁγίου καὶ Μαρίας τῆς παρθένου, καὶ ἐνανθρωπήσαντα.

OT: Exod. 14:2, 13; Pss. 27:1; 69:1; 113:4; 118:25; Isa. 7:14; 25:9
NT: Luke 1:31–35; 2:30–32; 19:10; John 1:14; 3:13; 6:33, 38; 12:47; Gal. 4:4–6; 1 Tim. 1:15; Heb. 2:14–17
Catechism: the incarnation of the Word, 456–83; motherhood of Mary, 484–507

1. See appendix 1 for a comparison of these creeds.
2. Hubertus Drobner, *The Fathers of the Church: A Comprehensive Introduction*, trans. Siegfried S. Schatzmann (Grand Rapids: Baker Academic, 2007), 292.

Theological Exposition

For Us Men and for Our Salvation

It is important to recognize the narrative quality of this section of the Creed. We are entering upon the "career" of the Word made flesh, and the first act of that work is the incarnation. This opening line, "for us men and for our salvation," communicates three things: (1) the *recipients* of the Son's work (those for whom he came); (2) the *purpose* of the Son's work (why he came); and (3) the opening *act* of that work (how he came).

It may seem obvious, but the Creed says that the Son came "for us men," a phrase inclusive of all men and women—that is, the entire human race. Jesus came not for a select group of people in the past or for a special few today but for "us"—all of us. This is the first time in the Creed that "we" are mentioned since the opening line, "I/we believe." When we confess that Jesus came into the world, we are personally implicated: he came "for us." The Letter to the Hebrews underlines this point when it says that the Son came to save not the angels but rather the descendants of Abraham. He came to save us, and so he was made flesh and blood like us (Heb. 2:14–17).

But for what purpose did he come? He came for "our salvation." The word "salvation" calls to mind a rich vein of biblical expression that spans the length and breadth of both the Old and the New Testament. The Hebrew words for "save" (*yasha'*) and "salvation" (*yeshu'ah*) have a common, everyday meaning: "to save" means to rescue or to deliver or to give help in time of need. In the Scriptures, God saves his people from all kinds of distress: from serious illness, from the attack of enemies, from the grief of exile, and from the threat of death. "Turn, O LORD, save my life; deliver me for the sake of your merciful love" (Ps. 6:4 RSV-2CE). "Save me, O God! For the waters have come up to my neck" (69:1). "Save us, we beg you, O LORD! O LORD, we beg you, give us success!" (118:25 RSV-2CE). This salvation was demonstrated preeminently when God delivered his people from the Egyptians at the Red Sea: "And Moses said to the people, 'Fear not, stand firm, and see the salvation of the LORD, which he will work for you today'" (Exod. 14:13). Isaiah beautifully expresses the hope of God's people who wait for their salvation: "It will be said on that day, 'Lo, this is our God; we have waited for him, that he might save us. This is the LORD; we have waited for him; let us be glad and rejoice in his salvation'" (Isa. 25:9). But for the people of Israel, "salvation" is not just a matter of being delivered from trouble; it also expresses *an ongoing relationship* with the Lord, who always remains their savior. "The LORD is my light and my salvation" (Ps. 27:1). "Restore to me the joy of your salvation, and uphold me with a willing spirit" (51:12 RSV-2CE). "I will lift up the cup of salvation and call on the name of the LORD" (116:13).

In the New Testament, words for "salvation" sometimes carry the general meaning of deliverance from any peril (see Matt. 8:25; 14:30), but normally salvation is focused on the work of Jesus to deliver us from our sins and bring us to eternal life. Importantly, Jesus's overall ministry is characterized by saving *people*: "For the Son of man came to seek and to save the lost" (Luke 19:10); "For I did not come to judge the world but to save the world" (John 12:47). The angel, speaking to Saint Joseph, describes Jesus's mission in terms of saving people from their sins: "[Mary] will bear a son, and you shall call his name Jesus, for he will save his people from their sins" (Matt. 1:21). This summing up of Jesus's mission in terms of salvation is confirmed by the apostle Paul: "The saying is sure and worthy of full acceptance, that Christ Jesus came into the world to save sinners" (1 Tim. 1:15). Jesus is uniquely the bringer of full salvation and the very personification of God's salvation. The apostle Peter proclaims Jesus as the one true source of salvation: "And there is salvation in no one else, for there is no other name under heaven given among men by which we must be saved" (Acts 4:12). And Simeon points to Jesus himself as the visible presence of God's salvation on earth: "My eyes have seen your salvation which you have prepared in the presence of all peoples, a light for revelation to the Gentiles, and for glory to your people Israel" (Luke 2:30–32 RSV-2CE).

When we confess in the Creed that the Son came "for us . . . and for our salvation," this full sense of God's deliverance is included. The phrase "for our salvation" serves as a summary statement of the *entire* work of Christ on our behalf. Its function is not limited or narrow but encompasses everything that Jesus did to deliver us and bring us new life.

The Importance of Salvation

The short phrase "for our salvation" could easily be overlooked, causing us to miss the centrality and importance of "salvation" for the Creed and the Christian faith. There has been a tendency to interpret the Nicene Creed as concerned primarily with the doctrines of the Trinity and the incarnation and only marginally concerned with salvation. On this reading, the Church became overly preoccupied with technical matters of natures and persons and seemed to forget that the core of the gospel is the story of our salvation. But this is to misunderstand why the Church was so concerned with the person of Christ. In brief, all of its clarifications were at the service of guarding and amplifying the saving work of God—Father, Son, and Holy Spirit. The whole point was to clarify how it is that "in Christ God was reconciling the world to himself" (2 Cor. 5:19). "The controversies which produced the doctrines which reached formal definition were often fired by concern that the gospel of salvation be safeguarded."[3]

It is true that the Nicene Creed does not offer an analytical description of our salvation. It does not attempt to say exactly *how* we are saved by the life, death, and resurrection of Jesus, nor does it attempt to harmonize the various scriptural images (e.g., salvation, redemption, sacrifice) that convey Christ's saving work. But this does not mean that the Creed ignores or downplays "our salvation." Quite the contrary: the clarification of Jesus's full divine identity and his genuine incarnation is entirely at the service of "our salvation."

Jesus is truly the Messiah (the Christ), the human son of Adam and the son of David, who was born to save the world. He is our true high priest—a human being—who has offered the perfect sacrifice for our sins. But Jesus is also "God with us" (Matt. 1:23; cf. Isa. 7:14); he is the "good shepherd" (John 10:11), God himself, who has come down from heaven to save us. Jesus *is* the eternal Son of God—the Word of God—begotten by the Father eternally, who has been born humanly through Mary and so is a real and true human being. He is God and man at once and so can truly act as our Savior.

Delivering us from the power of sin is at the core of what Jesus came to do, but he also delivers us from the power of death and from the dominion of the devil (see Eph. 2:1–6). And yet this deliverance from sin, death, and the devil is for a greater purpose—namely, that we might share God's own eternal life now and in the age to come. Christ's work of salvation and redemption is ordered to a greater positive good: that we might become partakers of the divine nature (2 Pet. 1:4) and be formed in the image and likeness of the Son through the Spirit (Rom. 8:29). When the Creed refers to "our salvation," this entire work of God is intended and included.

He Came Down from Heaven

We know *who* the Son came to save: he came for the entire human race. And we know the primary reason he came: for our salvation. Now we confess the decisive movement of the Son toward us: *he came down from heaven.*[4]

3. Frances Young, *The Making of the Creeds* (Harrisburg, PA: Trinity Press International, 1991), 80.
4. The Creed of Nicaea states simply that "he came down." The Nicene Creed (381) adds the phrase "from heaven," presumably to clarify that the Son came down directly from God the Father, who is in heaven.

The word "heaven" in the Bible has two primary senses. First, it refers to the upper part of the *created* world, including everything from the sky (the lower heavens), where the birds fly, to the stars and planets (the upper heavens). In this sense, God created "the heavens and the earth" (Gen. 1:1)—this is all part of the created world.[5] "The heavens" (in the plural) refers to the multiple levels of the heavens, from the lower to the upper. The apostle Paul himself points to this understanding when he says that he was transported in a vision and "caught up to the third heaven" (2 Cor. 12:2).

Second, the Bible also speaks of the dwelling of God in relation to "the heavens" or to "heaven." The idea is that God has his dwelling "above" the heavens—that is, higher and more exalted than the highest part of the created world. "The LORD is high above all nations, and his glory above the heavens!" (Ps. 113:4). "Be exalted, O God, above the heavens! Let your glory be over all the earth!" (57:5 RSV-2CE). "Praise him, you highest heavens, and you waters above the heavens!" (148:4). We see this expressed again in the apostle Paul, who says that in his ascension Christ "ascended far above all the heavens" (Eph. 4:10). The Letter to the Hebrews captures this same idea when it says that Christ, our high priest, has been "exalted above the heavens" (Heb. 7:26).

God's dwelling in relation to the heavens is also communicated more simply by saying that God acts "from heaven" and that he dwells "in heaven." This becomes the common way of speaking in both the Old and the New Testament. From the Psalms: "The LORD looks down from heaven upon the children of men" (Ps. 14:2); "Turn again, O God of hosts! Look down from heaven, and see" (80:14). In the Gospel of Matthew, Jesus repeatedly refers to "your Father who is in heaven" (Matt. 5:16, 45; 6:1; 7:11), and strikingly in the Lord's Prayer, Jesus invites us to call upon God as "our Father who art in heaven" (Matt. 6:9). In the same way, Jesus is said to have ascended into heaven (Mark 16:19; Luke 24:51; Acts 1:11; 1 Pet. 3:22), such that Stephen, in a vision, "gazed into heaven and saw the glory of God, and Jesus standing at the right hand of God" (Acts 7:55). The Father speaks "from heaven" (Matt. 3:17), the Holy Spirit is said to descend from heaven (Mark 1:10), and Jesus will return again in glory from heaven: "This Jesus, who was taken up from you into heaven, will come in the same way as you saw him go into heaven" (Acts 1:11).

5. For God creating the heavens, see also Pss. 33:6; 96:5; 121:2; Isa. 65:17; Jer. 32:17. In Hebrew, references to "heaven" are almost always in the plural ("the heavens"). The Greek and Latin translations of the Bible normally follow suit, but sometimes the plural in Hebrew ("heavens") is rendered by a singular in Greek and Latin ("heaven").

The language of the Creed, that the Son came down from heaven, draws especially on the Gospel of John: "No one has ascended into heaven but he who descended from heaven, the Son of man" (John 3:13). Jesus describes

LEX ORANDI

The Incarnation

The hymn "Let All Mortal Flesh Keep Silence" captures the drama of the incarnation, as the Word descends from heaven to take on our full humanity, while with the hosts of heaven we watch in reverent wonder.

> Let all mortal flesh keep silence,
> And with fear and trembling stand;
> Ponder nothing earthly-minded,
> For with blessing in his Hand,
> Christ our God to earth descendeth,
> Our full homage to demand.
>
> King of kings, yet born of Mary,
> As of old on earth He stood,
> Lord of lords, in human vesture,
> In the body and the blood;
> He will give to all the faithful
> His own self for heav'nly food.
>
> Rank on rank the host of heaven
> Spreads its vanguard on the way,
> As the Light of light descendeth
> From the realms of endless day,
> That the pow'rs of hell may vanish
> As the darkness clears away.
>
> At His feet the six-winged seraph,
> Cherubim with sleepless eye,
> Veil their faces to the presence,
> As with ceaseless voice they cry:
> "Alleluia, alleluia,
> Alleluia, Lord Most High!"[a]

a. Gerard Moultrie, trans., "Let All Mortal Flesh Keep Silence," Timeless Truths, accessed January 21, 2023, https://library.timelesstruths.org/music/Let_All_Mortal _Flesh_Keep_Silence/.

himself as "the bread of God . . . which comes down from heaven" (6:33) and announces, "I have come down from heaven, not to do my own will, but the will of him who sent me" (6:38). When we confess in the Creed that the Son "came down from heaven," we are reflecting this biblical understanding that the Son, with the Father, dwells eternally "in heaven" (that is, above all the created world) and that he descended from there when he became man in the incarnation. We are not presuming that "heaven" is located in our space-time world, just above the planets and the stars. "'Heaven' is being used here as a symbol for the transcendence of God, for his otherness to the world of conditioned objects and events."[6] God has his own special dwelling place that is not part of this created order. The language of "descent" communicates that God is higher and more glorious than we are and that he humbled himself, descending from his heavenly dwelling, in order to redeem the human race.

And by the Holy Spirit Was Incarnate of the Virgin Mary, and Became Man

This is the great and central truth of the Christian faith: the eternal Son of God, by the power of the Holy Spirit, took on our flesh—that is, became a full and complete human being—through the Virgin Mary. Here in the Creed, we confess the human birth—the incarnation—of the eternal Son of God. The Son, eternally begotten by the Father, was born humanly from a woman.

The original Greek of this sentence differs slightly from the Latin version. The Greek text reads, literally, "And [the Son] became flesh from the Holy Spirit and Mary the Virgin." The Spirit and the Virgin Mary are identified as the two coordinate sources of the incarnation of the Son. The Latin translation clarifies the distinct roles: "And [the Son] was incarnate *by* the Holy Spirit *from* the Virgin Mary."[7] It is *by* the power of the Holy Spirit that Christ became incarnate *from* the human flesh of the Virgin Mary.

The Creed of Nicaea (325) simply says he "was incarnate." The Nicene Creed (381) notably adds "from the Holy Spirit and the Virgin Mary." We can only speculate why those who composed the later Creed added these phrases, but it is likely that they wanted to underline both the divine power at work in the incarnation (the Holy Spirit) and the genuine human birth of the Son (from the Virgin). Jesus was not a mere man, but neither was he a pure spirit

---

6. Robert Barron, *Light from Light: A Theological Reflection on the Nicene Creed* (Park Ridge, IL: Word on Fire Academic, 2021), 59.

7. Our translation from the Latin.

who only appeared as a man. He is the true divine Son, who by the power of the Spirit was truly born of a woman (Gal. 4:4).

All this closely reflects the narrative of the birth of Jesus in the Gospel of Luke. The angel Gabriel says to Mary, "You will conceive in your womb and bear a son, and you shall call his name Jesus" (Luke 1:31). When Mary asks Gabriel how this will happen, since she has not had sexual relations with a man, Gabriel replies, "The Holy Spirit will come upon you, and the power

WITNESS TO THE TRADITION

Irenaeus on the Incarnation Leading to Deification

Saint Irenaeus, an eloquent teacher of the incarnation from the second century, explains how the incarnation of the Word reveals our destiny to become sons and daughters of God who share in the very life of God (deification):

> But again, those who assert that He was simply a mere man, begotten by Joseph, remaining in the bondage of the old disobedience, are in a state of death; having been not as yet joined to the Word of God the Father, nor receiving liberty through the Son, as He does Himself declare: "If the Son shall make you free, you shall be free indeed" [John 8:36]. But, being ignorant of Him who from the Virgin is Emmanuel, they are deprived of His gift, which is eternal life; and not receiving the incorruptible Word, they remain in mortal flesh, and are debtors to death, not obtaining the antidote of life. To whom the Word says, mentioning His own gift of grace: "I said, you are all the sons of the Highest, and gods; but you shall die like men" [Ps. 82:6–7]. . . . For it was for this end that the Word of God was made man, and He who was the Son of God became the Son of man, that man, having been taken into the Word, and receiving the adoption, might become the son of God. For by no other means could we have attained to incorruptibility and immortality, unless we had been united to incorruptibility and immortality. But how could we be joined to incorruptibility and immortality, unless, first, incorruptibility and immortality had become that which we also are, so that the corruptible might be swallowed up by incorruptibility, and the mortal by immortality, that we might receive the adoption of sons?[a]

a. Irenaeus, *Against Heresies* 3.19.1 (*ANF* 1:448–49).

of the Most High will overshadow you; therefore the child to be born will be called holy, the Son of God" (1:35). The conception will occur *by* the power of the Holy Spirit, but the child will be born *from* the flesh of Mary. Because it is the power of God himself that brings about this miraculous conception, the son to be born will be truly "the Son of God." But because the son to be born is also genuinely born humanly of Mary, he will also truly be Mary's son.

In bold language, the apostle Paul witnesses to this human birth of the Son of God from Mary: "But when the time had fully come, God sent forth his Son, born of woman, born under the law, to redeem those who were under the law, so that we might receive adoption as sons" (Gal. 4:4–5). It is *God's* Son, sent forth from the Father, who was born, yet the birth was a genuine *human* birth from the Virgin Mary. This is the great mystery of the incarnation: the divine Son—a divine person—was conceived in Mary's womb by the power of the Spirit and was born in time as a human being.

The verb that appears here, "was incarnate," does not occur in the New Testament, but it directly expresses the great biblical text on the incarnation, John 1:14: "And the Word became flesh and dwelt among us."[8] The Word, who was God and who dwelt with the Father (1:1–3), "became flesh" (Greek *sarx egeneto*; Latin *caro factum est*). What it means for the Word to become incarnate for us and for our salvation is clarified in the phrase that follows: "and became man." In Latin, this is literally "and was made man/human" (*et homo factus est*); in Greek, this is all contained in one verb, *enanthrōpeō* (to become man/human). But this would seem obvious, that the Word assumed a genuine human nature and became man. Why do we need to state that the Son, born of the Virgin Mary by the power of the Spirit, actually became a human being?

Early in the life of the Church (in the second century), a teaching appeared on its margins—in various forms—that denied that Christ actually took flesh and became a human being. We call this teaching by the general term "Docetism."[9] Docetists claimed that Christ only *appeared* in human form for our sake, but he never really became a human being and he certainly did not die on a cross. In their view, Christ came to save us from this material world, and so he would never have condescended to take on a true human body. They believed in an entirely spiritual view of salvation that rejected the body and denied the incarnation of the Word. This Docetist view of Christ

---

8. The Greek verb used here in the Creed, "to become flesh" (*sarkoō*), and the corresponding noun "incarnation" (*sarkōsis*), appear very early in the Christian tradition—for example, in the writings of Irenaeus of Lyons in the late second century (see *Against Heresies* 3.19.1).

9. The term comes from the Greek verb *dokeō*, which means "to seem" or "to appear."

was rejected as incompatible with the clear scriptural teaching that the Word actually became flesh and was born as a human being. This human birth was not an appearance but a reality.

LEX ORANDI

Hymns to the *Theotokos*

In the liturgies of the Church, both West and East, Mary is honored for being the mother of God (*Theotokos*). In the first selection below, from the Roman liturgy, the Fourth Eucharistic Prayer reflects the language of the Creed and echoes key biblical texts that witness to the birth of Christ from Mary by the power of the Spirit. In the second selection, taken from the Byzantine liturgy of Saint John Chrysostom, Mary is acknowledged as the *Theotokos*.

> And you so loved the world, Father most holy,
> that in the fullness of time
> you sent your Only Begotten Son to be our Savior.
> Made incarnate by the Holy Spirit
> and born of the Virgin Mary,
> he shared our human nature
> in all things but sin.
> To the poor he proclaimed the good news of salvation,
> to prisoners, freedom,
> and to the sorrowful of heart, joy.
> To accomplish your plan,
> he gave himself up to death,
> and, rising from the dead,
> he destroyed death and restored life.[a]

> Only-begotten Son and Logos of God, being immortal, You condescended for our salvation to take flesh from the holy Theotokos and ever-virgin Mary and, without change, became man. Christ, our God, You were crucified and conquered death by death. Being one with the Holy Trinity, glorified with the Father and the Holy Spirit: Save us.[b]

a. *Roman Missal*, 657.
b. "The Divine Liturgy of St. John Chrysostom," Greek Orthodox Archdiocese of America, accessed January 22, 2023, https://www.goarch.org/-/the-divine-liturgy-of -saint-john-chrysostom. Used with permission.

But if some people denied that the divine Christ really became a human being, others believed that when Christ became a man, he had to set aside his divinity. In their view, the Son had to cease being God in order to truly become a man. There is a perennial tendency to interpret Paul's statement that Jesus "emptied himself" (Phil. 2:7) as meaning that the eternal Word somehow laid aside his divinity and ceased being divine—at least in part—in order to become a human being. But if this were so, then the promise of a virgin conceiving and bearing a son named Immanuel, "God with us" (Isa. 7:14), would prove false. It would no longer be God who was man, but one who *used to be God* who now existed as a man. But then the whole point of the incarnation, as revealed in the Scriptures, unravels. What the human race needed was God himself to come and save us. In the incarnation, the person of the Son has appeared as a true human being in order to represent and redeem the human race. The eternal Word emptied himself, not by ceasing to be God but by humbling himself to take on our limited and time-bound human nature. The wonder of the incarnation is that the unbounded divine Word appears on earth as a human being—and that, in that assumed human nature, he wins our salvation.

Mary Theotokos, the Mother of God

In the period following the compilation of the Nicene Creed in 381, the Church wrestled with the question of *how* the divine Word "became flesh" without compromising his divinity or our humanity. How can a divine person be born and live as a genuine human being while remaining divine? How is the divinity related to the humanity?

Among the answers given to these questions, two positions emerged that would prove deeply inadequate concerning the mystery of the incarnation. The first, proposed by Apollinaris, the bishop of Laodicea, offered a "replacement" theory of the incarnation. In this view, the Word of God "replaced" the intellectual human soul of Christ by a kind of possession of Christ's human body. This seemed promising: the sinful human soul is surgically removed, and the Word comes to take its place, operating through the "flesh" of Christ to accomplish our salvation on earth. The major problem with this model is that Christ does not possess a full humanity. There is no higher soul or human intellect in Christ. For Apollinaris, the Christ we meet in the pages of the Gospels is a kind of "product" of two parts: he is part Word (who runs things from the center) and part human (with the intellectual soul removed). As Gregory of Nazianzus famously stated in rejecting this model,

"The unassumed is the unhealed."[10] If Christ did not assume a full human nature, including a human soul, then we have not been saved.

The second position, proposed by Nestorius, the archbishop of Constantinople, described the incarnation as a kind of special indwelling. For Nestorius, the divine Word did not became a human being—this would have compromised his divine nature—but he came to *dwell* in a special way within "the man." Nestorius proposed a strongly dualistic view of the incarnation that viewed Christ as the combination of the Word dwelling in the man, allowing for the close cooperation of humanity and divinity, but that kept the divine and human in their proper and separate spheres. Nestorius denied that he was teaching a doctrine of "two sons," but it is hard to avoid the conclusion that there are two distinct "who's" in his depiction of Christ. The major problem with this model is that it does not provide a single personal identity in Christ. For Nestorius, Jesus is not simply the Word now existing as a human being, but the conjunction of "the Word" dwelling in a special way in "the man," a kind of product of two parts. Yet our Christian confession boldly declares that Jesus *is* the divine Word who now exists as a human being. He is the eternal Son who has assumed a human nature and so has *become man*.

Because he viewed the incarnation as "the Word" dwelling in "the man," Nestorius rejected the title *Theotokos* for the Virgin Mary. *Theotokos*—literally, "God-bearer"—is normally rendered in the Western tradition as "the Mother of God." Nestorius rightly pointed out that Mary did not give birth to the divine nature, but he wrongly concluded from this that she should not be hailed as *Theotokos*. In response, Cyril of Alexandria argued that, though of course Mary did not give birth to *the divine nature*, she did give human birth to *the divine Son* and so is rightly identified as *Theotokos*. Mary gave human birth not to "the man" in whom the Word came to specially dwell but to the one who is God.[11] This answers the fundamental question, *Who* is Jesus? Jesus is the divine Son, the eternal Word of God, who has genuinely assumed our human nature and become man, and Mary is the mother of the Son who received a human nature (body and soul) in her womb.

In the end, through a long series of debates and controversies, the Church confirmed the language of the Nicene Creed but clarified that the Word really did assume our human nature with all its properties, excluding sin—he

---

10. Gregory of Nazianzus, *First Letter to Cledonius* (*Letter* 101.5), in *On God and Christ: The Five Theological Orations and Two Letters to Cledonius*, trans. Lionel Wickham, PPS 23 (Crestwood, NY: St. Vladimir's Seminary Press, 2002), 158.

11. The Council of Ephesus in 431 upheld the title *Theotokos* for Mary and rejected the indwelling model of the incarnation put forward by Nestorius.

became a genuine human being, inclusive of human birth and growth—but that he remained fully divine at the same time. In the mystery of the incarnation, the Word's becoming flesh did not compromise his divinity in any way. The divinity of the Word was veiled as the Word became flesh but was in no way cast off or laid aside. The one who appears in the pages of the Gospels—Jesus of Nazareth—is the Word made flesh, at one and the same time fully divine and fully human. "Jesus is not two separate beings, nor is he a mere human person in an intimate rapport with God, in the manner of a great saint. Rather, in the unity of one person, he is both divine and human."[12]

Living the Mystery

One way we can honor the great event of the incarnation is to stand in reverent awe and thanksgiving for this great act of love and condescension on God's part. "God so loved the world that he gave his only-begotten Son" (John 3:16 RSV-2CE). Each year, especially at the time of the Nativity of Jesus (Christmas), we celebrate in readings, carols, and visual images the marvelous and unthinkable action of God, who actually became one of us, fully assuming our nature, to win our salvation.

But we can also—in our own way—seek to imitate the great humility of the Word. The Creed speaks of a *descent*, a *coming down* of the Word from heaven. This is powerfully captured by Paul's great hymn in Philippians 2:5–11, which depicts a double "descent" or humbling. The first unthinkable descent was God humbling himself to become man. He descended and lowered himself to take on our sin-impacted nature (Rom. 8:3), to redeem our nature and bring us eternal life. The second descent was a further and equally unthinkable humbling: the Son, now as a man, humbled himself even to an ignominious, shameful, painful death on a cross. And he suffered this, not for anything he did or deserved, but to take our place and bear the suffering that was due to us.

In a symbolic way, the Lord Jesus acts out this double descent on the night before he died. Gathered with his disciples, he strips off his garments and adopts the posture of a servant. This is symbolic of the incarnation, of the divine Son emptying himself and taking the form of a servant and becoming man. And then, *as a servant*, he washes the feet of his disciples, one by one. This is symbolic of his sacrificial death, which cleanses us from all sin. Crucially, the Lord Jesus calls his disciples to "do as he did" and wash one another's feet. And so another significant way that we can respond to the incarnation of the

12. Barron, *Light from Light*, 64.

Word is to imitate Christ's lowliness and his sacrificial love by humbly "washing the feet" of those around us, even to the point of giving away our lives.

For Our Sake He Was Crucified

For our sake he was crucified under Pontius Pilate, he suffered death and was buried.	Crucifixus etiam pro nobis sub Pontio Pilato, passus et sepultus est.	σταυρωθέντα τε ὑπὲρ ἡμῶν ἐπὶ Ποντίου Πιλάτου καὶ παθόντα καὶ ταφέντα.

OT: Pss. 16:8–11; 22; Isa. 42:1–4; 50:4–9; 52:13–53:12; Jon. 1:17

NT: Mark 8:31; Luke 22:15; 24:44–46; John 3:14; 12:32–33; Acts 2:36; 4:10; 1 Cor. 1:23; 2:2; 15:3–4; 1 Tim. 6:13

Catechism: Jesus's passion, death, and burial, 571–73, 595–637

Theological Exposition

The Suffering, Death, and Resurrection of Christ according to the Scriptures

The narrative of the Creed now moves directly from Jesus's incarnation to his redemptive suffering and death. This does not minimize the importance of Jesus's earthly ministry or his teaching—his acts and words—that we find in the pages of the Gospels. These are implicitly taken up and included here. But the Creed confesses only the primary events that provide the central narrative of the entire scope of Christ's earthly ministry. And so we move directly to his crucifixion, sacrificial death, burial, and resurrection. The Creed's focus on these events reflects Paul's own summary of what was handed to him as the central events of our faith: "For I delivered to you as of first importance what I also received, that Christ died for our sins in accordance with the Scriptures, that he was buried, that he was raised on the third day in accordance with the Scriptures" (1 Cor. 15:3–4).

At this point, it is helpful to recognize that the testimony of the Gospels, even in the infancy narratives, points forward to Jesus's death and resurrection.[13] In other words, Christ's suffering and death was not a misstep or an

---

13. In Luke, the aged Simeon prophesies to Mary and Joseph that their child will cause the rising and fall of many in Israel and that a sword will also pierce Mary's own heart because of the destiny of this child (Luke 2:25–35). In Matthew, the Magi bring gifts, among which is

unexpected turn of events that God somehow used to bring about his purposes: "Jesus' violent death was not the result of chance in an unfortunate coincidence of circumstances, but is part of the mystery of God's plan."[14] *From the beginning*, the Son was born to suffer and die according to the testimony of the Scriptures. What Moses and the prophets declared in mystery was fulfilled in Christ's suffering, death, and resurrection. Jesus gives his own testimony to this on Easter Day when he tells his disciples that "'everything written about me in the law of Moses and the prophets and the psalms must be fulfilled.' Then he opened their minds to understand the Scriptures, and said to them, 'Thus it is written, that the Christ should suffer and on the third day rise from the dead'" (Luke 24:44–46). Strikingly here, Jesus sums up his own life in terms of his suffering, death, and resurrection. He points to these events as the central realities that accomplish the salvation he came to win on our behalf. Peter echoes the same truth in his speech before the Sanhedrin: "But what God foretold by the mouth of all the prophets, that his Christ should suffer, he thus fulfilled" (Acts 3:18). And Paul adds his own testimony in his speech before King Agrippa, claiming that he is "saying nothing but what the prophets and Moses said would come to pass: that the Christ must suffer, and that, by being the first to rise from the dead, he would proclaim light both to the people and to the Gentiles" (Acts 26:22–23). In presenting these events for our belief and confession, the Creed closely follows the testimony of the Bible.

For Our Sake He Was Crucified under Pontius Pilate[15]

The Creed begins the narrative of Christ's passion by saying, "For our sake . . ." Once again, we are reminded that Christ did all this "for us" or "on our behalf." We are the recipients of his great and undeserved mercy. The Creed then adds that Jesus "was crucified." We all know something of this gruesome punishment employed by the Romans to execute their enemies in the most fearsome manner. But why would the first Christians draw attention to this grim form of death that befell their revered Lord? We would expect them to hide or at least minimize the fact that he died in the most awful way possible, executed as a criminal. Instead, they made the cross and the

---

myrrh, commonly used in the anointing at burials. Both of these signal that Jesus is destined for suffering and even death (Matt. 2:7–11).

14. *CCC* 599.

15. This line is absent from the Creed of Nicaea (325). The authors of the Nicene Creed (381) clearly wanted to underline the historical setting and reality of Jesus's death on the cross, following the example of the Acts of the Apostles.

crucifixion a central element in their narrative of Christ (in the Gospels) and highlighted the fact of his crucifixion in their preaching.

Jesus himself, early in his ministry, announced that his destiny was to be "lifted up" for the salvation of the world: "And as Moses lifted up the serpent in the wilderness, so must the Son of man be lifted up, that whoever believes in him may have eternal life" (John 3:14–15). On the eve of his death, Jesus returns to this figure, which is linked directly to his imminent death: "'And I, when I am lifted up from the earth, will draw all men to myself.' He said this to show by what death he was to die" (12:32–33). On numerous occasions, Jesus challenged his disciples to take up their cross and follow him, in imitation of himself (Matt. 10:38; 16:24; Mark 8:34; Luke 9:23; 14:27). This obvious reference to crucifixion must have puzzled and alarmed his followers, who only later understood just how literally this would be fulfilled.

The apostle Paul seems to revel in the cross of Christ, not only in his preaching but also in the way he viewed his own life in Christ. Knowing that the crucifixion was a stumbling block to the Jewish people and a source of folly in the eyes of the gentiles, Paul nonetheless insisted on preaching Christ crucified (1 Cor. 1:23), declaring to the Corinthians, "For I decided to know nothing among you except Jesus Christ and him crucified" (2:2). Christ's crucifixion also appears in early summaries of the faith in the Acts of the Apostles. Preaching on the day of Pentecost, Peter does not spare his listeners: "Let all the house of Israel therefore know assuredly that God has made him both Lord and Christ, this Jesus whom you crucified" (Acts 2:36). He makes the same charge against the gathered Sanhedrin shortly afterward (4:10).

But why add "under Pontius Pilate" to the statement of faith in the Creed? Pilate, the Roman procurator who governed Judea on behalf of the Roman emperor, was clearly a key figure in the prosecution and death of Jesus. It was by his authority that the crucifixion occurred, and all four Gospels give ample testimony to how he was pressured by the Jewish authorities to consign Jesus to death by crucifixion.[16] But even more, Pilate represents a historical anchor in Jesus's life and death (see Luke 3:1). Jesus's trial and death happened not in the backwoods but under the eye and authority of the great power of the day (Rome). It is striking that in the book of Acts, Pilate is named on three separate occasions in connection with the death of Jesus (Acts 3:13; 4:27; 13:28). Paul even names Pilate in his First Letter to Timothy, where he speaks of "Christ Jesus who in his testimony before Pontius Pilate made the good confession" (1 Tim. 6:13). In short, when the Creed says that Christ "was

16. For Pilate's role in the death of Jesus, see Matt. 27; Mark 15; Luke 23; and John 18–19.

crucified under Pontius Pilate," it sums up the early Christian confession, found in the Scriptures, as a witness to how God has acted in history, bringing about the salvation of the human race through the paradoxical and gruesome death of his Son on the cross.

He Suffered Death and Was Buried

The Creed, in both Greek and Latin, literally says "he suffered and was buried." The verb "to suffer," when applied to Jesus, often contains within it the reality of death (see Luke 22:15; 24:46). The Letter to the Hebrews calls this "the suffering of death" (Heb. 2:9). We derive our word "passion" from the verb "to suffer"; Jesus's passion, then, refers to his suffering and death.

Jesus told his disciples on several occasions that he would suffer and die in Jerusalem: "And he began to teach them that the Son of man must suffer many things, and be rejected by the elders and the chief priests and the scribes, and be killed, and after three days rise again" (Mark 8:31; see also Matt. 16:21; Luke 9:22). Peter grasped clearly enough what Jesus meant and rebuked him, only to be rebuked by Jesus in return for standing (like Satan) in the path of God's plan: "And Peter took him and began to rebuke him, saying, 'God forbid, Lord! This shall never happen to you.' But he turned and said to Peter, 'Get behind me, Satan! You are a hindrance to me; for you are not on the side of God, but of men'" (Matt. 16:22–23). When Jesus addresses the disciples at the start of the Last Supper, he alerts them that the time for his suffering is at hand: "I have earnestly desired to eat this Passover with you before I suffer" (Luke 22:15).

Peter's rebuke reflected the Jewish expectation of his day: the Messiah of Israel was not supposed to suffer and die; he was meant to lead his people to victory over their enemies and bring about the peaceful reign of God in the land of promise. But Jesus understood that the "servant" passages in Isaiah revealed a different destiny for himself. He knew he was the Lord's servant, his chosen one, anointed by the Spirit to bring God's covenant to the people and light to the nations (Isa. 42:1–4; 49:6). He knew that the servant of the Lord was to suffer beatings and insults (50:4–6). Most of all, he understood that he was the servant who was chosen to suffer and die for the people, to take their punishment upon himself, that they might be free:

> Surely he has borne our griefs
> and carried our sorrows;
> yet we esteemed him stricken,
> struck down by God, and afflicted.

But he was wounded for our transgressions,
    he was bruised for our iniquities;
upon him was the chastisement that made us whole,
    and with his stripes we are healed.
All we like sheep have gone astray;
    we have turned every one to his own way;
and the LORD has laid on him
    the iniquity of us all. (Isa. 53:4–6 RSV-2CE)

LEX ORANDI

The Veneration of the Cross

During the veneration of the cross on Good Friday, the choir typically sings the mournful verses called "the reproaches." These short verses express how we treated Christ shamefully, who had given everything to us.

My people, what have I done to you?
    Or how have I grieved you? Answer me!
I scourged Egypt for your sake with its firstborn sons,
    and you scourged me and handed me over.
I led you out from Egypt as Pharaoh lay sunk in the Red Sea,
    and you handed me over to the chief priests.
I opened up the sea before you,
    and you opened my side with a lance.
I went before you in a pillar of cloud,
    and you led me into Pilate's palace.
I fed you with manna in the desert,
    and on me you rained blows and lashes.
I gave you saving water from the rock to drink,
    and for drink you gave me gall and vinegar.
I struck down for you the kings of the Canaanites,
    and you struck my head with a reed.
I put in your hand a royal scepter,
    and you put on my head a crown of thorns.
I exalted you with great power,
    and you hung me on the scaffold of the Cross.
My people, what have I done to you?
    Or how have I grieved you? Answer me![a]

a. *Roman Missal*, 331–33.

In what ways, then, did Jesus "suffer" on our behalf? In the first place, he suffered—knowingly and willingly—grievous physical punishment and torture, among the worst imaginable, through the scourging, crowning, and crucifixion that led to his death. Second, he suffered the grief of betrayal, denial, and abandonment from his closest followers, though he announced ahead of time that he knew this would happen. Third, he suffered mocking and insults not only from the Roman soldiers but also from the Jewish leaders who opposed him. Jesus went to his death with his opponents believing that he was a fraud and abandoned by God. Finally, he suffered—in a way unimaginable to us—the weight and grief of our sin. By bearing the full weight of our sin, Jesus suffered a spiritual anguish far greater than anything we can conceive. He truly was the Lamb of God, led to the slaughter, who bore our offenses and tasted death for us (Heb. 2:9).[17] Despite all these forms of suffering, the Letter to the Hebrews tells us that Jesus endured the suffering and shame of the cross willingly and with the expectation of joy because of love for his Father: "who for the joy that was set before him endured the cross, despising the shame, and is seated at the right hand of the throne of God" (12:2).

Jesus not only suffered death, but he was really and truly buried in the earth. Each of the Gospels recounts the burial of Jesus in some detail.[18] The Roman centurion, by piercing his side with a spear, confirmed that Jesus was actually dead (John 19:33–34). Joseph of Arimathea, a rich man, asked Pilate for the body and placed it in his own tomb nearby (19:38). Jesus was placed in the tomb on Friday, just before the opening of the Sabbath; he lay in the tomb all of Saturday; and on the third day (early on Sunday), he rose from the dead. Jesus himself predicted his own burial, likening it to the three days that Jonah spent in the belly of the whale (Matt. 12:40). And Paul includes the burial of Jesus as part of the fundamental †kerygma that he received and handed on: "For I delivered to you as of first importance what I also received, that Christ died for our sins in accordance with the Scriptures, *that he was buried . . .*" (1 Cor. 15:3–4). The burial of Jesus is not only a recorded fact; it underscores that Jesus truly died and was put in the earth. He did not temporarily swoon and then recover; he truly died and was buried, his body truly a corpse. Jesus *really died*, and his burial is proof of his bodily death.

17. Thomas Joseph White sums up the suffering of Christ under three headings: "Jesus' suffering is varied, and pertains to his spiritual faculties, his emotions or passions, and to his physical body" (*The Trinity: On the Nature and Mystery of the One God* [Washington, DC: Catholic University of America Press, 2022], 644).

18. See Matt. 27:57–66; Mark 15:42–47; Luke 23:50–56; John 19:38–42.

The Nicene Creed does not make reference to Christ's descent to the place of the dead (to "hell"), as we find in the Apostles' Creed. But the conviction, grounded in the Scriptures, that Christ descended to the place of the dead was widespread in the early Church, both East and West. According to this view, because Jesus really died and his soul was separated from his body at death, his soul went to the place of the dead (in biblical terms, Sheol or Hades). But as the *Catechism* says, "He descended there as

WITNESS TO THE TRADITION

Pope Leo the Great on Christ's Passion

Leo the Great preached year after year on the passion, death, and resurrection of Christ. In this homily, he draws our attention especially to how Christ assumed our nature—our weakness—in order to win redemption for our nature and bring us to share in the very life of God.

Among all the works of God's mercy, dearly beloved, which from the beginning have been devoted to the salvation of mortals, none is more wonderful, none more sublime, than that Christ was crucified for the world. All the mysteries of former times serve this mystery. . . . "God was in Christ reconciling the world to himself" (2 Cor. 5:19), and the Creator himself was bearing the humanity that was about to be restored to the image of its Maker. . . . Jesus knew that the time for the fulfillment of his glorious Passion was at hand and said, "My soul is sorrowful even unto death" (Matt. 26:38), and . . . "Father, if it is possible, let this cup pass away from me" (Matt. 26:39). Since these words express a certain fear, he cured the emotion of our weakness by participating in it, and drove away the anxiety in the experience of suffering by undergoing it. In us, therefore, the Lord trembled with our terror, that he might clothe himself by the putting on of our weakness, and wrap our inconstancy in the firmness of his strength. . . . He had entered the economy of salvation in a wonderful interchange, receiving our state and giving us his own, giving honors for insults, health for pain, life for death.[a]

a. Leo the Great, *Sermon* 54.1, 4, in *Sermons*, trans. Jane P. Freeland and Agnes J. Conway, FOTC 93 (Washington, DC: Catholic University of America Press, 1996), 232–35.

LEX ORANDI

Christ's Passion

The opening prayer for the celebration of Good Friday asks for the grace of the passion of Christ to transform our lives, so that we might reflect the image of Christ, the new Adam:

> O God, who by the Passion of Christ your Son, our Lord,
> abolished the death inherited from ancient sin
> by every succeeding generation,
> grant that just as, being conformed to him,
> we have borne by the law of nature
> the image of the man of earth,
> so by the sanctification of grace
> we may bear the image of the Man of heaven.[a]

a. *Roman Missal*, 315.

Savior, proclaiming the Good News to the spirits imprisoned there."[19] The descent to the place of the dead both confirms Christ's real death and completes his saving work. According to this tradition, Christ entered Hades, bound Satan the strong man (Matt. 12:28–29), and broke the devil's power of death over the human race. By proclaiming the gospel to the dead (1 Pet. 4:6), Christ completed the proclamation of the good news to all, and he brought away with him those who were eagerly waiting for his appearing. As the *Catechism* explains, "Jesus did not descend into hell to deliver the damned, nor to destroy the hell of damnation, but to free the just who had gone before him."[20]

Living the Mystery

We know that Jesus's suffering and death was uniquely effective. As Paul says, Christ is the new Adam whose death brought about the true and perfect sacrifice to atone for our sins: "For if many died through one man's trespass, much more have the grace of God and the free gift in the grace of that one

---

19. CCC 632, referring to 1 Pet. 3:18–19.
20. CCC 633.

man Jesus Christ abounded for many" (Rom. 5:15). The *Catechism* explains this unique sacrifice for sins as the work of the Trinity:

> This sacrifice of Christ is unique; it completes and surpasses all other sacrifices. First, it is a gift from God the Father himself, for the Father handed his Son over to sinners in order to reconcile us with himself. At the same time it is the offering of the Son of God made man, who in freedom and love offered his life to his Father through the Holy Spirit in reparation for our disobedience.[21]

We "live this mystery" first of all by receiving it in faith: "So we are ambassadors for Christ, God making his appeal through us. We beg you on behalf of Christ, be reconciled to God" (2 Cor. 5:20 RSV-2CE). By believing the gospel and turning away from our sin, we receive the new life that comes from Christ's sacrifice. We also live the mystery by participating in the liturgy and receiving the Eucharist. Through both word and sacrament, Christ's unique sacrifice is made present, and his grace is poured out anew.

But we also live this mystery by participating in a mysterious way in the suffering of Christ. Paul especially identifies this suffering with Christ as part of what it means to be sons and daughters of God, filled with the Spirit: "When we cry, 'Abba! Father!' it is the Spirit himself bearing witness with our spirit that we are children of God, and if children, then heirs, heirs of God and fellow heirs with Christ, *provided we suffer with him* in order that we may also be glorified with him" (Rom. 8:15–17). Peter also tells us that suffering with and for Christ is part of what it means to be his disciple: "Beloved, do not be surprised at the fiery ordeal which comes upon you to prove you, as though something strange were happening to you. But rejoice in so far as you share Christ's sufferings, that you may also rejoice and be glad when his glory is revealed" (1 Pet. 4:12–13).

This is a part of the Christian life that most of us would gladly bypass. It does not sound like "good news." Christ's work of redemption delivers us from sin, frees us from the fear of death, and sets us free to live a new life in the Spirit. But in his generosity, Christ also invites us to share in his suffering, to join our suffering to his, and to offer our suffering back to him, so that in a mysterious way it may contribute to the good of others and the salvation of the world (see 2 Cor. 4:11–12). Christ uniquely died for the sins of the whole world, but we can join our suffering and even our death to the suffering and death of the one who died for us: "For this reason we . . . are taken up into

---

21. CCC 614.

the mysteries of his life, . . . associated with his sufferings as the body with its head, suffering with him, that with him we may be glorified."[22]

And Rose Again on the Third Day

| And rose again on the third day in accordance with the Scriptures. | Et resurrexit tertia die secundum Scripturas, | καὶ ἀναστάντα τῇ τρίτῃ ἡμέρᾳ κατὰ τὰς γραφάς, |
| He ascended into heaven and is seated at the right hand of the Father. | et ascendit in caelum, sedet ad dexteram Patris. | καὶ ἀνελθόντα εἰς τοὺς οὐρανούς, καὶ καθεζόμενον ἐν δεξιᾷ τοῦ πατρός. |

OT: Ps. 16:8–11; Isa. 53:10–11; Hosea 6:2
NT: Matt. 12:40; Luke 24:44–46; Acts 2:31–33; Rom. 1:4; 1 Cor. 15:20–21; 2 Cor. 5:4–8; Eph. 1:20; 5:1; Rev. 1:17–18
Catechism: the resurrection of Jesus, 638–58; the ascension of Jesus, 659–67

Theological Exposition

Christ's resurrection and ascension are discrete events in Scripture—and we celebrate them liturgically on different days—but they belong together as two parts of one fundamental action. Christ rose from the dead in order to ascend to heaven and sit as Lord at the right hand of the Father. When Paul writes that "God has highly exalted [Jesus] and bestowed on him the name which is above every name" (Phil. 2:9), he is including in one sweeping action both the resurrection and the ascension. When the Letter to the Hebrews, speaking of Christ, says, "When he had made purification for sins, he sat down at the right hand of the Majesty on high" (Heb. 1:3), it moves directly from the cross to Christ's glorious ascension and enthronement in heaven. The resurrection is assumed in this one movement. The two events—resurrection and ascension—are sometimes joined together in one statement of God's work. In Ephesians, Paul states that the Father "accomplished [his work] in Christ when he raised him from the dead and made him sit at his right hand in the heavenly places" (Eph. 1:20). And in Acts, Peter proclaims that "this Jesus God raised up" and immediately adds that Jesus is "exalted at the right hand of God" (Acts 2:32–33).

22. CCC 793.

At the same time, Christ's resurrection and ascension make no sense apart from his suffering and death. The suffering, death, resurrection, and ascension of Jesus all form part of one act, one saving work—and this is why the Creed highlights these events and binds them together in our common confession of the faith.

And Rose Again on the Third Day in accordance with the Scriptures

The resurrection of Christ is the lynchpin of our faith. The *Catechism* calls it "the crowning truth of our faith in Christ."[23] According to Bishop Robert Barron, "The Resurrection of Jesus Christ from the dead is the fulcrum on which all of Christian faith turns."[24] Paul makes this forcefully clear when he says, "If Christ has not been raised, then our preaching is in vain and your faith is in vain. We are even found to be misrepresenting God" (1 Cor. 15:14–15). He goes on to show that if the resurrection did not really occur, then as Christians we live a false and pitiable life: "If Christ has not been raised, your faith is futile and you are still in your sins. . . . If for this life only we have hoped in Christ, we are of all men most to be pitied" (15:17, 19).

Why is this so? Because if Christ died and remained dead (in the tomb), then his claims about himself and his work would be crushed. He would be (at best) a teacher and prophet who may have said some good and lasting things about human life. But his extraordinary claims about his relationship with his Father (e.g., that in him God is present) and his promise that he would provide eternal life to those who believe in him—all this and more would be proved false and ungrounded. By raising Jesus from the dead, the Father vindicates and confirms all that Jesus said and did. As Paul says, Jesus was "designated Son of God in power according to the Spirit of holiness by his resurrection from the dead" (Rom. 1:4).

But the resurrection of Jesus is much more than the Father's stamp of approval on Jesus's words and actions. It is also the breaking in of the new creation and the establishment of Jesus as the Lord of all creation. As the book of Revelation depicts so powerfully, Jesus is the one who "lives": "I am the first and the last, and the living one; I died, and behold I am alive for evermore, and I have the keys of Death and Hades" (Rev. 1:17–18). Jesus is not like a superhero who returns to his home after a successful campaign in

---

23. CCC 638.
24. Barron, *Light from Light*, 88.

the world. Jesus returns to the Father but now *in our nature*, as the glorified Son of Man. In Christ our nature has received a new birth. It is now a human being who sits on God's very throne, the Word made flesh now glorified in our human nature. And because he is there, so we are with him when we become joined to his body. This is the profound significance of the resurrection and ascension of Jesus to the right hand of the Father.

Testimony to the resurrection of Jesus appears prominently in all four Gospels.[25] The empty tomb of Jesus provides a kind of negative evidence for the resurrection: his body is no longer there, and no one can produce it to show that he is still dead. But it is the many resurrection appearances, beginning with Mary Magdalene and other women at the tomb, that provide the positive testimony to Jesus being bodily alive again and that empower the early Christians to proclaim Jesus as risen from the dead. To their utter amazement, they saw him alive again—and this they proclaimed. In fact, being a witness to the resurrection is one of the main qualifications for being an apostle. When Peter addresses the other apostles about the need to replace Judas, he says that they must choose one of those who have gone about with them, because "one of these men must become with us a witness to his resurrection" (Acts 1:22). The apostles are the primary witnesses to his resurrection, but these witnesses also include James, Paul himself, and up to five hundred brothers and sisters at one time (1 Cor. 5:5–8).

As the *Catechism* clarifies, the resurrection of Jesus was both an event in human history and an event that goes beyond normal human history. It took place in time—three days after his death—and was empirically experienced by many who saw Jesus, touched him, shared a meal with him, and even put their hands in his wounds. At the same time, Jesus rose to a new and different life not restricted by the parameters of our world. According to Pope Benedict XVI, "Jesus' resurrection was about breaking out into an entirely new form of life, into a life that is no longer subject to the law of dying and becoming, but lies beyond it—a life that opens up a new dimension of human existence."[26]

The resurrection of Jesus is not the resuscitation of a corpse but the beginning of a new kind of life—the eternal life of God's kingdom. Jesus's body (his corpse) was no longer in the tomb—he was bodily raised from the dead. But his body was transformed and made new through the power of God.

25. See Matt. 28; Mark 16; Luke 24; John 20–21.
26. Pope Benedict XVI, *Jesus of Nazareth*, part 2, *Holy Week: From the Entrance into Jerusalem to the Resurrection*, trans. Vatican Secretariat of State (San Francisco: Ignatius, 2011), 244.

In his resurrected body, Jesus interacted and ate with the disciples, and he still bore the wounds of his passion and death, but he could also appear at will. According to the *Catechism*, Christ's resurrected body is "not limited by space and time but able to be present how and when he wills; for Christ's humanity can no longer be confined to earth and belongs henceforth only to the Father's divine realm."[27]

The Creed confesses that Jesus "rose again on the third day *in accordance with the Scriptures*" (emphasis added). We would all like to have been part of the Bible study that Jesus held on Easter Day, when he explained to the apostles how "everything written about me in the law of Moses and the prophets and the psalms must be fulfilled" (Luke 24:44). Jesus then adds, "Thus it is written, that the Christ should suffer and on the third day rise from the dead" (24:46).

While we do not have a transcript of what Jesus said that day, we have reliable clues about what passages from the Old Testament speak of Jesus's resurrection. Peter himself, preaching on the day of Pentecost, points to Psalm 16 as biblical evidence, claiming that David "foresaw and spoke of the resurrection of the Christ" (Acts 2:31). We can also see an indication of Christ's resurrection in the conclusions of both Psalm 22 and Isaiah 53. These two texts point powerfully to Christ's suffering and death, but they also indicate that the one who suffers returns to new life (see Ps. 22:22, 29–30; Isa. 53:10–11). What about Christ rising "on the third day"?[28] Is there any indication of this from the Old Testament? It was on the third day that the Lord appeared of old on Mount Sinai; this was a "theophany" (a divine manifestation) of the Lord in glory (Exod. 19:10–11). But the passage most commonly referenced by scholars is from the prophet Hosea: "On the third day he will raise us up, that we may live before him" (Hosea 6:2). In addition, Jesus refers to the three days of Jonah in the belly of the whale as representing his burial in the earth, signifying his resurrection after three days (Matt. 12:40).

In summary, the confession that Jesus rose again on the third day is a central part of the Church's kerygma, as we see in Paul's own summary statement of the basic gospel: "He was raised on the third day in accordance with the Scriptures" (1 Cor. 15:4). To announce that Jesus died but then rose from the dead, never to die again, was a core element of the preaching of the early Church and remains the same for us today.

27. CCC 645.
28. The New Testament refers to Christ rising on the third day especially in Matthew (16:21; 17:23; 20:19) and Luke (9:22; 18:33; 24:7) but also in Acts 10:40 and 1 Cor. 15:4.

He Ascended into Heaven and Is Seated at the Right Hand of the Father [29]

We have already noted that Christ's ascension is intimately connected to his resurrection. The ascension is the completion of the resurrection, the exaltation of the risen Son to the right hand of the Father, where he reigns as Lord. The event of the ascension appears in Mark (16:19) but is especially developed in Luke and Acts. The closing of the Gospel of Luke describes this event: "Then he led them out as far as Bethany, and lifting up his hands he blessed them. While he blessed them, he parted from them, and was carried up into heaven" (Luke 24:50–51; see also Acts 1:9–11). In the Gospel of John, Jesus speaks frequently about his imminent "going to the Father," and shockingly, he tells his disciples that "it is to your advantage that I go away." Why is this an advantage? "For if I do not go away, the Counselor will not come to you; but if I go, I will send him to you" (John 16:7). The ascension of Christ is also closely linked to the outpouring of the Spirit, as Peter confirms in his speech on Pentecost day: "Being therefore exalted at the right hand of God, and having received from the Father the promise of the Holy Spirit, he has poured out this which you see and hear" (Acts 2:33).

The early Christian confession of Christ's ascension and enthronement is grounded in two Old Testament passages. The first is Psalm 110:1: "The LORD says to my lord: 'Sit at my right hand, till I make your enemies your footstool.'" Peter cites this verse in his Pentecost preaching (Acts 2:34–36) to show that what the people are experiencing is the fulfillment of this enthronement passage from Psalm 110. Paul makes reference to this verse when he says that Christ "must reign until he has put all his enemies under his feet" (1 Cor. 15:25). Hebrews, too, refers to this verse with respect to Christ's ascension and enthronement, saying that Christ "sat down at the right hand of the Majesty on high" (Heb. 1:3).[30]

The second passage is Daniel's powerful vision of the Son of Man appearing on the clouds of heaven. This figure "came to the Ancient of Days and was presented before him. And to him was given dominion and glory and kingdom" (Dan. 7:13–14). Christ applies this to himself in his confession

---

29. The reference to Christ sitting at the right hand of the Father is not in the Creed of Nicaea (325) but was added by those who composed the Nicene Creed (381). This addition—Christ seated at the Father's right hand—underscores the ongoing distinction between the Father and the Son even in heaven, and so it tacitly rejects the modalism (the merging of the Father and the Son) that was current in the mid-fourth century.

30. Jesus applies Ps. 110:1 to himself in Matt. 22:41–46; Mark 12:35–37; Luke 20:41–44.

LEX ORANDI

Christ's Ascension

The collects for the Feast of the Ascension underline the meaning of Christ's ascension and lift our hearts to embrace the grace of this mystery. Christ's ascension is also our exaltation; even now, in this life, we may dwell with him there in spirit.

Gladden us with holy joys, almighty God,
and make us rejoice with devout thanksgiving,
for the Ascension of Christ your Son
is our exaltation,
and, where the Head has gone before in glory,
the Body is called to follow in hope.

Grant, we pray, almighty God,
that we, who believe that your Only Begotten Son, our Redeemer,
    ascended this day to the heavens,
may in spirit dwell already in heavenly realms.
Who lives and reigns with you in the unity of the Holy Spirit,
God, for ever and ever.[a]

a. *Roman Missal*, 432 (modified).

before the high priest: "Again the high priest asked him, 'Are you the Christ, the Son of the Blessed?' And Jesus said, 'I am; and you will see the Son of man seated at the right hand of Power, and coming with the clouds of heaven'" (Mark 14:61–62). It is this vision that Saint Stephen saw as he was being stoned to death: "Behold, I see the heavens opened, and the Son of man standing at the right hand of God" (Acts 7:56). The book of Revelation portrays the fulfillment of Daniel's vision when depicting the ascension and enthronement of Christ. The Son, the Lamb of God, comes to the throne of his Father and receives the scroll that reveals the unfolding of human history. And all the heavenly host join in praise and worship of God and the Lamb: "Worthy is the Lamb who was slain, to receive power and wealth and wisdom and might and honor and glory and blessing!" (Rev. 5:12). This is a vision from the "other side" of the ascension. The disciples witness Jesus departing into heaven; Revelation presents his glorious arrival in heaven and enthronement with the Father.

WITNESS TO THE TRADITION

John of Damascus on Christ's Ascension

The *Catechism* cites the great Eastern Church Father Saint John of Damascus (d. 750) to show how the eternal Son who is God is now seated bodily at the Father's right hand:

> Henceforth Christ is *seated at the right hand of the Father*: "By 'the Father's right hand' we understand the glory and honor of divinity, where he who exists as Son of God before all ages, indeed as God, of one being with the Father, is seated bodily after he became incarnate and his flesh was glorified."[a]

a. CCC 663 (quoting John of Damascus, *An Exposition of the Orthodox Faith* 4.2).

In summary, the ascension of Christ completes the great work of redemption and re-creation. "Being seated at the Father's right hand signifies the inauguration of the Messiah's kingdom, the fulfillment of the prophet Daniel's vision concerning the Son of man."[31] With Christ, the Lamb of God, seated on the throne, there is now "a man" on the throne who is also God the Son. Christ died for our redemption and rose to give us new life, and by his presence with the Father he is now able to rule as Lord over all creation.

Living the Mystery

Paul provides a clue to how we can live the mystery of Christ's resurrection and ascension. He writes to the church in Rome, "We were buried therefore with him by baptism into death, so that as Christ was raised from the dead by the glory of the Father, we too might walk in newness of life" (Rom. 6:4). What does Jesus's resurrection equip us to do? *To walk in newness of life.* Christians are often criticized for talking a lot about redemption but failing to look redeemed. If we proclaim that Jesus has died and risen again, then this should result in a way of life that reflects the power of the risen Christ. If we consistently fail to show this newness of life, then we are justly critiqued for being hypocrites.

31. CCC 664.

Paul also speaks of his desire to know Christ and "the power of his resurrection" (Phil. 3:10). This is not a hope for the next life but a power to live for Christ *in this life*. The preeminent source for living a new way of life is the gift of the Spirit. We "live this mystery," then, especially by living the new way of life in Christ by the power of the Spirit.

What does this mean? It means a new way of *acting*, especially the overcoming of sin. For Paul, the power of Christ's resurrection comes to us so that "we might no longer be enslaved to sin" (Rom. 6:6). What a great joy it is when we experience sinful patterns giving way and the fruit of the Spirit blossoming in our lives!

It means a new way of *thinking*, our minds being transformed in Christ: "Do not be conformed to this world but be transformed by the renewal of your mind" (Rom. 12:2). Through Christ's Spirit our minds can be genuinely renewed and sanctified, so that we are led to ponder the things of God that are worthy of praise (Phil. 4:8).

To walk in newness of life also means a new way of *loving*. Because God's own love has been poured into our hearts through the Holy Spirit (Rom. 5:5), we are now equipped to begin to love the way God loves. This means loving others from the heart with a sincere love (1 Pet. 1:22). It brings about a readiness to lay down our lives for one another, even to death if the occasion arises (John 15:13).

A beautiful verse from Paul's Letter to the Ephesians sums up what it means to live this mystery by walking in newness of life: "Therefore be imitators of God, as beloved children. And walk in love, as Christ loved us and gave himself up for us, a fragrant offering and sacrifice to God" (Eph. 5:1–2).

He Will Come Again in Glory

He will come again in glory to judge the living and the dead, and his kingdom will have no end.	et iterum venturus est cum gloria, iudicare vivos et mortuos: cuius regni non erit finis.	καὶ πάλιν ἐρχόμενον μετὰ δόξης, κρῖναι ζῶντας καὶ νεκρούς· οὗ τῆς βασιλείας οὐκ ἔσται τέλος.

OT: Pss. 9:7–8; 96:12–13; Isa. 11:3–4

NT: Matt. 25:31–46; John 5:22, 28–29; 14:3; Acts 10:42; 17:31; 1 Cor. 15:24–28; 2 Cor. 5:10; 2 Tim. 4:1; Heb. 9:28; 1 Pet. 1:17; Rev. 3:3; 21:22–23

Catechism: the second coming of Jesus and the final judgment, 668–82

Theological Exposition

He Will Come Again in Glory to Judge the Living and the Dead

This closing statement points to the final act of the story of redemption: Jesus's glorious return to bring the kingdom of God to its consummation. We believe and confess that Christ has risen and ascended to heaven, where he now reigns as Lord, but we also know from divine revelation that this same Jesus will return again in glory to bring a final reckoning (judgment) to all people. The promise of Christ's return in glory is not just something added to our faith as a kind of appendix, or something boxed away and put into the attic until needed. The return of the Lord is an essential part of the gospel message; it brings to completion the work of redemption (Rom. 8:19–23).

It is helpful to recognize that the Creed splits the account of "last things" into two parts. In this first part here, the focus is on Jesus himself returning in glory to judge all people (living and dead). In the second part—the final sentence of the Creed—we hear about the resurrection of the dead and eternal life in the world to come. Together they comprise our confession that this world is not all that there is: we await the bodily return of Christ, the resurrection of our bodies, the final judgment, and the renewal of the whole creation.

Jesus himself alerts his disciples that he will be going away but will return again: "And when I go and prepare a place for you, *I will come again* and will take you to myself, that where I am you may be also" (John 14:3). The Letter to the Hebrews speaks of the two comings of Christ, the first to deal with sin (on the cross), the second to save those who are waiting for him: "Christ, having been offered once to bear the sins of many, will appear a second time, not to deal with sin but to save those who are eagerly waiting for him" (Heb. 9:28).

The promise that Jesus will come again appears widely throughout the New Testament. Speaking through parables and plain statements, Jesus promises that he will come a second time to bring a time of judgment and full renewal. Unlike his first coming, which happened in secret and was revealed only to a few, his second coming will be public and glorious: "For as the lightning comes from the east and shines as far as the west, so will be the coming of the Son of man" (Matt. 24:27). Paradoxically, though the last days before Jesus's coming will be accompanied by signs of the end (24:32–33), the actual coming of Jesus will arrive unexpectedly, like a thief in the night (24:43–44; 1 Thess. 5:2; 2 Pet. 3:10). In Revelation, John hears Jesus say, "I will come like a thief, and you will not know at what hour I will come upon

LEX ORANDI

Waiting for Christ's Return in Glory

The collects for the first week of the Advent season express with special clarity our active waiting and eager longing for Christ's return. These prayers teach us how to be disposed to the grace of Advent as we wait for Christ.

> Grant your faithful, we pray, almighty God,
> the resolve to run forth to meet your Christ
> with righteous deeds at his coming,
> so that, gathered at his right hand,
> they may be worthy to possess the heavenly Kingdom.
>
> Keep us alert, we pray, O Lord our God,
> as we await the advent of Christ your Son,
> so that, when he comes and knocks,
> he may find us watchful in prayer
> and exultant in his praise.
>
> Prepare our hearts, we pray, O Lord our God,
> by your divine power,
> so that at the coming of Christ your Son
> we may be found worthy of the banquet of eternal life
> and merit to receive heavenly nourishment from his hands.[a]

a. *Roman Missal*, 139, 140, 142.

you" (Rev. 3:3). In the same way, Jesus cautions his followers to live as faithful servants until the day of his return (Matt. 24:45–51).

The Creed draws our attention to one essential component of Jesus's return in glory—namely, the judgment of the living and the dead. The notion that God will judge his people and the whole world did not begin with the New Testament, but has deep roots in God's word to his people Israel in the Old Testament. The point of God's judgment is not only a reckoning, a kind of balance sheet of how each individual has done, but also a rectifying of all evil. There will come a time when God will put all things right, punish all evil, and bring to pass his full and direct reign. The Psalms especially communicate this judgment by which God will rule over his people and the world: "But the LORD sits enthroned for ever, he has established his throne for judgment; and he judges the world with righteousness, he judges the peoples with equity" (Ps. 9:7–8). When the Lord God comes to judge, it will bring great joy to the whole creation: "Then shall all the trees of the wood sing for joy before the LORD, for he comes, for he comes to judge the earth. He will judge the world with righteousness, and the peoples with his truth" (96:12–13).

A truly striking claim made by Jesus himself is that God will judge the world through the Son, through *this man* who is walking on the earth: "The Father judges no one, but has given all judgment to the Son" (John 5:22). Speaking of himself as the Son of Man, Jesus makes this astounding claim about his role in judgment: "Do not marvel at this; for the hour is coming when all who are in the tombs will hear his voice and come forth, those who have done good, to the resurrection of life, and those who have done evil, to the resurrection of judgment" (5:28–29). In contrast to human judgment, which is always partial and subject to error, this final judgment will be utterly true and right because Jesus sees the heart truly and knows how to judge perfectly (see Isa. 11:3–4).

The final judgment by Jesus became a central part of the apostolic kerygma. When Peter proclaims the good news to Cornelius and his household, he includes Christ's role in judgment in his preaching: "And he commanded us to preach to the people, and to testify that he is the one ordained by God to be judge of the living and the dead" (Acts 10:42; see also 1 Pet. 4:5). Paul incorporates the final judgment in his preaching to the Athenians: "He has fixed a day on which he will judge the world in righteousness by a man whom he has appointed, and of this he has given assurance to all men by raising him from the dead" (Acts 17:31). And Paul underlines the place of the final judgment when charging Timothy to continue in faithful ministry: "I charge you in the presence of God and of Christ Jesus who is to judge the living and the dead, and by his appearing and his kingdom . . ." (2 Tim. 4:1). When the Creed confesses that Jesus will come again to judge the living and the dead, it closely reflects the New Testament's testimony to the certainty of this judgment.

Though heaven and hell are not named explicitly in this context, the promise of judgment implies that these are the two possible destinations for human beings. There are two options: eternal life either with God or without God. The solemn final judgment described by Christ himself, when he will separate "the sheep" from "the goats" (Matt. 25:31–46), stands as a sober witness to the reality that each of us will be judged according to what we have done during our earthly lives: "For we must all appear before the judgment seat of Christ, so that each one may receive good or evil, according to what he has done in the body" (2 Cor. 5:10). And though the final judgment will occur only

WITNESS TO THE TRADITION

Justin Martyr on the Return of Christ and the Final Judgment

Writing in about the year 150, Saint Justin Martyr gives witness to the early tradition in the Church that Christ will come a second time to raise the dead and judge all human beings. Justin frames this testimony as prophecy that has yet to be fulfilled. Just as Christ fulfilled many prophecies from the Old Testament in his first coming, so we can be confident that he will come again and fulfill those prophecies that have not yet come to pass. Justin laid his life down for this faith, dying as a martyr for Christ in about the year 165.

> Since then we show that all things that have already happened had been proclaimed through the prophets before they came to pass, it must necessarily be believed also that those things that were similarly predicted, but are not yet come to pass, will certainly take place. . . . For the prophets have proclaimed before two comings of His: one, which has already happened, as that of a dishonored and suffering man; and the second, when, as has been proclaimed, He will come from heaven with glory with His angelic host; when also He will raise the bodies of all the people who have lived, and will clothe the worthy with incorruption, but will send those of the wicked, eternally conscious, into the fire with the wicked demons.[a]

a. *First Apology* 52, in *St. Justin Martyr: The First and Second Apologies*, trans. Leslie William Barnard, Ancient Christian Writers (New York: Paulist Press, 1997), 59.

when Christ returns in glory, the Church, confirming the scriptural witness, teaches that our eternal state is already determined at physical death: "Each man receives his eternal retribution in his immortal soul at the very moment of his death, in a particular judgment that refers his life to Christ."[32]

And His Kingdom Will Have No End

The phrase "and his kingdom will have no end," not found in the Creed of Nicaea (from 325), arose within the specific historical context of the Arian controversy of the fourth century. As debates raged back and forth about

32. CCC 1022.

how to understand and confess Christ as truly God, Marcellus, the bishop of Ancyra, a supporter of the Council of Nicaea, began to formulate his own peculiar explanation of Jesus's relation to the Father.[33] Marcellus believed that God was singular in himself, so he did not believe that the Son and the Spirit were eternally discrete "persons." Rather, in order to create the world and to redeem the world, the Father effectively appeared in a new form through his internal Word in the incarnation. But this was a temporary arrangement lasting only until the work of "the Son" was accomplished. Basing his teaching on the apostle Paul's timetable of God's plan in 1 Corinthians 15:24–28, Marcellus proposed that Jesus's role as king over the world would come to an end at some point, and the Word would then retract back into the singularity of the Father. Paul writes, "Then comes the end, when he delivers the kingdom to God the Father after destroying every rule and every authority and power" (1 Cor. 15:24). Marcellus interpreted this passage to mean that once the work of the Son in the world is completed, the Son himself will hand the kingdom back to the Father and (in effect) will be merged back into the Father. Thus he taught that Christ's kingdom was not eternal but provisional and temporary.

The Council Fathers at Constantinople in 381 clearly wished to reject this "modalist" interpretation of the Son and the kingdom of God, so they added the clause "and his kingdom will have no end." By saying this, they are confirming that the Son exists in his own person eternally; he is not just a temporary mode of God's presence. And they also affirm that the kingdom of the Son will exist for eternity. By handing over the kingdom to the Father, the Son does not relinquish his role as king but expresses that the battle for the kingdom of God is now complete and the work is accomplished. As the book of Revelation so powerfully conveys, the eternal city of God, the new Jerusalem, is centered on God and the Lamb together: "And I saw no temple in the city, for its temple is the Lord God the Almighty and the Lamb. And the city has no need of sun or moon to shine upon it, for the glory of God is its light, and its lamp is the Lamb" (Rev. 21:22–23).

Living the Mystery

How can we today "live the mystery" of Christ's glorious return and the promise of his judgment of the living and the dead? There is a sober, cautionary

---

33. For an overview of Marcellus's modalist theology, see Khaled Anatolios, *Retrieving Nicaea: The Development and Meaning of Trinitarian Doctrine* (Grand Rapids: Baker Academic, 2011), 26, 86–92.

CONTEMPORARY ISSUES

The Uniqueness of Jesus Christ

There is a strong current in our contemporary culture that wants to acknowledge many paths to God. Because of a desire to be inclusive of all peoples and their religious traditions, many conclude that every person must find his or her own way to God—and that many roads can lead to the same goal.

How does this square with the words of Jesus, "I am the way, and the truth, and the life; no one comes to the Father, but by me" (John 14:6)? Or with the words of Peter when he proclaims, "And there is salvation in no one else, for there is no other name under heaven given among men by which we must be saved" (Acts 4:12)? Do these claims automatically eliminate non-Christians from the sphere of salvation?

The Catholic Church teaches that Jesus Christ is the unique Son of God, who has offered the single and unique sacrifice for sins.[a] There is a strongly *inclusive* quality to salvation through Christ: God the Father desires that all people attain salvation (1 Tim. 2:4), and Christ has offered the way of salvation to every person. The good news is that "Jesus is the Savior of all men, that all need salvation, and that salvation is offered to all through Christ."[b]

The Catholic Church also teaches that God, in ways known to himself alone, can bring to salvation those who are outside the Church and who may not know Christ explicitly in this life: "Those also can attain to salvation who through no fault of their own do not know the Gospel of Christ or His Church, yet sincerely seek God and moved by grace strive by their deeds to do His will as it is known to them through the dictates of conscience."[c] But this does not in any way relativize the role of Jesus Christ or make him expendable. There may be many paths to God, but all of them lead to Christ (explicitly or implicitly), and it is through Christ alone that we have eternal life—for he is himself eternal life. "And this is the testimony, that God gave us eternal life, and this life is in his Son. He who has the Son has life; he who has not the Son of God has not life" (1 John 5:11–12).

When we confess in the Creed Christ's work of salvation—his incarnation, passion and death, resurrection and ascension, and glorious return— we are confessing the uniqueness of Jesus as the way to salvation and eternal life in God open to all people.

a. *CCC* 618.
b. *CCC* 389.
c. Pope Paul VI, *Lumen Gentium* 2.16, November 21, 1964, https://www.vatican.va/archive/hist_councils/ii_vatican_council/documents/vat-ii_const_19641121_lumen-gentium_en.html.

side to this mystery. The Scripture communicates a clear sense of warning, so that we might be prepared when Jesus returns. The parable of the wise and the unwise virgins and the story of the servant who was ill prepared for his master's return are intended to awaken us so that we take seriously the call to be prepared. There is a place here for a proper "fear of the Lord" (traditionally one of the gifts of the Spirit; see Isa. 11:2–3). As Peter says, "If you invoke as Father him who judges each one impartially according to his deeds, conduct yourselves with fear throughout the time of your exile" (1 Pet. 1:17). This is a godly, filial fear that knows the Lord God but also is aware of the great seriousness of what is at stake. We treat our salvation with earnestness and sobriety because God does.

But even more, we can approach the coming of the Lord and our appearing before him with joy and longing. This is not incompatible with the fear of the Lord. Here, in this life, we have already "tasted the kindness of the Lord" (1 Pet. 2:3). We wait expectantly for Christ's return, like the ten wise virgins, so that when he appears we will hear the cry, "Behold, the bridegroom! Come out to meet him" (Matt. 25:6). Jesus assures his disciples, "So you have sorrow now, but I will see you again and your hearts will rejoice, and no one will take your joy from you" (John 16:22). Yes, we live in sobriety and the fear of the Lord, but because we already know God, because we already taste and see his goodness now, our overall disposition is one of joyful anticipation, to receive in fullness what we already possess in part—participation in the divine life (2 Pet. 1:4).

CHAPTER 5

GOD *the* HOLY SPIRIT

Introduction

The statement on the Holy Spirit in the Nicene Creed (381) is the most significant addition to the original Creed of Nicaea (325). That earlier creed simply stated, "We believe in the Holy Spirit." In the reformulation found in the Nicene Creed, the confession of faith in the Holy Spirit is considerably expanded.

In the controversy over the teaching of Arius (318–25), the pivotal question originally centered on the full divinity of Jesus: Is Jesus a created being, or is he genuinely "true God from true God"? The Council of Nicaea gave a definitive answer to this question in support of Jesus's full divinity, though a full understanding of *how* to understand Jesus's divinity in relation to the Father occupied the Church for the next fifty years. Later (beginning in the 350s), a new question arose: Is the Holy Spirit as revealed in the New Testament also truly God, or is the Spirit a created power that serves God?

This second controversy is not as well known as the earlier Arian controversy, but it was just as decisive for defining what the Christian faith is. If the Spirit is not truly God, then Christian faith becomes "binitarian," not "trinitarian": the Father and the Son are recognized as fully and coequally divine, but the Spirit is relegated to the position of a ministering creature. In response to those who were rejecting the Spirit's divinity, one of the primary tasks that faced the Fathers at the Council of Constantinople in 381 was to find a form of words, closely reflecting the scriptural witness, that would uphold and declare that the Spirit was fully and coequally God with the Father and the Son.

In this section we will explore the Nicene Creed's statement on the Holy Spirit as the condensed expression of the Church's faith. We will also seek to understand why the arguments put forward against the full divinity of the Spirit proved to be unpersuasive, and in so doing, we will gain a greater understanding of the Spirit's relation to the Father and the Son and of his distinctive mission in the world.

I Believe in the Holy Spirit, the Lord, the Giver of Life

I believe in the Holy Spirit, the Lord, the giver of life.	Et in Spiritum Sanctum, Dominum et vivificantem.	καὶ εἰς τὸ πνεῦμα τὸ ἅγιον, τὸ κύριον καὶ ζωοποιόν.

OT: Gen. 1:2; Exod. 34:28–35; Isa. 11:2; 42:1; 61:1; Ezek. 36:26–27; Joel 2:28–29

NT: Matt. 1:18, 20; Luke 1:35; 4:14–18; John 14:16–17; 16:7; Acts 1:4; 2:1–4; Rom. 5:5; 1 Cor. 2:10–14; 3:16; 12:3–13; 2 Cor. 13:14

Catechism: the procession of the Spirit, 243–48; the Holy Spirit in the economy of salvation, 683–747

Theological Exposition

The Holy Spirit in the Bible

As we begin this section on the Holy Spirit, it will be useful to focus our attention first on the biblical revelation (the Old and New Testaments) regarding the Holy Spirit. To put this in the form of a question: How is the Holy Spirit (or the Spirit of God) revealed in the Bible? Is the revelation of the Spirit something that occurs only in the New Testament, or do we find testimony to the Spirit's presence and activity also in the Old Testament?[1] We will begin by looking at the clear manifestation of the Spirit in the New Testament and then inquire about the presence and activity of the Spirit in the Old Testament.

The Holy Spirit as an "actor" in the divine drama of salvation shows up in the Gospel stories that narrate Jesus's infancy. In the opening scene in his

---

1. For helpful surveys of the Holy Spirit in the Bible, see Yves Congar, *I Believe in the Holy Spirit*, trans. David Smith (New York: Crossroad, 1997), 3–62; and Anthony C. Thiselton, *The Holy Spirit—In Biblical Teaching, through the Centuries, and Today* (Grand Rapids: Eerdmans, 2013).

Gospel, Matthew tells us that Mary was "found to be with child of the Holy Spirit" (Matt. 1:18). Wondering about this, Joseph is told by the angel of the Lord to take Mary as his wife because "that which is conceived in her is of the Holy Spirit" (1:20). Likewise, in Luke's Gospel the angel Gabriel tells Mary she will conceive by the power of the Holy Spirit: "The Holy Spirit will come upon you, and the power of the Most High will overshadow you" (Luke 1:35). Throughout Luke's narrative of Jesus's infancy, the Spirit appears as a primary *actor* in the story (1:41, 67; 2:25–27).

When Jesus's public ministry begins, there we find the Spirit present and active alongside him. All four Gospels identify the Spirit's role in Jesus's baptism (Matt. 3:11, 16; Mark 1:8, 10; Luke 3:16, 21–22; John 1:32–33). The Spirit also plays a central role in the personal life of Jesus himself, leading him into the desert to be tested: "And Jesus, full of the Holy Spirit, returned from the Jordan, and was led by the Spirit for forty days in the wilderness, tempted by the devil" (Luke 4:1–2; see also Matt. 4:1; Mark 1:12). Jesus begins his Galilean ministry under the anointing of the Spirit (Luke 4:14–18), and the Spirit continues to accompany Jesus's ministry in various ways (see Matt. 12:28; Luke 10:21).

Notably, Jesus *himself* speaks of the Spirit as a divine person, distinct from himself, who will be given to the faithful and guide them from within: "The Holy Spirit will teach you in that very hour what you ought to say" (Luke 12:12; see also 11:13). Especially in the Farewell Discourse in John's Gospel, Jesus instructs the apostles about the coming of the Holy Spirit: he will be "another Counselor" who will dwell within them and lead them into all truth (John 14:16, 26). To clarify the distinctive person of the Spirit, Jesus utters the shocking words that it will be to their advantage that Jesus himself goes away to the Father, for then he will send the Spirit to them in power (16:7).

The presence and action of the Holy Spirit becomes even more pronounced in the Acts of the Apostles. Called to "wait for the promise of the Father" (Acts 1:4), the apostles, along with the Virgin Mary, experience the Spirit coming to them in power, with a great wind and tongues of fire (2:1–4). This is not just a *power* but a *person* who comes upon them and anoints them. This outpouring of the Spirit, occurring initially on the day of Pentecost, occurs several more times as the apostles carry the mission of Jesus out into the world (see 8:14–17; 9:17–18; 10:44–48; 19:1–7). More generally, the Spirit leads the early Christians in mission (8:29; 11:28; 13:2; 16:6–7) and guides them as they seek to resolve difficult issues in the Christian community (15:28).

The New Testament letters enlarge this picture of the activity and gift of the person of the Holy Spirit. Paul speaks of the indwelling Spirit as the one who pours out the love of God into our hearts (Rom. 5:5), who witnesses to us from within that we are truly sons and daughters of God (8:14–17). The Spirit not only distributes a multitude of gifts to the members of the Christian community (1 Cor. 12:3–13), but even reveals to us the mind of God (2:10–14). The Spirit is the one who dwells within us and sanctifies us in both body and soul (3:16). Significantly, Paul indicates the full divinity of the Spirit by including the Spirit in a closing prayer ("†doxology"), linking the Spirit with the Father and the Son: "The grace of the Lord Jesus Christ and the love of God and the fellowship of the Holy Spirit be with you all" (2 Cor. 13:14).

The Holy Spirit, however, not only appears in the New Testament but is clearly present and active in the Old Testament as well. We find an important but veiled reference to the Spirit in the opening verses of Genesis—the Spirit hovers over the void from which God will bring forth creation (Gen. 1:2). We see the Spirit of God active in equipping the people of Israel to construct the temple (Exod. 31:1–5; 35:30–33) and even more so in anointing the prophets to speak the word of the Lord (1 Sam. 10:6; 2 Chron. 15:1; Ezek. 2:2; Mic. 3:8).

Of great significance is the activity of the Spirit foretold in the coming Messiah (Isa. 11:2) and in the obedient servant of the Lord who will bring God's life and light to the nations (42:1). Jesus himself quotes Isaiah (61:1) when manifesting his own identity: Jesus "opened the book and found the place where it was written, 'The Spirit of the Lord is upon me, because he has anointed me to preach good news to the poor'" (Luke 4:17–18).

And crucially, it is the promise of the gift of the Spirit in the Old Testament that sets the stage for the gift of the Spirit in the New Testament. Ezekiel promises a day to come when God will put his Spirit inside his people and change their hearts: "A new heart I will give you, and a new spirit I will put within you; and I will take out of your flesh the heart of stone and give you a heart of flesh. And I will put my spirit within you" (Ezek. 36:26–27). The prophet Joel likewise proclaims a day when the Spirit of God will be poured out on "all flesh" (Joel 2:28–29)—and it is this promise that Peter says is being fulfilled on the day of Pentecost (Acts 2:16–21).

In summary, we see in the New Testament the Holy Spirit revealed as a divine actor whom Jesus himself treats as a distinct divine person to be sent upon his followers (John 20:22; Acts 1:5, 8; 2:33). This manifestation of the Spirit is grounded in the Old Testament, which testifies to the presence and activity of God's Holy Spirit and promises a day to come when a new gift of

LEX ORANDI

"Come, Holy Spirit"

The following popular, traditional prayer to the Holy Spirit calls upon the Spirit to fill the hearts of the faithful with God's love, and it also displays the person and the gifts of the Holy Spirit that are made available to the faithful:

> Come, Holy Spirit, fill the hearts of your faithful and kindle in them the fire of your love.
>
> Send forth your Spirit and they shall be created. And you shall renew the face of the earth.
>
> O, God, who by the light of the Holy Spirit, did instruct the hearts of the faithful, grant that by the same Holy Spirit we may be truly wise and ever enjoy his consolations.
>
> Through the same Christ Our Lord. Amen.[a]

a. "Prayer to the Holy Spirit," United States Conference of Catholic Bishops, accessed January 23, 2023, https://www.usccb.org/prayers/prayer-holy-spirit.

the Spirit will be given to transform the hearts of God's people. This wide biblical testimony to the reality and person of the Spirit deeply shaped the confession of faith concerning the Spirit that we find in the Nicene Creed.

The Meaning of the Name "Holy Spirit"

As we turn now to consider the significance of the Creed's statement "I believe in the Holy Spirit," the first question that naturally arises is this: Why does the Bible call the Third Person of the Trinity by the name "Holy Spirit," a name that seems equally applicable to the Father and the Son? Why were these two words combined to designate this particular person? While we cannot say definitively why any name for God or for the persons of the Trinity is given in the inspired Scriptures, we can inquire about the appropriateness and fittingness of the name.

In both Hebrew and Greek, the term for "spirit" (*ruakh* and *pneuma*, respectively) has multiple senses. It can refer to (1) the wind, (2) human breath, or (3) the "spirit" that is the animating life principle in a human being. Jesus makes use of these multiple meanings when he speaks of the Spirit as comparable to a wind that blows wherever it wills (John 3:8). And in a striking passage, Jesus *breathes* on his disciples in the upper room on Easter Day, saying to them, "Receive the Holy Spirit" (20:22). The Spirit is the "breath" of God, his own life sent forth to animate and enliven his people. The name "Spirit," then, is especially appropriate to the person who comes invisibly to live inside us and who communicates to us the life-giving "breath" of God.

The adjective "holy" plainly applies to all three persons of the Trinity, but there is a specially appropriate sense of identifying the Spirit as holy because it is principally through the effective indwelling of the Spirit that we are *made* holy. Paul names the third person "the Spirit of holiness" (Rom. 1:4) and speaks of the offering of the gentiles as "sanctified by the Holy Spirit" (15:16)—that is, "made holy" through the power of the Spirit. For Paul, because the Spirit has come to dwell within us, when we give way to sin we "grieve the Holy Spirit of God" (Eph. 4:30), who dwells within us and calls us to holiness.

Recognizing that "Holy" and "Spirit" apply to all three divine persons, Saint Augustine adds that "it is not to no purpose that he is specially called the Holy Spirit; for because he is common to both [Father and Son], he is specially called that which both are in common."[2] Saint Thomas Aquinas offers a further reason for the fittingness of the title "Holy Spirit": "For the name spirit in things corporeal seems to signify impulse and motion; for we call the breath and the wind by the term spirit. Now it is a property of love to move and impel the will of the lover towards the object loved."[3] Because the Scriptures identify the Spirit particularly with the love of God (see Rom. 5:5), Aquinas concludes that it is fitting that we call this †procession of love by the name "Spirit." In a summary statement on the name "Holy Spirit," the *Catechism* explains what the Creed declares: "'Holy Spirit' is the proper name of the one whom we adore and glorify with the Father and the Son. The Church has received this name from the Lord and professes it in the Baptism of her new children."[4]

Historical Context for the Creed's Statement on the Holy Spirit

We can profitably ask, Why does the creedal statement on the Holy Spirit open with the descriptive titles "Lord" and "giver of life"? To answer this

---

2. Augustine, *The Trinity* 15.19.37 (*NPNF*[1] 3:219).

3. Thomas Aquinas, *Summa Theologica* I.36.1, trans. Fathers of the English Dominican Province, 2nd ed. (New York: Benziger Brothers, 1920), https://www.ccel.org/a/aquinas/summa /FP/FP036.html#FPQ36OUTP1.

4. CCC 691.

question, we need to return to the historical setting in which the Creed of 381 was formulated. As noted already, in the late 350s a new controversy arose concerning whether the Holy Spirit is genuinely God. Between 358 and 360, Saint Athanasius composed three letters to his friend and cobishop, Serapion, who had asked for Athanasius's help in responding to people who were claiming that the Holy Spirit was simply a creature.[5] In these impressive letters Athanasius presents numerous arguments from Scripture to show that the Holy Spirit must be God—and not a creature—because he does things only God can do (e.g., he gives life, he sanctifies us, he makes us divine).

Just a few years later (374–75), Saint Basil the Great wrote a treatise, *On the Holy Spirit*, likewise to show that the Holy Spirit should be ranked as truly God, a distinct divine person, who is consubstantial with the Father and the Son. Basil argues both from the Scriptures and from the liturgical texts of the Church to demonstrate the Spirit's full divinity. Basil, too, was responding to those *in the Nicene coalition* who denied the Spirit's divinity on the grounds that Scripture never calls the Spirit "God." For them, the role the Spirit plays is akin to that of an angel, a special messenger of God. Basil rejects this position and argues that it reflects neither the inspired Scriptures nor the pattern of prayer manifested in the Church's liturgy.[6]

Basil's close friend and coworker, Saint Gregory of Nazianzus, also took up his pen just five years later and delivered an oration dedicated to the Holy Spirit, in which he proclaims with great force that the Holy Spirit is a divine person (*hypostasis*), truly and fully God, consubstantial with the Father and the Son: "*What, then? Is the Spirit God?* Certainly. *Is he consubstantial? Yes, if he is God.*"[7] He was opposing a group, known at this point as the †Macedonians,[8] who affirmed the full divinity of the Son but rejected the full divinity of the Spirit. Gregory delivered this oration in the city of Constantinople in 380, shortly before the opening of the council that produced the Nicene Creed.

---

5. Athanasius calls those who deny the Spirit's divinity "Tropikoi" (from the Greek word *tropos*), because in his view they were misusing and misinterpreting biblical passages (or "tropes") to argue that the Spirit is a creature.

6. Basil identifies this group that denies the Spirit's divinity as "Pneumatomachians," meaning "those who fight against the Spirit."

7. Gregory of Nazianzus, *Oration 31.10*, in *On God and Christ: The Five Theological Orations and Two Letters to Cledonius*, trans. Lionel Wickham, PPS 23 (Crestwood, NY: St. Vladimir's Seminary Press, 2002), 123 (emphasis original).

8. The name "Macedonian" derives from a former bishop of Constantinople (i.e., Macedonius) who supported the view that the Spirit was not God.

This set the stage for the council itself. More than thirty "Macedonian" bishops arrived to participate in the council, but when they perceived that Gregory and a majority at the council vigorously upheld the full divinity of the Spirit, they quickly abandoned the council and left the city. The challenge to the Spirit's divinity by the Macedonian bishops helps explain why the statement in the Creed on the Holy Spirit was so carefully worded. The Fathers at the council were committed to teaching the Spirit's full divinity but were also hoping to persuade the Macedonian contingent to agree, and so they used careful scriptural language rather than proclaiming outright in the Creed that the Spirit is "God" and consubstantial with the Father. Their

WITNESS TO THE TRADITION

Gregory of Nazianzus on the Holy Spirit

Gregory of Nazianzus offered an explanation for why the full personhood and divinity of the Holy Spirit was revealed last in order, after the Father and the Son. For Gregory, the Bible first reveals God as Father, then manifests the Son, and finally shows the full reality of the person of the Holy Spirit. Gregory sees in this gradual revelation of the three persons a providential divine pedagogy to instruct us about the triune God.

> In this way, the old covenant made clear proclamation of the Father, a less definite one of the Son. The new covenant made the Son manifest and gave us a glimpse of the Spirit's Godhead. At the present time, the Spirit resides amongst us, giving us a clearer manifestation of himself than before. It was dangerous for the Son to be preached openly when the Godhead of the Father was still unacknowledged. It was dangerous, too, for the Holy Spirit to be made (and here I use a rather rash expression) an extra burden, when the Son had not been received. . . . No, God meant it to be by piecemeal additions, "ascents" as David called them, by progress and advance from glory to glory, that the light of the Trinity should shine upon more illustrious souls. This was, I believe, the motive for the Spirit's making his home in the disciples in gradual stages proportionate to their capacity to receive him.[a]

a. Gregory of Nazianzus, *Oration* 31.26, in *On God and Christ: The Five Theological Orations and Two Letters to Cledonius*, trans. Lionel Wickham, PPS 23 (Crestwood, NY: St. Vladimir's Seminary Press, 2002), 137.

efforts at winning over the Macedonians apparently failed, but the wording they crafted remains the fundamental creedal statement on the Spirit's divinity.

The Lord, the Giver of Life

We can now return to our original question: Why does the creedal statement open with the short titles "Lord" and "giver of life"? Because in combination they show that the Spirit is fully God and worthy of common adoration with the Father and the Son. The primary scriptural location for both titles comes from 2 Corinthians 3:6–18. In this richly complex passage, Paul is contrasting the giving of the law with the gift of the Spirit, and he speaks of his own role as being a minister "of a new covenant, not in a written code but in the Spirit; for the written code kills, but the Spirit gives life" (2 Cor. 3:6). Here we see the Spirit depicted as the "life giver." Paul then describes the new covenant as "the dispensation of the Spirit" (3:8). Clearly for Paul, Jesus came to bring new life in the Holy Spirit and to usher in a new covenant in which the law of God will be written on our hearts (Ezek. 36:26).

But then, strikingly, Paul says, "Now the Lord is the Spirit" (2 Cor. 3:17; cf. v. 18), and immediately he relates this to our freedom in Christ: "and where the Spirit of the Lord is, there is freedom" (3:17). This is the *only* instance in the Bible where the Spirit is given the title "Lord," and in context this is clearly a divine title. Paul has been recounting the scene with Moses on Mount Sinai in the presence of the Lord (Exod. 34:28–35), so he clearly intends the title "Lord" here to refer to the divine name. And so in this one passage, Paul identifies the Spirit as "the giver of life" and as "the Lord." Only God can rightly be called "Lord," and only God can truly give life. Through the use of these two titles, then, the Creed confesses the true and full divinity of the Spirit.

In the Old Testament, the title "Lord" is normally reserved for the God of Israel, but in the New Testament it is widely applied to Jesus himself. The Father and the Son are equally "the Lord" and so are equally God. By assigning this title to the Holy Spirit, the Creed is equating the status of the Spirit with that of the Father and the Son. And the scriptural warrant for this title comes from Paul himself: "The Lord is the Spirit."[9] In the face of the claim by the Macedonians that the Bible never calls the Spirit "God," the use of

---

9. Biblical interpreters disagree over whether Paul is referring to the person of the Holy Spirit in 2 Cor. 3:17–18; some believe this is a reference to God the Father, and others to Jesus the Son. But the Creed reasonably understands Paul as referring to the Holy Spirit when he says, "The Lord is the Spirit."

the title "Lord" shows this to be false. The Spirit is indeed truly "the Lord" in the same sense as the Father and the Son.

In the same way, by referring to the Spirit as "the giver of life," the Creed reveals that the Spirit must be truly God. The Greek term in the Creed, *zōopoion*, which means "life giver" or "one giving life," is closely related to the form found in John 6:63, which could be rendered "the Spirit is the life giver [*to zōopoioun*]." But if the Spirit genuinely gives life, then he must be God because only one who is God can truly give life: "See now that I, even I, am he, and there is no god beside me; I kill and I make alive; I wound and I heal" (Deut. 32:39). When the king of Israel was asked to heal Naaman of his leprosy, he reasonably acknowledged his inability to give life: "Am I God, to kill and to make alive?" (2 Kings 5:7). No created being can truly give life.

As God the Father has life in himself, so too does the Son: "For as the Father has life in himself, so he has granted the Son also to have life in himself" (John 5:26). Jesus is the one who truly gives life—abundant and eternal life—because he is God now appearing in the flesh: "I came that they may have life, and have it abundantly" (10:10).[10] But equally, Scripture affirms that the Spirit too is a giver of life (6:63; 2 Cor. 3:6). When the Creed confesses the Spirit to be "the Lord, the giver of life," it is claiming unambiguously that the Spirit is truly and fully God along with the Father and the Son.

Living the Mystery

We are accustomed to thinking about *Jesus as Lord* because this truth is so clearly underlined in the Scriptures. According to Paul, every creature will one day confess "that Jesus Christ is Lord, to the glory of God the Father" (Phil. 2:11), and Paul adds that "no one can say 'Jesus is Lord' except by the Holy Spirit" (1 Cor. 12:3). And so one of the primary works of the Holy Spirit is to reveal to us the lordship of Jesus Christ.

But here in the Creed we are confronted with the truth that the Spirit too is Lord. Does this truth make any difference in the way that we relate to the Holy Spirit? This confession of the Spirit as Lord secures the truth that the Spirit is fully divine. If the Spirit is "Lord," then the Spirit is God. But in addition to this, if the Spirit is truly Lord, then we have an obligation to follow the Spirit and be utterly receptive to him. Just as we obey Jesus as Lord and

---

10. For the Spirit as the giver of divine life, see also Rom. 8:11 and 1 Pet. 3:18.

"Veni, Sancte Spiritus"

For the Feast of Pentecost, the Church invokes this marvelous prayer to the Holy Spirit, sung before the proclamation of the gospel:

Come, Holy Spirit, come!
And from your celestial home
Shed a ray of light divine!

Come, Father of the poor!
Come, source of all our store!
Come, within our bosoms shine.

You, of comforters the best;
You, the soul's most welcome guest;
Sweet refreshment here below;

In our labor, rest most sweet;
Grateful coolness in the heat;
Solace in the midst of woe.

O most blessed Light divine,
Shine within these hearts of thine,
And our inmost being fill!

Where you are not, we have naught,
Nothing good in deed or thought,
Nothing free from taint of ill.

Heal our wounds, our strength renew;
On our dryness pour your dew;
Wash the stains of guilt away:

Bend the stubborn heart and will;
Melt the frozen, warm the chill;
Guide the steps that go astray.

On the faithful, who adore
And confess you, evermore
In your sevenfold gift descend:

Give them virtue's sure reward;
Give them your salvation, Lord;
Give them joys that never end.[a]

a. *Compendium of the Catechism of the Catholic Church* (Washington, DC: United States Conference of Catholic Bishops, 2006), 187–88 (modified).

follow him wherever he leads (Rev. 14:4), so too we should follow the Spirit, who is also our Lord.

Here we can take a cue from Jesus's own words, when he says, "If you love me, you will keep my commandments. And I will ask the Father, and he will give you another Counselor, to be with you for ever, even the Spirit of truth, whom the world cannot receive, because it neither sees him nor knows him; you know him, for he dwells with you, and will be in you" (John 14:15–17 RSV-2CE). The Spirit is the †Paraclete, or "another Counselor"—that is, one who guides, leads, encourages, and admonishes. It is not as if we now have two masters, Jesus and the Spirit, in competition with each other. The lordship of the Son is perfectly aligned with the lordship of the Spirit, but the two persons come to us in two distinct †missions and lead us in distinctive ways.

How does the lordship of the Spirit function in us? It is especially oriented to shaping and forming us inwardly, according to the image of Christ, through the Spirit's gifts and fruits. As we are receptive to the Spirit's working and cooperate actively with his grace, we "are being transformed into the same image from one degree of glory to another; for this comes from the Lord, the Spirit" (2 Cor. 3:18 NRSV). One of the chief ways that we live the mystery of the Spirit's lordship is by being responsive to his full working within us. By doing so, we will bear much fruit and so please the Father (John 15:4–8).

The special prayer on the Feast of Pentecost (see the sidebar "Veni, Sancte Spiritus") displays this inward working of the Spirit in our lives. Not only does the Spirit refresh us and give us life within; he also leads us and shapes us by his work. The final lines of the prayer tellingly recognize the Spirit's lordship, which leads us to joy unending: "Give them your salvation, *Lord*; give them joys that never end."

Who Proceeds from the Father and the Son

| who proceeds from the Father and the Son, | qui ex Patre Filioque procedit, | τὸ ἐκ τοῦ πατρὸς ἐκπορευόμενον, |

OT: Gen. 2:7
NT: John 14:17–23; 15:26; 20:22; 1 Cor. 2:12; Gal. 4:4, 6; Rev. 22:1
Catechism: the *Filioque*, 246–48

Theological Exposition

The Procession of the Spirit

In the early Church, all parties recognized that the Scriptures had little to say about the procession of the Spirit. The biblical testimony paints a vivid portrait of the unique identity and activity of the Spirit of God, but it speaks minimally about the Spirit's origin. From where (and from whom) does the Spirit come? The Macedonian party (see above) argued that the Spirit was a creature, a kind of super-angel, that served the purposes of God (the Father and the Son). Their answer to the question of the Spirit's origin was simple: the Spirit is a creature made by God to serve divine purposes in the world. The Nicene Creed seeks to give a different account of the Spirit's origin, one that reveals the Spirit not as a creature but as truly God. In this section we will explore the original language of the Spirit's procession in the Nicene Creed in the context of key testimonies of the Spirit's procession in both the East and the West. In the following section we will take up the vexed and complex question of the addition of the Latin term †*Filioque* (and the Son) to the Nicene Creed in the West.

The original Greek text of the Creed simply says "who proceeds from the Father." The verb "proceeds" (*ekporeuomai*) is a nontechnical word that means "to go from/forth" or "to come from/forth." The preposition "from" (*ek*) shows derivation: the Spirit "comes forth *from* the Father."[11] The Father, then, is the source and origin of the Spirit. The Spirit is not "from nothing" (*ex nihilo*), as the rest of creation is. Significantly, the choice of this verb links the creedal statement to the clearest statement in the New Testament on the Spirit's procession, John 15:26: "But when the Counselor comes, whom I shall send to you from the Father, even the Spirit of truth, who proceeds [*ekporeuomai*] from the Father, he will bear witness to me." The creedal statement is simply a rephrasing of Jesus's own testimony to the Spirit's origin: the Spirit "comes forth from the Father."

The New Testament has much to say about the mission of the Spirit, but most of these testimonies apply to the activity of the Spirit *in the world* and do not directly address the question of the Spirit's ultimate origin. So, for example, Jesus himself in John 15:26 says that he will "send" the Spirit to his disciples, even as he points to the Father as the ultimate origin of the Spirit. Jesus also says that *the Father* will send the Spirit to the disciples in Jesus's

---

11. In the Greek, the preposition *ek* is doubled, appearing also as a prefix attached to the verb: "to go forth *from*."

name (14:26). Plainly, both the Father and the Son cooperate in sending the Spirit into the world. Paul too describes the sending forth of the Spirit to make us adopted sons and daughters of God: "And because you are sons, God has sent the Spirit of his Son into our hearts, crying, 'Abba! Father!'" (Gal. 4:6). Peter witnesses to this outpouring of the Spirit in his preaching on Pentecost day: "Being therefore exalted at the right hand of God, and having received from the Father the promise of the Holy Spirit, he has poured out this which you see and hear" (Acts 2:33).

There is minimal biblical testimony, however, to the Spirit's ultimate origin. Beyond the key passage from John 15:26, we have Paul's testimony that "we have received not the spirit of the world, but the Spirit which is from [*ek*] God" (1 Cor. 2:12). So the Spirit is plainly *from God* and *comes forth from the Father*. But what does this "coming forth" (procession) mean? How is the Spirit's procession from the Father different from the Son's generation from the Father? This is a question that occupied the teachers of the fourth century as they sought to give testimony to the Spirit's unique divine person.

Among the Eastern Fathers, there was a clear commitment to speak cautiously about the procession of the Spirit, restricting descriptions to what the Scriptures plainly revealed. Defending the full divinity of the Spirit, Saint Basil the Great offers a careful statement about the procession of the Spirit as the breath of God: the Spirit is "said to be 'of God' [1 Cor. 2:12]; not indeed in the sense in which 'all things are of God' [1 Cor. 11:12], but in the sense of proceeding out of God, not by generation, like the Son, but as Breath of His mouth."[12] For his part, Saint Gregory of Nazianzus cautions against prying into the mystery of God by trying to figure out what the "procession" of the Spirit means:

> Insofar as he proceeds from the Father, he is no creature; inasmuch as he is not begotten, he is no Son; and to the extent that procession is the mean between ingeneracy and generacy, he is God. . . . What, then, is "proceeding"? You explain the ingeneracy of the Father and I will give you a biological account of the Son's begetting and the Spirit's proceeding—and let us go mad the pair of us for prying into God's secrets.[13]

Among the Western Fathers, there was likewise a recognition that we do not really understand what the procession of the Spirit is, but they saw in the

---

12. Basil the Great, *On the Holy Spirit* 18.46 (NPNF² 8:29). For an exploration of how to better understand the Spirit as breathed by the Father (and the Son), see Etienne Vetö, *The Breath of God: An Essay on the Holy Spirit in the Trinity* (Eugene, OR: Cascade Books, 2019).

13. Gregory of Nazianzus, *Oration* 31.8 (Wickham, 122).

LEX ORANDI

Byzantine Hymn to the Holy Spirit

This simple but profound prayer to the Holy Spirit appears in the Byzantine liturgy for the Feast of Pentecost:

> Heavenly King, Comforter, the Spirit of truth, everywhere present and filling all things, Treasury of blessings and Giver of Life, come and dwell in us; cleanse us of every stain and save our souls, gracious One.[a]

a. "The Great Vespers of Pentecost," Greek Orthodox Archdiocese of America, accessed January 23, 2023, https://www.goarch.org/-/the-great-vespers-of-pentecost, under "The Doxastikon." Used with permission.

scriptural revelation a clear link between the Spirit and the Son and tried to give expression to what this link might mean. In particular, they linked the Spirit to the reality of divine love and so described the procession of the Spirit in terms of "love proceeding" from the Father and the Son. As we shall see, this notion of the Spirit as "love" proceeding is closely linked to the Western confession that the Spirit proceeds from the Father *and the Son*.

In summary, the creedal confession that the Spirit "proceeds from the Father" was intended to distinguish the Spirit from all created beings and to identify the Spirit as a unique divine person. In the Catholic understanding of the procession of the Spirit, the Spirit is understood to proceed principally from the Father, who is the ultimate source, but also from the Son, to whom is given an active role along with the Father in the spiration of the Spirit. As Thomas Joseph White explains, "The Father is always and ever the fontal principle of both the Son and the Spirit, even if he gives the Son eternally to be with him the source of the Spirit."[14]

Historical Context: The Nicene Creed and the Filioque

A discerning reader will quickly observe a significant difference between the original statement of the Nicene Creed in Greek ("who proceeds from the Father") and the profession of the Western Catholic tradition ("who proceeds from the Father *and the Son*"). The addition consists of one word (*Filioque*,

---

14. Thomas Joseph White, *The Trinity: On the Nature and Mystery of the One God* (Washington, DC: Catholic University of America Press, 2022), 483.

"and the Son") inserted into the Latin form of the Creed. In this section we will explore the distinctive theological accounts of the Spirit's procession in the East and West and survey the complex history of the insertion of this word into the Creed in the West and the controversy this provoked with the Eastern Byzantine Church.

It is important to realize that the Catholic Church recognizes and affirms the original language of the Nicene Creed in Greek and that it has neither added the words "and the Son" to the Greek form of the Creed nor required Eastern Catholics who confess the Creed in Greek to add the words "and the Son" (though they are required to believe what these words convey). How, then, did it come about that the Western Catholic Church added the word *Filioque* to the confession of the Nicene Creed? What were the causes of this addition, and how was it explained and defended theologically?

First, the Nicene Creed of 381 was not broadly known until the Council of Chalcedon in 451. It was at this point that the Western Church received and recognized this creed as an authoritative expansion of the original Creed of Nicaea (325). In an important sense, the Nicene Creed became the ecumenical expression of the Church's faith through Chalcedon's explicit acceptance and publication of it. By this time, however, the Western theological tradition had already developed an understanding of the Spirit's procession from the Father and the Son (or *through* the Son). In order to understand the insertion of the *Filioque* into the Latin form of the Creed and the controversy with the East that followed, it will be helpful to grasp the distinctive Eastern and Western understandings of the procession of the Spirit.

In the Greek East, two primary ways of speaking about the Spirit's procession emerged.[15] The first is represented by Gregory of Nazianzus, who, following the plain sense of John 15:26, confesses simply that the Spirit proceeds from the Father. Due to Gregory's enormous influence, this became the most common way to describe the Spirit's procession in the Eastern tradition. A second way appears in Gregory's two Cappadocian friends and companions (Basil the Great and Gregory of Nyssa), who on occasion speak in terms of the Spirit's procession from the Father *through* the Son. In the words of Basil, "One, moreover, is the Holy Spirit, and we speak of him singly, conjoined as he is to the one Father through the one Son, and through himself completing the adorable and blessed Trinity."[16] We find a similar teaching on the Spirit's

---

15. There is also a third expression found in the Eastern Fathers and in the later Byzantine tradition—namely, that the Spirit proceeds from the Father and *rests on* or *reposes in* the Son.

16. Basil the Great, *On the Holy Spirit* 18.45 (NPNF[2] 8:28).

procession *through the Son* in three major Eastern Fathers of the Church: Cyril of Alexandria, Maximus the Confessor, and John of Damascus. Cyril writes in one instance that "the Spirit proceeds from the Father and the Son," but normally he teaches that the Spirit proceeds from the Father *through* the Son.[17] According to Saint Maximus the Confessor, "Just as the Holy Spirit by nature and according to essence exists of God the Father, so too by nature and according to essence is the Spirit of the Son, insofar as the Spirit proceeds essentially from the Father ineffably through the begotten Son."[18] For his part, John of Damascus clearly upholds that the Spirit proceeds from the Father but also adds that the Spirit comes from the Father through the Son: "I say that God is always Father since he has always his Word coming from himself, and through his Word, having his Spirit issuing from him."[19]

The roots of the Western understanding of the Spirit's procession go all the way back to Tertullian,[20] but the developed expression of the Son's role in the Spirit's procession emerges in the fourth century. Writing in about 360, Saint Hilary of Poitiers addresses the Father in language that confesses the Spirit's origin coming from the Father *through* the Son: "So I hold fast in my consciousness the truth that your Holy Spirit is from you and through him, although I cannot by my intellect comprehend it. . . . May I receive your Spirit who takes his being from you through your only Son."[21] By all accounts, it is Saint Ambrose who first states explicitly the teaching that the Spirit proceeds from the Father *and* the Son.[22] But it is Augustine who gives a thorough and sophisticated explanation for the Spirit proceeding from both the Father and the Son as one principle, and he anchors this in the conviction that the Spirit is best understood as "love proceeding," the mutual love of the Father and the Son:

> And the Holy Spirit proceeds from the Father principally [*principaliter*], the Father giving the procession without any interval of time, yet in common from

---

17. Cyril of Alexandria, *Thesaurus* 34 (*Patrologia Graeca* 75:585A).

18. Maximus the Confessor, *Responses to Thalassios* 63, in *On Difficulties in Sacred Scripture: The Responses to Thalassios*, trans. Maximos Costa, FOTC 136 (Washington, DC: Catholic University of America Press, 2018), 470.

19. John of Damascus, *Dialogue against Manichaeus* 5, trans. The Pontifical Council for Promoting Christian Unity, "The Greek and Latin Traditions regarding the Procession of the Holy Spirit" (1995), http://www.christianunity.va/content/unitacristiani/en/documenti/altri-testi/en1.html.

20. For Tertullian's speculation on the procession of the Spirit, see *Against Praxeas* 4.

21. Hilary of Poitiers, *On the Trinity* 12.56–57 (NPNF[2] 9:233).

22. Ambrose, *On the Holy Spirit* 1.11.115.

WITNESS TO THE TRADITION

Maximus the Confessor on the *Filioque*

The great Byzantine theologian Saint Maximus the Confessor encountered the Latin teaching on the *Filioque* when acting as a theologian for Pope Martin I in Rome. Though he acknowledged that the Latin teaching on the Spirit's procession from the Father and the Son was not the same as the Eastern view, he defended the Latin teaching, arguing that, properly understood, the *Filioque* was consistent with the fundamental Eastern understanding of the Spirit's procession.

> For the procession they (the Romans) brought the witness of the Latin Fathers, as well, of course, as that of St. Cyril of Alexandria in his sacred study on the Gospel of St. John. On this basis they showed that they themselves do not make the Son Cause . . . of the Spirit. They know, indeed, that the Father is the sole Cause of the Son and of the Spirit, of one by generation and of the other by [procession]—but they explained that the latter comes . . . through the Son, and they showed in this way the unity and the immutability of the essence.[a]

a. Maximus the Confessor, *Letter to Marin of Cyprus*, trans. The Pontifical Council for Promoting Christian Unity, "The Greek and Latin Traditions regarding the Procession of the Holy Spirit" (1995), 11–12, http://www.christianunity.va/content/unitacristiani/en/documenti/altri-testi/en1.html.

both [Father and Son]. But he would be called the Son of the Father and of the Son, if—a thing abhorrent to the feeling of all sound minds—both had *begotten* Him. Therefore the Spirit of both is not begotten of both, but proceeds from both.[23]

Notably, Augustine underlines that the Father is the one from whom the Spirit *principally* proceeds, even as he recognizes the Son's role in the Spirit's proceeding. This theological trajectory, finding its climax in Augustine, became the common view of the Spirit's procession in the West.

The actual insertion of the *Filioque* into the Latin Nicene Creed came in stages. In fact, the first creedal statement of the Spirit's procession from the Father and the Son appears not in the Nicene Creed but in the so-called

23. Augustine, *The Trinity* 15.25.47 (NPNF[1] 3:225).

The *Filioque* in Orthodox-Catholic Relations

Discussion and debate over the *Filioque* illustrates the problems and concerns that have historically characterized theological investigation and dialogue between the Eastern Orthodox churches and the Catholic Church.[a] There are two related but distinct issues raised by the Eastern Orthodox. First, is the *Filioque* theologically sound? Second, even if it is theologically defensible, was the Western Church justified in introducing this phrase unilaterally into the ecumenical Creed of the Church without consulting with the Orthodox East?

Among Eastern Orthodox theologians today, there are two primary stances regarding the Western teaching of the *Filioque*. The first position considers the *Filioque* to be simply incorrect and heretical—it attempts to say more than divine revelation reveals and so disfigures a true understanding of the Trinity. The second position regards the *Filioque* as the theological opinion of the Western tradition and can find elements that work in harmony with Orthodox teaching about the Spirit's procession. Those who hold the second position do not think that, properly understood, the *Filioque* is church-dividing, but they reject the view that the *Filioque* should be the defined dogma of the Church. Across the board, the Orthodox believe that it was improper for the Western Church to insert a new word unilaterally into the Creed, and they typically request that the Catholic Church remove the public confession of the *Filioque* for the sake of ecumenical unity.[b]

The Catholic Church holds to the dogmatic definition of the *Filioque* but recognizes that theological descriptions of the *Filioque* have not always been thorough; it also holds that new understandings have led to greater points of agreement between the East and the West.[c] As Thomas Joseph White explains, "For its part, the Roman Catholic Church does not presently require that Eastern rite churches in communion with Rome pronounce the *Filioque* in the liturgical recitation of the Creed and does not consider the doctrine a Church-dividing issue."[d] The Catholic Church does, however, require its own members to accept the truth of the *Filioque* and requests that the Orthodox churches not denounce the *Filioque* as theologically false.

In terms of theology, two areas of common ground between the two traditions have come to occupy an important place in explaining the *Filioque* in a theologically convergent way. The first is the Father as the principle source of the Spirit's procession. This truth is underlined by Augustine and found explicitly in the teaching of Thomas Aquinas: "The Holy Spirit proceeds equally from both, although sometimes he is said to proceed principally or properly from the Father, because the Son has this power from the Father."[e] The second point of convergence is the expression common to the two traditions, that the Spirit proceeds from the Father *through* the Son. This too is upheld in the teaching of Saint Thomas: "Therefore, because the Son receives from the Father that the Holy Spirit proceeds from him, it can be said that the Father spirates the Holy Spirit through the Son, or that the Holy Spirit proceeds from the Father through the Son."[f]

The *Catechism* offers a contemporary statement of the Catholic understanding of the *Filioque* that seeks to take into account the growing consensus between the East and the West: "For the eternal order of the divine persons in their consubstantial communion implies that the Father, as 'the principle without principle,' is the first origin of the Spirit, but also that as Father of the only Son, he is, with the Son, the single principle from which the Holy Spirit proceeds."[g]

a. The North American Orthodox-Catholic Theological Consultation published an agreed statement entitled "The *Filioque*: A Church-Dividing Issue?" (Oct. 5, 2003), https://www.usccb.org/resources/filioque-a-church-dividing-issue.

b. The 2003 joint statement of the North American Orthodox-Catholic Theological Consultation (see previous note) represents this second position—namely, that the *Filioque* should not be seen as a church-dividing issue but that "the Catholic Church, as a consequence of the normative and irrevocable dogmatic value of the Creed of 381, use the original Greek text alone in making translations of that Creed for catechetical and liturgical use."

c. At the request of Pope John Paul II, the Pontifical Council for Promoting Christian Unity published a study entitled "The Greek and the Latin Traditions regarding the Procession of the Spirit" (Sept. 20, 1995), which sought to show greater commonality between the two traditions. See http://www.christianunity.va/content/unitacristiani/en/documenti/altri-testi/en1.html.

d. White, *The Trinity*, 491.

e. Aquinas, *Summa Theologica* I.36.3, reply 2 (trans. Fathers of the English Dominican Province, modified), https://www.ccel.org/a/aquinas/summa/FP/FP036.html#FPQ36A3THEP1.

f. Aquinas, *Summa Theologica* I.36.3 (trans. Fathers of the English Dominican Province, modified), https://www.ccel.org/a/aquinas/summa/FP/FP036.html#FPQ36A3THEP1.

g. CCC 248.

Athanasian Creed. This creed, though attributed to Athanasius (and, over-all, faithful to his teaching), originated in the West and was composed and promulgated in late fifth-century Gaul. Following this, the Third Council of Toledo (589) gave dogmatic sanction to the *Filioque*, and subsequently the *Filioque* was inserted locally into the Creed, first in Spain and then in Gaul. It was only in the year 1014 that Pope Benedict VIII agreed to the recitation of the Nicene Creed, inclusive of the *Filioque*, in the liturgy of the Mass, a prac-tice that has continued to the present day. In the centuries that followed, the Second Council of Lyons (1274) and the Council of Florence (1439) declared the procession of the Spirit from the Father and the Son to be a dogmatic teaching of the Catholic Church.

At various points, the inclusion of the *Filioque* into the Nicene Creed gave rise to controversies between the Latin West and the Byzantine East. In the ninth century, disagreement over the truth of the *Filioque*, as well as arguments over the warrant for inserting it into the Latin Creed, played a central role in the Photian Schism (863–67) and also figured in the schism of 1054 that led to mutual excommunications between the pope and the ecumenical patriarch. The *Filioque* was also a central topic of discussion and debate at the Council of Florence in 1439. At that council, the Eastern Orthodox delegation signed a statement of agreement with the *Filioque*, but the Orthodox Church as a whole rejected this agreement, leaving the *Filioque* as a significant point of dispute between East and West.

Though the *Filioque* remains an important difference and point of conten-tion between the Catholic and Eastern Orthodox churches, significant strides have been made toward seeing the Eastern and Western teachings on the pro-cession of the Spirit as complementary rather than contradictory—and as no longer church-dividing.[24]

Living the Mystery

The question of the procession of the Spirit can appear as something far removed from real life, an issue that theologians debate but that has little application for normal Christians from day to day. But in fact the core truth has profound implications for the way we live our lives. The Holy Spirit is not a creature, like an angel, who goes about doing things for God. *The Spirit is*

---

24. For a thorough study of the *Filioque* in history and in contemporary theology, see Mat-thew Levering, *Engaging the Doctrine of the Holy Spirit: Love and Gift in the Trinity and the Church* (Grand Rapids: Baker Academic, 2016), 113–68.

God himself. He comes forth from the Father and the Son (or through the Son) in a unique way. He is the breath of God breathed into us to give us new life. Through the Spirit the love of God is poured into our hearts. He is himself the preeminent gift of God, from whom all other gifts flow.

One of the most striking testimonies to the relationship between the Son and the Spirit occurs when the risen Jesus appears to his disciples in the upper room on Easter Day. In John's narrative, Jesus appears to them, shows them his wounds, wishes them peace, and then sends them out. But then it says, "And when he had said this, he breathed on them, and said to them, 'Receive the Holy Spirit'" (John 20:22). Jesus himself breathes on them and imparts to them not his human breath but the very gift of the Spirit to dwell within them. This scene recalls the creation of Adam, when God breathes into his nostrils the breath of life (Gen. 2:7). Jesus—who is the Son of God—now breathes the Holy Spirit into his followers. Jesus says that he himself will send the Spirit from the Father—for the Spirit proceeds from the Father (John 15:26)—and this is fulfilled when he breathes on them the gift of the Holy Spirit to bring about a new and profound indwelling.

When we confess that the Spirit proceeds from the Father and the Son (or that he proceeds from the Father *through* the Son), we are acknowledging that the Spirit that has come to dwell in us is truly God and that by virtue of the Spirit dwelling in us, the Father and the Son have come to make their home in us (John 14:17, 23). The goal of the Christian life is not just to be delivered from sin and death by God's saving work, though this is absolutely crucial. The goal is not just to live a good way of life in imitation of God himself, though this too is centrally important. God's purpose for us is that we should be brought into the very communion of the Father, Son, and Spirit: "For you did not receive the spirit of slavery to fall back into fear, but you have received the spirit of sonship. When we cry, 'Abba! Father!' it is the Spirit himself bearing witness with our spirit that we are children of God, and if children, then heirs, heirs of God and fellow heirs with Christ" (Rom. 8:15–17).

The Spirit who comes forth from the Father and the Son is the very one who comes to dwell effectively in us, leading us into a deifying communion through a mutual indwelling with the Father and the Son: "In that day you will know that I am in my Father, and you in me, and I in you. . . . If a man loves me, he will keep my word, and my Father will love him, and we will come to him and make our home with him" (John 14:20, 23). As Scott Hahn eloquently says, "The giving of the Holy Spirit is the reason for the incarnation. Pentecost is

the reason for Christmas and Good Friday and Easter and the Ascension. . . .
It is only by the Spirit that we can know God."[25]

Who with the Father and the Son Is Adored and Glorified

| Who with the Father and the Son is adored and glorified, who has spoken through the prophets. | Qui cum Patre et Filio simul adoratur et conglorificatur, qui locutus est per prophetas. | τὸ σὺν πατρὶ καὶ υἱῷ συμπροσκυνούμενον καὶ συνδοξαζόμενον, τὸ λαλῆσαν διὰ τῶν προφητῶν. |

OT: Exod. 20:3; Ezek. 11:5
NT: Matt. 28:19; Rom. 8:15–17, 26; 1 Cor. 12:3; 2 Cor. 13:14; Eph. 2:18; 4:4–7; Rev. 2:7
Catechism: the divinity and identity of the Spirit, 245, 685, 691–93; the Spirit speaking through the prophets, 702, 719; the Spirit and prayer, 2664–72

Theological Exposition

This final section on the Holy Spirit confirms the full divinity of the Spirit as adored and glorified along with the Father and the Son, and it identifies a central activity of the Spirit—namely, his speaking "through the prophets" (that is, through the inspired Scriptures).

The Creed has already named the Spirit "Lord" and "giver of life," titles that indicate the full divinity of the Spirit. But now in a way that cannot be sidestepped or explained away, the Spirit is confessed to be fully God. How so? Because only God is worthy of adoration and glory. By confessing the Spirit as worthy of adoration and glory along with the Father and the Son, the Creed proclaims the Spirit as a distinct divine person who is fully God.

The worship of the one true God alone is, in fact, the core meaning of the first commandment: "You shall have no other gods before me" (Exod. 20:3). In the long history of Israel, the plunge into idolatry was a constant temptation, and the prophets constantly called Israel back to follow and worship only the Lord, the one true God. As the *Catechism* explains, "Idolatry not only refers to false pagan worship. It remains a constant temptation to faith. Idolatry consists in divinizing what is not God."[26] And so, according to the

25. Scott Hahn, *The Creed: Professing the Faith through the Ages* (Steubenville, OH: Emmaus Road, 2016), 132.
26. CCC 2113.

Creed, true worship of the one God means honoring the Father, the Son, *and the Spirit* with one common adoration.

With the Father and the Son Is Adored and Glorified

The Creed employs two compound verbs to express the Spirit's being adored with the Father and the Son.[27] Translated literally (from the Greek), the Creed says, "Who *with* the Father and the Son is worshiped-*with* and glorified-*with*." The repetition of the word "with" (Greek *syn*) underlines the truth that our relation to the Spirit is identical to our relation with the Father and the Son. The Spirit does not receive a lesser honor, but there is one common and equal worship and glorification of the Father, Son, and Spirit. In the historical context of the forging of the Nicene Creed, where a group of bishops was teaching that the Spirit was merely a creature, this statement expressed in plain and unambiguous language that the Spirit was fully God, to be worshiped in one adoration with the Father and the Son.

The scriptural foundation for this claim—that the Spirit is worthy of adoration with the Father and the Son—was laid down by several Church Fathers in the years leading up to the Council of Constantinople in 381.[28] They typically made use of three complementary means to show from the Scriptures that the Spirit was truly and fully God. First, the *titles* accorded to the Spirit in the New Testament align with the titles used for the Father and the Son, thus showing the Spirit to be God. In the explanation of Basil the Great,

> He is called Spirit, as "God is a Spirit" (John 4:24). . . . He is called holy, as the Father is holy, and the Son is holy. . . . He is called good (Ps. 143:10) as the Father is good, and He who was begotten of the Good is good. . . . He is called upright (Ps. 51:10), as "the Lord is upright" (Ps. 92:15). . . . He is called Paraclete (John 14:16), like the Only begotten. . . . Thus names are borne by the Spirit in common with the Father and the Son.[29]

---

27. The first verb, "to worship together with" (*symproskyneō*), does not appear in the New Testament, but it does occur in the Fathers of the Church to describe the common worship due to the Father, Son, and Holy Spirit. The second verb, "to glorify together with" (*syndoxazō*), appears once in the Bible (Rom. 8:17), where it refers to our being glorified with Jesus in heaven through our resurrection from the dead.

28. The main writings come from Athanasius in his three letters to Serapion (358–60); from Didymus the Blind, *On the Holy Spirit* (ca. 360–65); from Basil the Great, *On the Holy Spirit* (375); and from Gregory of Nazianzus, *Oration* 31, on the Holy Spirit (380).

29. Basil the Great, *On the Holy Spirit* 19.48 (NPNF[2] 8:30).

Second, the *activities* of the Spirit—what the Spirit does—show that the Spirit is God, because only one who is God could do what the Spirit does. Therefore, because he does these things, this shows that he is God. Saint Athanasius highlights the Spirit's role in deifying us as conclusive evidence that he is fully God:

> But if we become sharers of the divine nature (2 Pet. 1:4) by partaking of the Spirit, someone would have to be insane to say that the Spirit has a created nature and not the nature of God. For it is because of this that those in whom the Spirit dwells are divinized. And if he divinizes, there can be no doubt that his nature is of God.[30]

Finally, the *doxologies* to the Father, Son, and Spirit together show that the Spirit is truly God. For the Fathers, the biblical passages that most clearly show the Spirit's full divinity are the brief doxologies where the Spirit is aligned with the Father and the Son. The passage that stands out comes from the end of Matthew's Gospel, where Jesus says, "Go therefore and make disciples of all nations, baptizing them in the name of the Father and of the Son and of the Holy Spirit" (Matt. 28:19). The sacramental act of baptism is accomplished in the "name" of the Father and of the Son and of the Spirit. Notably, "name" is singular—there is one name into which people are baptized into new life, and this name includes all three persons. More than any other biblical passage, this reference to the single *name* demonstrates the equality of the three trinitarian persons and shows their codivinity. We are baptized not into a creature but into God, and this one God *is* the Father, the Son, and the Holy Spirit.

Paul's prayer at the close of his Second Letter to the Corinthians also witnesses to the coequality of the Father, Son, and Spirit, as worthy of one common adoration: "The grace of the Lord Jesus Christ and the love of God and the fellowship of the Holy Spirit be with you all" (2 Cor. 13:14). Grace is referred to the Son (our Lord Jesus Christ), love is referred to the Father, and fellowship (communion, *koinōnia*) is referred to the Spirit. But the three are linked in one closing prayer, a doxology. Doxologies are not offered to creatures. By offering this prayer that requests the blessing of the Father, Son, and Spirit, Paul shows that he considers them equally God, though also clearly distinct from one another.[31]

---

30. Athanasius, *Letters to Serapion* 1.24.3, in *Works on the Spirit: Athanasius the Great and Didymus the Blind*, trans. Mark DelCogliano, Andrew Radde-Gallwitz, and Lewis Ayres, PPS 43 (Yonkers, NY: St. Vladimir's Seminary Press, 2011), 90.

31. See also Eph. 2:18, where Paul describes our access to God in terms of the Father, Son, and Spirit: "Through him we . . . have access in one Spirit to the Father." In Eph. 4:4–7, Paul groups together the Father, Son, and Spirit as the source of all good things that come to us.

Who Has Spoken through the Prophets

We might ask, Why would the Creed include a statement on the Spirit speaking through the prophets? Why draw attention to *this* activity of the Spirit? And who exactly are "the prophets" to whom the Creed refers?

To address the last question first, the prophets referred to here are preeminently the prophets of the Old Testament (e.g., Isaiah, Jeremiah, Ezekiel). An example of the Spirit speaking through a prophet appears in the early ministry of Ezekiel, when the Spirit "falls upon" the prophet and tells him what words to speak: "And the Spirit of the Lord fell upon me, and he said to me, 'Say, Thus says the Lord'" (Ezek. 11:5).

But it is important to see that, by "the prophets," the Creed means to point us to the inspired Scriptures—the canonical Bible. As the *Catechism*

WITNESS TO THE TRADITION

Basil the Great on the Glory of Adoration Given to the Holy Spirit

In his influential treatise on the Holy Spirit (written ca. 375), Basil the Great maintains that the Spirit is worthy of the same glory and honor that are given to the Father and the Son. The emphasis he places on this common glory appears prominently in the Nicene Creed, written just six years afterward. Speaking about the Holy Spirit, he writes,

> Shall we not then highly exalt Him who is in His nature divine, in His greatness infinite, in His operations powerful, in the blessings He confers, good? Shall we not give Him glory? And I understand glory to mean nothing else than the enumeration of the wonders which are His own. . . . While then so many things are glorified, do you wish the Spirit alone of all things to be unglorified? Yet the Apostle says "the ministration of the Spirit is glorious" [2 Cor. 3:8]. How then can He Himself be unworthy of glory? . . . What reason is there for robbing of His share of glory Him Who is everywhere associated with the Godhead; in the confession of the Faith, in the baptism of redemption, in the working of miracles, in the indwelling of the saints, in the graces bestowed on obedience? For there is not even one single gift which reaches creation without the Holy Spirit.[a]

a. Basil the Great, *On the Holy Spirit* 23.54; 24.55 (*NPNF*² 8:35, modified).

clarifies, "By 'prophets' the faith of the Church here understands all whom the Holy Spirit inspired in living proclamation and in the composition of the sacred books, both of the Old and the New Testaments."[32] So while the individual prophets convey in a particularly focused way the inspired speech of the Holy Spirit, the entirety of the Bible, inspired by the Spirit, is included in the creedal statement.

The fact that the Spirit "has spoken through the prophets" conveys to us important truths about the Spirit's person and role. First, it points to the fact that the Spirit is a divine person *who can speak*. The Spirit is not just a force or a power or an aura that acts invisibly in the world. The Spirit genuinely speaks and communicates with human beings—in this case, through the anointed and inspired prophets who spoke God's word. It is easy to forget that the Spirit has the capability to speak to us. We know through the abundant testimony of the Gospels that Jesus, the incarnate Son—who is God's very Word—speaks living words. We also hear on special occasions the voice of the Father himself, especially when giving testimony to his beloved Son (Matt. 3:17; 17:5; John 12:28). But the Spirit also has a voice and can speak.

Jesus himself tells his disciples to expect the activity of the Spirit, who will speak to them the very words of the Son: "When the Spirit of truth comes, he will guide you into all the truth; for he will not speak on his own authority, but whatever he hears he will speak, and he will declare to you the things that are to come" (John 16:13). When Agabus the prophet warns Paul of the dangers to come, it is the Holy Spirit speaking through him: "And coming to us he took Paul's belt and bound his own feet and hands, and said, 'Thus says the Holy Spirit'" (Acts 21:11 RSV-2CE). Paul tells us that it is by the Spirit that we can proclaim the lordship of Jesus: "No one speaking by the Spirit of God ever says 'Jesus be cursed!' and no one can say 'Jesus is Lord' except by the Holy Spirit" (1 Cor. 12:3). Seven times in the book of Revelation, John declares, "He who has an ear, let him hear what the Spirit says to the churches" (e.g., Rev. 2:7).[33]

The unique quality of the Spirit's "speaking" is that the Spirit always makes use of a human being (and a human voice or pen) to speak. We never hear the Spirit's words coming down the wind or out of the blue—the Spirit speaks, but he always speaks *through* the words of a human being.

There is a further significance to the Creed pointing to this activity of the Spirit: the prophets of the Old Testament, inspired by the Spirit, announced

32. CCC 702.
33. For references to the Spirit speaking, see also 1 Tim. 4:1; Heb. 3:7–8; and Rev. 14:13.

beforehand the coming of the Messiah and predicted all that was fulfilled in the life, death, and resurrection of Jesus. In other words, the Spirit of God, acting through the prophets, declared ahead of time the coming and work of Christ. This prophetic announcement, highlighted throughout the four Gospels, plays an important part in showing the divine quality of the gospel. What Jesus did for our salvation was announced in prophecy through the Spirit's action, and this demonstrates both the divine nature of the Spirit and the divine quality of the gospel message.

Further, by linking the confession of our faith to the testimony of "the prophets," the Creed links our faith in Christ explicitly to the Old Testament. This is the clearest place in the Creed where the Church is linked to the people of Israel. As we noted when speaking about the doctrine of

CONTEMPORARY ISSUES

The Inspiration of the Bible

Since the rise of the period of the Enlightenment in the West (that is, since the seventeenth century), the question of the inspiration of the Bible has been a constant and contentious issue. Earlier periods in Church history witnessed debates over the meaning of what was contained in the Bible, but all sides generally believed that the Bible was inspired by the Spirit. The key question for them was this: What does the inspired Scripture mean?

But with the Enlightenment came deep doubts about the inspiration of the Bible itself. Were the various authors and editors who wrote down the books of the Bible over many years really "inspired" by the Spirit to write what they wrote? How did this inspiration work, and how can we know what is really from God (if anything)?

The famous "Scopes Monkey Trial" of 1925, dealing with the issue of whether Darwinian evolution could be taught in public schools, was debated in part over a literal interpretation of the first chapters of Genesis. The rise of fundamentalism in the twentieth century was at root an effort, however flawed, to uphold the truth of the (literal) inspiration of the Bible.

At the Second Vatican Council, the Catholic Church engaged the contested question of the inspiration of the Bible and offered a firm but nuanced affirmation of divine inspiration. The council declared that all the canonical books of the Old and New Testaments, "in

creation, the Church fought a long, hard battle against various Gnostic groups to uphold the Old Testament as the true and inspired witness to Jesus. By naming the Spirit as the one who spoke through the prophets, the Creed binds the Old and New Testaments together and ensures that our understanding of Jesus comes to us "in accordance with the Scriptures" (1 Cor. 15:3).

Living the Mystery

The Creed tells us that the Spirit is "adored and glorified" along with the Father and the Son. One result of this is that we can (and should) pray to the Holy Spirit, offering worship and entreating the help of the Spirit for our

their entirety, with all their parts," were written under the inspiration of the Spirit and so can be said to have "God as their author,"[a] citing the well-known passage from 2 Timothy 3:16: "All scripture is inspired by God." The council readily acknowledged that the human authors who wrote the books of the Bible made use, under the Spirit's inspiration, of all their own powers and abilities—there is a genuine *human* authorship of the Scriptures. This activity of the Spirit that guides the sacred authors does not overwhelm or dominate them (like demonic possession), but makes use of their full powers and free will to communicate the words of God.

Consequently, the council affirmed that "the books of Scripture must be acknowledged as teaching solidly, faithfully and without error that truth which God wanted put into sacred writings . . . for the sake of salvation."[b] And so the Church confirms and explains what the Nicene Creed more briefly expresses—namely, that the Spirit truly inspired the sacred authors (the prophets) and that through these words the Spirit spoke and continues to speak. In consequence, we can rely upon these inspired books to tell us the truth about God and how he has acted in the world to redeem us in Christ.

a. Pope Paul VI, *Dei Verbum* 3.11, November 18, 1965, accessed January 24, 2023, https://www.vatican.va/archive/hist_councils/ii_vatican_council/documents/vat-ii _const_19651118_dei-verbum_en.html.
b. Pope Paul VI, *Dei Verbum* 3.11.

needs. Learning how to pray *with* the Spirit, *in* the Spirit, and *to* the Spirit is part of growing into maturity in relationship with God.

The most common instance when we adore and glorify the Spirit with the Father and the Son occurs in the traditional doxology that Catholics pray in many contexts: "Glory be to the Father, and to the Son, and to the Holy Spirit, as it was in the beginning, is now, and ever shall be, world without end. Amen."[34] Here we see the three persons given equal glory and praise. When we pray this doxology, we are offering adoration to all three persons equally, as the one true God.

In the liturgical worship of the Church, prayers are most commonly offered *to* the Father, *through* the Son, and *in* the Holy Spirit.[35] We see this pattern reflected in the closing doxology of the prayer for the consecration of the Eucharist: "Through [Christ], and with him, and in him, O God, almighty Father, in the unity of the Holy Spirit, all glory and honour is yours, for ever and ever. . . . Amen."[36] This orientation to the Father through the Son and in the Holy Spirit reflects the scriptural pattern of access to the triune God: "For through [the Son] we both have access in one Spirit to the Father" (Eph. 2:18).

Saint Basil explains these two forms of the doxology by distinguishing their aims. The first form, which offers adoration to all three persons equally, expresses the full divine dignity of the three persons (and so of the Spirit); the second form announces how the grace of God works in us: it is through the work and mediation of the Son and by the indwelling presence of the Spirit that we approach the Father and offer him praise.[37]

What does this mean for us when we pray? First, all Christian prayer is (in principle, even if not explicitly) offered *to* the Father, *to* the Son, and *to* the Spirit and, equally, all Christian prayer is offered *to* the Father, *through* the Son, and *in* the Spirit. These are not mutually exclusive or competitive ways of approaching God; rather, the two forms of prayer reveal the richness of our relationship with the three persons of the Trinity.

Second, because the Spirit is a fully divine person, we are authorized and encouraged to offer prayer directly to the Spirit. On the one hand, we know

34. The contemporary English version of this prayer simplifies the language: "Glory to the Father, and to the Son, and to the Holy Spirit, as it was in the beginning, is now, and will be for ever. Amen."

35. CCC 2665: "Even though her prayer is addressed above all to the Father, it includes in all the liturgical traditions forms of prayer addressed to Christ."

36. Irish Catholic Bishops' Conference, *The Order of Mass*, accessed January 24, 2023, https://www.catholicbishops.ie/wp-content/uploads/2011/02/Order-of-Mass.pdf.

37. Basil the Great, *On the Holy Spirit* 27.68.

LEX ORANDI

"Come, Holy Ghost, Creator Blest"

The following traditional hymn to the Holy Spirit, translated from the ninth-century hymn by Rabanus Maurus, calls upon the Spirit to take up his dwelling in us and to pour out upon us the multitude of graces that flow from him.

> Come, Holy Ghost, Creator blest,
> and make our hearts your place of rest;
> come with your grace and heav'nly aid,
> and fill the hearts which you have made.
>
> To you, the Counselor, we cry,
> to you, the gift of God most high,
> the fount of life and fire of love,
> the soul's anointing from above.
>
> Praise we the Father and the Son
> and Holy Spirit, with them One,
> and may the Son on us bestow
> the gifts that from the Spirit flow.[a]

a. Edward Caswall, "Come, O Creator Spirit Blest," Hymnary.org, accessed March 6, 2023, https://hymnary.org/text/come_holy_ghost_creator_blest.

that the Spirit lives within us and (as Paul says) "helps us in our weakness; for we do not know how to pray as we ought" (Rom. 8:26). We can freely call upon the Holy Spirit to help us in our prayer and to aid us in our weakness. On the other hand, we can also call upon the Spirit to bless us and to pour out his gifts upon us and on the Church. "Since he teaches us to pray by recalling Christ, how could we not pray to the Spirit too? That is why the Church invites us to call upon the Holy Spirit every day, especially at the beginning and the end of every important action."[38] The Spirit is the very presence of God—God in person—living in us and working in our hearts. He is the inexhaustible Gift who is the bestower of all grace.

38. CCC 2670.

CHAPTER 6

LIFE *in the* TRINITY

Introduction

When comparing the Creed of Nicaea (325) with the developments at Constantinople (381), we find not only the clarification about the divinity of the Holy Spirit, but a burst of dogmatic professions about the Church, baptism, and eternal life. While there has been abundant reflection on the meaning of this part of the Creed, there is surprisingly little commentary on how this part originated. In one magisterial survey of this period, R. P. C. Hanson writes, "The inclusion in Constantinople of the reference to the church, baptism and resurrection can only be due to the fact that these items happened to be in the original creed taken by the council of 381 to express its doctrine. We can be sure that they also figured in all other creeds of the time whether Arian, Macedonian or Apollinarian."[1] In other words, there was no immediate controversy about these matters that led to their inclusion in 381 but only a faithfulness to the source material the bishops were working with. While not without detractors at the time, the main doctrinal outlines of the Church, baptism, and resurrection were largely settled.

Still, it is fitting that these doctrines were appended to the creed that was destined to become standard throughout most of the Christian world. The controversy in 381 was about whether the Holy Spirit was divine and, consequently, whether he could give eternal life. At stake was salvation understood as sharing in the divine life. The one, holy, catholic, and apostolic Church is

1. R. P. C. Hanson, *The Search for the Christian Doctrine of God: The Arian Controversy, 318–381* (Grand Rapids: Baker Academic, 2005), 817.

the locus of that salvation, which happens through baptism and culminates in eternal life in the world to come. The doctrine of the Holy Spirit naturally flows into the doctrines of the Church, baptism, and resurrection.

For this reason, many commentators treat the final articles of the Creed as an extension of the article on the Holy Spirit. We could have called this chapter "Life in the Spirit." Alternatively, we could have also called this chapter "Life in Christ," for all of these doctrines could just as easily be framed christologically as †pneumatologically.[2] We have called it "Life in the Trinity" because we believe this reflects more closely the concerns and patterns of thinking of the early Church. As Augustine says, "The correct sequence of the Creed demanded that the Church be subjoined to the Trinity, as a dwelling to its Inhabitant, as a temple to God, and a city to its Founder."[3] The first part of the Creed treats the Trinity, whereas the second part treats our life in the Trinity. In this final chapter, we will consider how the Creed treats the Church, baptism, and resurrection, paying particular attention to the trinitarian dimension of these doctrines.

The Church

| I believe in one, holy, catholic and apostolic Church. | Et unam sanctam catholicam et apostolicam Ecclesiam. | Εἰς μίαν ἁγίαν καθολικὴν καὶ ἀποστολικὴν ἐκκλησίαν. |

OT: Deut. 7:6; 9:10

NT: one, John 13:35; 17:20–21; Acts 2; 1 Cor. 10:16–17; Gal. 3:27–28; Eph. 4:5–6; holy, Matt. 13:24–50; 1 Pet. 2:9; Rev. 15:4; catholic, Matt. 28:19; Acts 2:5; apostolic, Matt. 16:18; 18:18; John 20:22–23; Acts 15:28; Gal. 2:1–10; 2 Tim. 1:6

Catechism: the Church, 748–975

Theological Exposition

In Greek and Latin, the word for "church" is *ekklēsia/ecclesia*, which means "assembly" and especially the assembly of God's chosen people (e.g., Deut.

2. CCC 748 states, "The article of faith about the Church depends entirely on the articles concerning Christ Jesus." In the very next paragraph, the *Catechism* states, "The article concerning the Church also depends entirely on the article about the Holy Spirit, which immediately precedes it" (749).

3. Augustine, *Enchiridion* 15.56, in *St. Augustine: Faith, Hope, and Charity*, trans. Louis A. Arand, Ancient Christian Writers (New York: Newman, 1947), 59.

9:10 LXX).[4] Etymologically, *ecclesia* comes from the Greek *ek-kaleō*, which means "to call out of" or "to call forth." The Church consists of those who are called out of their normal way of life to be gathered together and set apart for God. They are called forth to become part of a new community and a new way of life. The English word "church," from the Greek *kyriakos* (via the German *Kirche*), means "of the Lord" or "belonging to the Lord." The Church has its origin *from* the Lord, and the Church is that people—or better, body—which properly *belongs to* the Lord.

In the first centuries, Christians certainly experienced themselves as a new and small community, yet, surprisingly, they consistently made rather grand claims about the Church. The Church, they said, "was created before the sun and moon."[5] According to one early second-century letter, "the relation of Christians to the world is that of a soul to the body."[6] The Church is the soul of the world, without which the world would be dead!

One reason Christians could say such things is that they saw the membership of the Church consisting not only of believers worldwide but also of the angels in heaven and the faithful of all time. The angels were the first creatures made, and their worship of God, revealed in Scripture and present in the liturgy, was a model and inspiration for believers. Worshiping the same God, we belong to the same holy assembly of God. As for the ancient historical reality of the Church, Augustine, for example, uses the striking image of the birth of Jacob (Gen. 25:26). Christ is the Head of the Church, but he does not appear first. Rather, like Jacob being born, the hand (Israel) appears first, tripping up Esau (the nations). Then emerges the Head (Christ) and finally the body (the Church). All the faithful, old and new, are one body. The Jews emerge first in time announcing the coming of Christ, but they are organically connected to the body, which emerges after the Head and is subordinate to it.[7] Augustine (and others) saw "God's servant Abel the just" (as we still hear in the eucharistic prayer)[8] as the first member of the Church (and as protomartyr and type of Christ).[9]

The New Testament offers a rich variety of images to describe the Church. The Church is Christ's body (Eph. 1:22; Col. 1:18) and bride (Eph. 5:25–27;

---

4. See "Believing the Church and Believing in the Church" in chap. 1 for a discussion of what it means to believe *in* the Church.

5. *Second Clement* 14 (ANF 9:254).

6. *Letter to Diognetus* 6, in *Early Christian Writings: The Apostolic Fathers*, trans. Andrew Louth (London: Penguin, 1987), 145.

7. See Augustine, *Instructing Beginners in Faith* 1.3.6.

8. This phrase comes from Eucharistic Prayer I in the *Roman Missal*, 641.

9. See, for example, Augustine, *City of God* 15.1.

Rev. 21:2); a virgin (2 Cor. 11:2) and a mother (Gal. 4:26); the building, temple, or household of God (1 Cor. 3:9; 2 Cor. 6:16; 1 Tim. 3:15); the vineyard that draws life from Christ the vine (John 15:5); the sheepfold with Christ as the shepherd (John 10:1–10); the kingdom of God (Matt. 16:18–19); and the new or heavenly Jerusalem (Rev. 21:2). Interestingly, the Creed does not invoke any of this rich imagery, though it is certainly presupposed. Instead, the Creed uses four terms to describe the Church: "one," "holy," "catholic," and "apostolic." The first two terms pick up on New Testament language for the Church, while the latter two pick up themes implicit in the biblical witness. All four terms respond to challenges faced in the early Church.

The terms "one," "holy," "catholic," and "apostolic" are traditionally called the four "marks" of the Church. Some contemporary theologians consider these marks as "ideals" for which the Church should strive. But to consider them merely as ideals reduces the Church to a sociological phenomenon. This is not how Scripture or the Tradition understands the Church. These marks are constitutive elements of the Church that describe her essence and are inseparable. They are characteristics that, on the one hand, can visibly distinguish the true Church from false imitations; but they are also characteristics that describe the deepest reality of the Church, despite the sociological status of the Church at any given time in history. So even in the fractiousness of the Reformation period, or the scandal of the clerical sexual-abuse crisis, or the small number of believers in the upper room at Pentecost, or the worldliness of the medieval episcopate, the Church is one, holy, catholic, and apostolic. It is true, of course, that the Church should always strive to more perfectly embody these marks, but in doing so she is striving to become what she already is—that is, she is striving to manifest her own nature.

One

Regardless of the actual situation on the ground, Christians have insisted repeatedly that the Church is one. "There is neither Jew nor Greek, there is neither slave nor free, there is neither male nor female; *for you are all one in Christ Jesus*," Paul says to the Galatian church (Gal. 3:28). The Galatians were not known for their unity: there were conflicts between Jews and Greeks, slaves and free people, and males and females, so it is all the more striking that Paul declares emphatically that they are *already* one in Christ.

Even a casual reading of the letters of Paul (or John or Peter or the Apostolic Fathers) suggests that the unity of the Church was never a sociological reality in any stable sense. Still, in the middle of the second century, a crisis point was reached as the Christian Church, now spread throughout the world, had to deal with the ever-present threat of Gnostic Christianity. Some Gnostics remained in local congregations, while others formed their own communities and evangelized from there. Gnostic Christians viewed themselves as the true Christians, while the bishops and theologians of the day viewed them as parasites on the Church. But their pesky presence brought to the surface serious questions about the unity of the Church that had been smoldering for some time. Does oneness arise from some kind of concord among Christians, like agreement in belief or getting along in a particular way? If there is disagreement or discord within a church or between churches, can they still be one? Is the oneness of the Church visible or invisible, institutional or spiritual? Or is the Church really many? Should we speak, as some scholars today advocate, of early *Christianities*, a widely divergent group of sects (churches?), each interpreting Jesus in its own way?

Irenaeus launched a full-scale attack against the Gnostics, and his criticisms show how early Christians came to understand the oneness of the Church. According to Irenaeus, the Gnostics "assemble in unauthorized meetings"[10] to practice different rituals or seemingly Christian rituals with very different meanings.[11] The Gnostics "overthrow the faith of many, by drawing them away, under a pretense of [superior] knowledge."[12] They consider themselves "wiser not merely than the presbyters, but even than the apostles, because they have discovered the unadulterated truth."[13] For Irenaeus, the Gnostics violate the unity of the Church because they do not preach the same faith, do not practice the same sacraments, and do not recognize the same apostolic authority, which is now represented by the bishops. For Irenaeus, common faith, sacraments, and ministry are the marks of unity.

These marks manifest and safeguard a deeper unity of the one Church, which Irenaeus roots in the presence of the one God in the Church.

> For where the Church is, there is the Spirit of God; and where the Spirit of God is, there is the Church, and every kind of grace; but the Spirit is truth. Those, therefore, who do not partake of Him, are neither nourished into life from the mother's breasts, nor do they enjoy that most limpid fountain which issues from the body of Christ.[14]

10. Irenaeus, *Against Heresies* 3.3.2 (ANF 1:415).
11. Irenaeus, *Against Heresies* 1.13, 25; 4.18.4–5.
12. Irenaeus, *Against Heresies* 1.Pref.1 (ANF 1:315).
13. Irenaeus, *Against Heresies* 3.2.2 (ANF 1:415).
14. Irenaeus, *Against Heresies* 3.24.1 (ANF 1:458).

As Christ's own body, the Church shares Christ's Spirit—that is, the Church partakes of the Spirit of God and shares it with others, bringing them into the unity of the Body of Christ. There is an ontological unity of the Church rooted in God's presence.

By presenting the unity of the Church in these ways, Irenaeus is synthesizing the biblical witness. "There is *one* body and *one* Spirit, just as you were called to the *one* hope that belongs to your call, *one* Lord, *one* faith, *one* baptism, *one* God and Father of us all, who is above all and through all and in all" (Eph. 4:4–6). The one Father of all is "through all and in all," making us one body in the one Lord and one Spirit, and we share the one baptism, one faith, and one hope. During the Last Supper, Christ prays, "I do not pray for these only, but also for those who believe in me through their word, that they may all be one; even as you, Father, are in me, and I in you, that they also may be in us, so that the world may believe that you have sent me" (John 17:20–21 RSV-2CE). Jesus is saying that the unity of the Church participates in the unity of the Father and the Son and, of course, the Holy Spirit, whom he promises to send to lead them into all truth (John 14:15–31; 16:13). This unity will be the source of salvation for the world.

We see the same ideas developed in the Pentecost narrative. The apostles receive the Holy Spirit and, in turn, call people from "every nation under heaven" (Acts 2:5) to be gathered into the communion of the Church.[15] "Repent, and be baptized," Peter tells this diverse crowd, "every one of you in the name of Jesus Christ for the forgiveness of your sins; and you shall receive the gift of the Holy Spirit" (2:38). Baptized into Christ, they belong to Christ's body and receive his Spirit; they share in the life of God. This ontological unity then becomes manifest in their practice. "And they held steadfastly to the apostles' teaching and fellowship, to the breaking of the bread and to the prayers" (2:42). Many see in this verse a description of the nascent Christian liturgy; if that is so, then we see all the elements of ecclesial unity that Irenaeus systematizes later on (faith, sacraments, ministry). Baptism gives entry into the life of the triune God, making all peoples part of the one Body of Christ and sharing in his Holy Spirit. Sharing in the life of the one God becomes

---

15. In Acts 2, Luke lists more than a dozen different nations that are present in Jerusalem. This long list of disparate nations would seem to represent the confusion of tongues and human division that even the chosen people suffer post-Babel. Yet after the Holy Spirit comes upon the apostles, "each one heard them speaking in his own language" (Acts 2:6). The scattering of Babel is reversed in the gathering of Pentecost. There is one language of the Holy Spirit, which all can understand, a true union of all peoples rather than the false unification of the tower of Babel.

manifest in coming under the apostles' authority to learn what to believe about Christ and to worship together, especially in the ritual of breaking bread.

Paul, too, argues that ecclesial unity is guaranteed and manifest in the eucharistic body of Christ. "The cup of blessing which we bless," he says, "is it not a participation in the blood of Christ? The bread which we break, is it not a participation in the body of Christ? Because there is *one* bread, we who are many are *one* body, for we all partake of the *one* bread" (1 Cor. 10:16–17). The Eucharist is a participation in Christ himself. We partake of one bread, which makes real our unity as the one Body of Christ. The unity that we have in baptism is made manifest in the communion we share at the table of the Lord. The Eucharist gives us a more profound union with Christ and therefore a more profound union with God and with each and every other person who is in Christ.

We will discuss the apostles and their successors, the bishops, in the "Catholic" and "Apostolic" sections below, but for now we can briefly note that for early Christians, the apostles and the bishops who succeeded them were tasked with safeguarding the truth of the faith, the integrity of the sacraments, and therefore the unity of the Church. It was the responsibility of the faithful to attune themselves to their bishops so that the whole Church would manifest the harmony of the Body of Christ. Ignatius of Antioch says,

> That is why it is proper for your conduct and your practices to correspond closely with the mind of the bishop. . . . [If you are] attuned to [your] bishop like the strings of a harp, . . . the result is a hymn of praise to Jesus Christ from

LEX ORANDI

One Church

In a section entitled "The Church on the Path to Unity," the *Roman Missal* offers a eucharistic prayer that recognizes that oneness is a present reality and a goal to be achieved by God:

> For by the word of your Son's Gospel
> you have brought together one Church
> from every people, tongue, and nation,
> and, having filled her with life by the power of your Spirit,
> you never cease through her
> to gather the whole human race into one.[a]

a. *Roman Missal*, 775.

minds that are in unison, and affections that are in harmony. . . . Let there be a whole symphony of minds in concert . . . so that [God] may hear you and know by your good works that you are indeed members of His Son's Body.[16]

Visible unity is the responsibility of bishops, who hold to the truth and offer the sacraments, but it is also the responsibility of all the baptized, who must manifest the new life of God within them. They do this by their fidelity to the successors of the apostles, but also by their Christlike way of life. "See how they love one another," Tertullian reports the pagans saying when they observed Christian unity.[17] That love is poured into their hearts by the Holy Spirit (Rom. 5:5). In fact, that love is the presence of God himself, for "God is love" (1 John 4:8). The Spirit works in the deepest parts of believers, groaning in prayer, healing their weakness, and aligning their wills with God's will (Rom. 8:26–27). When wills are aligned with God, there is concord with God and neighbor. The Holy Spirit conforms people to Christ, and the more Christlike they are, the more they show forth the presence of the Spirit and the unity of the Church. The unity of the Church is rooted in God's love, and the Church will be recognized by how it manifests that unity: "By this all men will know that you are my disciples," Jesus says on the night of the Last Supper, "if you have love for one another" (John 13:35).

Holy

In the year 250, the emperor Decius ordered everyone in the Roman Empire (Jews exempted) to offer sacrifice to the state gods for the well-being of the empire. Some Christians refused and were martyred; others bribed officials to get out of sacrificing; others sacrificed under torture, while some were tortured and still did not sacrifice; and finally, some sacrificed willingly to avoid trouble. Once the persecution was over, many of these apostate Christians wanted to return to the Church. How was the Church to treat each of these groups? Could confessors and apostates partake of the same bread and cup? Were they still part of the same assembly of God, or had some excluded themselves? If so, was this exclusion permanent or temporary? Ultimately, these questions all deal with how we understand the holiness of the Church: Do the members make the Church holy, or does the Church make the members holy? Is the Church a holy oasis containing only the pure, or is it a mixed

---

16. Ignatius, *Epistle to the Ephesians* 4, in Louth, *Early Christian Writings*, 62.
17. Tertullian, *Apology* 39 (ANF 3:46).

body of sinners and saints? And if the Church is mixed, what does it mean to be a "holy" Church?

These questions were made even starker in the next generation after the even more violent persecution of Emperor Diocletian (beginning in 303). Similar responses and questions arose, but a group of North African Christians called the Donatists made a vigorous response: the Church is the Church of the holy, where no sinner can abide. The Church is holy because the members are holy. Therefore, the validity of the sacraments depends on the holiness of the minister, for how could a sinful minister communicate forgiveness of

CONTEMPORARY ISSUES

Unity Today

Nearly a thousand years after the schism with the Orthodox and more than five hundred years after the Reformation, how is it possible to believe in "one Church"? Is it even meaningful to talk about unity when we seem so hopelessly divided? And can the Catholic Church still believe itself to be "the one true Church" in light of so many recent Catholic scandals and the presence of so many good non-Catholic Christians outside the visible boundaries of the Church?

In *Ut Unum Sint*, Pope Saint John Paul II affirms the ancient teaching that the Church is already one. True ecclesial unity, he says, is "constituted by the bonds of the profession of faith, the sacraments and hierarchical communion." He immediately goes on to show the trinitarian foundation of this unity: "For the Catholic Church, then, the *communion* of Christians is none other than the manifestation in them of the grace by which God makes them sharers in his own *communion*, which is his eternal life."[a]

What, then, does this mean for our Orthodox and Protestant brothers and sisters? John Paul II notes that there are many "elements of sanctification and truth" (e.g., faith, baptism, Scripture), which "in various ways are present and operative beyond the visible boundaries of the Catholic Church."[b] These elements propel us toward unity, for they all properly belong in the one Church that Christ willed and founded.

The Catholic Church has preserved the fullness of what Christ willed for the Church: faith, sacraments, and ministry. The Orthodox

sins, and how could an unholy priest offer a holy sacrifice? Christians who sinned gravely—especially those who denied Christ or handed over the holy things of the Church—could not be readmitted to the Church. They could only entrust themselves to God's mercy, outside the boundaries of the Church. Under a newly developed penitential discipline, the Catholic Church of Africa and Rome had readmitted these sinners, so their churches, according to the Donatists, were defiled and no longer could be considered part of the one holy Church Christ founded. The holy Church, they said, was now a remnant found only in a corner of North Africa among the Donatists and their successors.

Pushing back against the narrow (and, for Donatists in later generations, rather convenient) Donatist definition of holiness, Catholics argued that on

have preserved these as well, though they have not preserved communion with Peter and his successors. The Orthodox, then, are the one Church of Christ, lacking only full communion. Through baptism, Protestants are truly members of the Body of Christ, but "because of the lack of the Sacrament of Orders they have not preserved the genuine and total reality of the Eucharistic mystery."[c] Therefore, Protestant Christians have a real though imperfect communion with the Church. For this reason, Protestant denominations are called "ecclesial communities," a term that recognizes that while not preserving the fullness of what it means to be the Church, Protestants have true and sanctifying ecclesial elements.

As Western culture becomes increasingly hostile to Christianity, it is often the case that Catholics, Orthodox, and Protestants find they have common cause. Many ecumenical friendships, communities, and cultural endeavors have arisen in the past fifty years. Indeed, as many of their own members compromise on questions of truth or morality, Catholics, Orthodox, and Protestants often find themselves closer to each other than they do to certain members of their own communions. We must hope that in God's mysterious providence he will use these developments to bring the Church into the unity that Christ himself prayed for at the Last Supper.

a. Pope John Paul II, *Ut Unum Sint* 1.9, accessed August 8, 2022, https://www.vatican.va/content/john-paul-ii/en/encyclicals/documents/hf_jp-ii_enc_25051995_ut-unum-sint.html.

b. Pope John Paul II, *Ut Unum Sint* 1.12.

c. Pope John Paul II, *Ut Unum Sint* 2.67.

earth the Church is always a mixed body. Jesus himself taught this: the Church on earth is a mix of wheat and weeds (Matt. 13:24–43), good fish and bad fish (13:47–50), and Peters and Judases. God will sort out the good and the bad at the end of time, but for now we must live with a mixed Church. To try to separate out people before the proper time could be disastrous (13:29–30). The realities of human conversion mean that people require time and a place to repent and heal from sin. The development of the sacrament of penance in the third century had profound consequences both for the meaning of the Church's holiness and for how the boundaries of the Church were conceived.

If the Church is a *corpus permixtum*, "a thoroughly mixed body of Christ," what does that mean for the holiness of the Church? Much turns on how the Church came to understand the Bible's vision of holiness. God alone is holy (Rev. 15:4), which is why the seraphim surround God's throne, singing "Holy, holy, holy" (Isa. 6:3; Rev. 4:8). Anything or anyone else becomes holy only to the extent that they are "set apart" for God (the meaning of the Hebrew word *qadosh*, "holy"). They are holy insofar as they belong to God and participate in his holiness. God himself sets things apart to make them holy, such as the Sabbath (Gen. 2:2–3) and the Israelite people. "For you are a people holy to the LORD your God; the LORD your God has chosen you to be a people for his own possession" (Deut. 7:6). With the coming of Christ, this people becomes the Church, the *kyriakos*, "the ones belonging to the Lord." As Peter says, the Church is "a chosen race, a royal priesthood, a holy nation, God's own people" (1 Pet. 2:9).

The Church is holy, then, not due to the makeup of its members at any particular time, but because God is holy. The Church is holy because God has chosen it, set it apart, and communicated holiness to it. As we said above, the Church is Christ's body animated by the Holy Spirit. In the Gospel of Luke, the angel says that the Holy Spirit will overshadow Mary and that "the holy one who shall be born of you shall be called the Son of God" (Luke 1:35, our translation). The *Holy* Spirit forms a *holy* one in Mary's womb. Similarly, in baptism, the Holy Spirit makes us holy by uniting us to the holy Body of Christ. After baptism, we belong to God's holy body, and so we participate in God's holiness.

Of course, we are all painfully aware that being a member of the holy Church does not mean that the members necessarily act in a holy manner. The same Corinthian Christians whom Paul calls "saints"—*hagioi*, "holy ones" (1 Cor. 1:2; 6:1–2)—are the ones he rebukes for dividing the church, being sexually immoral, and desecrating the Eucharist (among other things).

The Holy Church

In the Mass for the Dedication of a Church, the priest prays a beautiful preface that powerfully communicates the sacramental, christological, pneumatological, and communal dimensions of the Church's holiness:

Here is prepared the table of the Lord,
where your children, fed by the Body of Christ,
are gathered into the one, the holy Church.

Here the faithful drink of your Spirit
from the streams that flow from Christ, the spiritual rock,
through whom they, too, become a holy oblation, a living altar.ᵃ

a. *Roman Missal*, 1232.

Our historical—and recent—scandals are a shameful reminder that despite being "saints," we are not yet "saints." This is why God commands holy people to be holy: "You shall be holy, for I am holy" (1 Pet. 1:16; cf. Lev. 19:2). Holiness is at once a given in our baptism and the working out of the grace of holiness in our lives.

To say that the Church is holy means that she is the source of holiness for the world. The Church—made up of wheat and weeds, saints and sinners—can communicate holiness to others because she participates in God. This occurs especially (though not exclusively) through the sacraments. Contrary to the Donatist claims, it is God who makes the sacraments holy, not the minister. (We will revisit this below in the baptism section.) In the sacraments, God communicates his divine life to us, and we are made holy to the degree that we allow God's grace to transform us.

The Church's mission is to communicate God's holiness to the whole world. Her mission is to draw all people into Christ's holy body so that everyone has the opportunity to belong to God. The Church is not a holy oasis amid the profane desert of the godless world. No, she is the leaven that permeates the whole and lifts it up (Matt. 13:33). The Church is God's holy body, which preserves the holy fire that can set others on fire. The one Church is holy because the one holy God made her holy. Her mission is to draw all people into God's holiness so that they might live into their dignity as those who belong to the Lord.

Catholic

The term "catholic" does not appear in the New Testament, let alone as a description of the Church, but the idea that the Church is universal is present from the start. The risen Christ tells the apostles to "make disciples of *all* nations, baptizing them in the name of the Father and of the Son and of the Holy Spirit" (Matt. 28:19). Christ's command here lays the foundation for what the term "catholic" will come to mean, for present here is the notion that the universality of the Church is intimately related to faith in the Trinity, moral instruction ("make disciples"), and the sacraments ("baptizing"). We see these same elements present in the Pentecost story, the traditional "birthday" of the Church. The newly inspired apostles preach Christ to "devout men from *every* nation under heaven" (Acts 2:5), after which they exhort these men to repent (morality) and be baptized in the name of Christ (faith, sacraments). From the very start, the Church was catholic and had a catholic mission rooted in the nature of God, faith, morality, and the sacraments.

The first person to use the term "catholic Church" is Ignatius of Antioch, writing in the early 100s. Arrested and on his way to Rome to be martyred, Ignatius wrote a letter to the Christians of Smyrna, whom he praises for having been "mercifully endowed with all the gifts of the Spirit, and filled with faith and love."[18] But he warns this young church to have nothing to do with the Docetists, who believe "everything our Lord did was only illusion."[19] Their rejection of the incarnation has profound consequences.

> They have no care for love, no thought for the widow and orphan, none at all for the afflicted, the captive, the hungry or the thirsty. They even absent themselves from the Eucharist and the public prayers, because they will not admit that the Eucharist is the self-same body of our Saviour Jesus Christ which suffered for our sins, and which the Father in His goodness afterward raised again.[20]

For Ignatius, to reject belief in Christ's physical body leads to the moral failure of not caring for the bodies of the poor. It also leads to dividing the Church body: the Docetists reject the eucharistic body of Christ, which is "the self-same body of our Saviour Jesus Christ," and so they separate from the ecclesial Body of Christ. For Ignatius, belief in Christ (as true God and true man), in his one Church, and in his sacraments leads to embracing all

---

18. Ignatius, *Epistle to the Smyrnaeans*, preface, in Louth, *Early Christian Writings*, 101.
19. Ignatius, *Epistle to the Smyrnaeans* 4 (Louth, 102).
20. Ignatius, *Epistle to the Smyrnaeans* 6–7 (Louth, 102).

people, even the weakest members of society. These things are essential to the meaning of what it means for the Church to be "catholic."

In the very next paragraph, Ignatius exhorts the Smyrnaean Christians to live out the oneness of the Church: "Abjure all factions," he says, and "follow your bishop . . . as obediently as Jesus Christ followed the Father."[21] Ignatius then uses the term "catholic Church" for the first time on record: "The sole Eucharist you should consider valid is one that is celebrated by the bishop himself, or by some person authorized by him. Where the bishop is to be seen, there let all his people be; *just as* where Jesus Christ is present, we have the catholic Church."[22] The bishop is the "nucleus" of this community, around whom the (baptized) people gather. They gather around the bishop because he is the guardian and teacher of the true faith about Christ, as well as the one who can offer a "valid" Eucharist—that is, a Eucharist that is "the self-same body" of Christ. The first part of the sentence about the bishop and his people leads logically to the next part: "*just as* where Jesus Christ is present, we have the catholic Church." For Ignatius, catholicity is rooted in being in communion with one's bishop, who makes Christ present in the Eucharist. And where Christ is present, there is the catholic Church.

The meaning of the term "catholic" in the Creed has been much debated, but Ignatius's formula suggests a couple of likely interpretations: "catholic" means "whole" or "complete" and also "universal." Because the Eucharist is "the self-same body" of Christ, every time a bishop (or a priest authorized by him) celebrates the Eucharist, Christ is present. The risen Christ transcends time and space, so it is not a *part* of Christ (since Christ is not divisible) but the *whole* of Christ that is present. Therefore, we can find the reality of the one, holy Church *completely* (that is, "catholically") present. Yet this same Christ is present in each and every place around the world where the bishop celebrates a valid Eucharist. It is universal. So the many different churches are not a federation of distinct entities, but one Body spread throughout the world, since the same indivisible Christ is present in each of them, making them one with himself and each other.

Ignatius gives us a profound vision of what the catholic Church looks like. The bishop safeguards and preaches the truth about Christ—namely, that "in him the whole fulness of deity dwells bodily" (Col. 2:9). The bishop provides the Eucharist to his baptized people so that the same body of Christ that died and rose is "re-presented," or made present again. Both of these—faith in

---

21. Ignatius, *Epistle to the Smyrnaeans* 8 (Louth, 103).
22. Ignatius, *Epistle to the Smyrnaeans* 8 (Louth, 103, emphasis added).

the incarnation and the grace of the Eucharist—commit us to care for the bodily needs of "the least of these my brethren," where Christ himself tells us that he is particularly present (Matt. 25:40). Christ is fully present where the people are gathered around their bishop celebrating the Eucharist, and this commits them to drawing all people, even the least among them, into the same communion. It commits them to loving one another as Christ loved them, another sign that both Christ and the Holy Spirit of Christ are present. The Church is fully present in every particular church, but it is also one with every other "catholic" church throughout the world because the same Christ and the same Spirit are present. And when we receive the Eucharist, we have communion with God and our bishop and with every other church throughout the world that has a bishop celebrating a valid Eucharist.

Apostolic

The Church is apostolic because it is founded upon the apostles (Eph. 2:19–20). Christ himself chose twelve apostles (representing the twelve tribes of Israel) as the base for his universal mission to bring all people into communion with himself. To put it rather boldly, it is only through the apostles that we have access to Christ and the salvation he won for us. "We have learned from none others the plan of our salvation," Irenaeus says, "than from those through whom the Gospel has come down to us, which they did at one time proclaim in public, and, at a later period, by the will of God, handed down to us in the Scriptures, to be the ground and pillar of our faith."[23] This is one of Irenaeus's strongest arguments against the Gnostic teachings about Christ. Christ founded a Church on the apostles and committed the truth to them. They committed their teaching to writing and appointed successors who received the same truth. The apostolic origin of this teaching ensures that we are as close as possible to Christ's own teachings. The Gnostics claim to have other, superior teachings, but these cannot be verified by any apostolic authority. One mark of the Church Christ founded is that its teachings accord with the teachings of the apostles, their writings, and their successors.

Christ gave the apostles the means to execute his plan of salvation by granting them his own divine authority to forgive sins, offer acceptable sacrifice to God, and teach faith and morals in a binding way. In one resurrection appearance, Christ breathes on his apostles, saying, "Receive the Holy Spirit. If you forgive the sins of any, they are forgiven; if you retain the sins of any, they are

---

23. Irenaeus, *Against Heresies* 3.1.1 (*ANF* 1:414).

retained" (John 20:22–23). At the Last Supper, the apostles are entrusted with the perfect sacrifice of Christ's body, of which they are told to partake and distribute to others (Luke 22:14–20). The apostles are also given the power to "bind and loose," a phrase that refers to their power to give authoritative interpretations of Scripture, morality, and doctrine and to hold people accountable to those interpretations.[24] These apostolic powers are the means of drawing all people into one holy communion.

This authority is passed on from the apostles to their successors. The Church is apostolic in another sense, then, because it preserves an apostolic ministry through what is called "†apostolic succession." Apostolic succession is the way that divine authority is passed on from one generation of leaders to the next. It is the idea that the authority Christ gave the apostles is passed on to successors who, through the gift of the Holy Spirit, stand in the place of the apostles. "I remind you to rekindle the gift of God that is within you through the laying on of my hands," Paul says to his successor, Timothy (2 Tim. 1:6). Through the laying on of hands, the Holy Spirit is passed on to those who succeed the apostles (and those who succeed them), who have the same apostolic authority to forgive sins, teach with authority, and offer sacrifice.[25]

One way this apostolic authority was exercised was in councils. In Acts 15, we see the apostles and elders gather in Jerusalem to discern a matter of faith, morals, and the interpretation of Scripture. Do non-Jews have to keep the Jewish law in the Church? The apostles exercise their divine authority in a remarkable way, telling the Church that the Jewish laws regarding food and circumcision—laws that are recorded in Scripture as coming directly from God—do not have to be kept by gentiles. In what might be called the first Post-Synodal Apostolic Exhortation, the apostles write, "For it has seemed good to the Holy Spirit and to us to lay upon you no greater burden than these necessary things" (Acts 15:28). The apostles, given the gift of the Spirit, gather in council to discern the Spirit's will. They interpret the Scriptures to give a binding decision on morality for the whole Church. The apostolic authority exercised in the Jerusalem Council is again exercised in the production of the creeds of Nicaea and Constantinople, when the truth about Christ and the Holy Spirit had to be taught authoritatively.

The Church is apostolic also because through apostolic succession the Church is faithful to what the apostles have handed on. The Church accepts

24. Peter is given the authority to bind and loose individually (Matt. 16:19), whereas the other apostles are given it collectively (18:18).

25. For an early description of apostolic succession, see *First Clement* 42–44.

as Scripture the writings of the apostles or the writings authorized by them. Irenaeus leaves us an early and important witness to this apostolic tradition:

> For, after our Lord rose from the dead, [the apostles] were invested with power from on high when the Holy Spirit came down [upon them], were filled from all [His gifts], and had perfect knowledge: they departed to the ends of the earth, preaching the glad tidings of the good things [sent] from God to us, and proclaiming the peace of heaven to men, who indeed do all equally and individually possess the Gospel of God. Matthew also issued a written Gospel among the Hebrews in their own dialect, while Peter and Paul were preaching at Rome, and laying the foundations of the Church. After their departure, Mark, the disciple and interpreter of Peter, did also hand down to us in writing what had been preached by Peter. Luke also, the companion of Paul, recorded in a book the Gospel preached by him. Afterwards, John, the disciple of the Lord, who also had leaned upon His breast, did himself publish a Gospel during his residence at Ephesus in Asia.[26]

The apostles—especially the three "pillars," Peter, James, and John (Gal. 2:9)—play a significant role in authenticating the stories about Jesus. God sends Paul to them in order to confirm the gospel he received from Christ and had been preaching for years (2:1–10). They extend "the right hand of fellowship" (2:9), confirming him as a true apostle. Most of the books of the New Testament are written by or come from the tradition of Paul and these three "pillars."

Believing in an "apostolic Church" is an extension of believing in the incarnation. Christ does not send angels to reveal his message to the world; he does not flash a sign in the sky that everyone can read; he does not reveal himself privately within the mind or heart of every single person. Instead, he entrusts the saving truth to twelve apostles, "treasure in earthen vessels" (2 Cor. 4:7). This is a risky plan, but Christ loves what he created and saves what he created and continues to work through what he created. Entrusting salvation to people makes us "God's fellow workers" (1 Cor. 3:9) and builds up love within the Church. We must go to others to learn the faith. We must trust the apostles and their successors, who have preached the truth; made disciples of others; written, copied, and translated Scripture; and given their lives for God and others. The apostles and their successors often fail, but believing in an apostolic Church means believing that Christ works through the frailty of human flesh.

---

26. Irenaeus, *Against Heresies* 3.1.1 (ANF 1:414).

WITNESS TO THE TRADITION

Irenaeus on the Primacy of Rome

While the early Church did not have a fully developed theology of the papacy, there was, from the beginning, a recognition that the Bishop of Rome had a special authority that was rooted in apostolic authority. The Church of Rome was founded and organized by Peter and Paul, both of whom were martyred there. The Bishop of Rome succeeded Peter and held the same authority among bishops as Peter had among the apostles; therefore, the Church of Rome held a preeminent authority. Irenaeus is an early witness to this:

> Since, however, it would be very tedious, in such a volume as this, to reckon up the successions of all the Churches, we do put to confusion all those who, in whatever manner, whether by an evil self-pleasing, by vainglory, or by blindness and perverse opinion, assemble in unauthorized meetings; [we do this, I say,] by indicating that tradition derived from the apostles, of the very great, the very ancient, and universally known Church founded and organized at Rome by the two most glorious apostles, Peter and Paul; as also [by pointing out] the faith preached to men, which comes down to our time by means of the successions of the bishops. For it is a matter of necessity that every Church should agree with this Church, on account of its preeminent authority.[a]

a. Irenaeus, *Against Heresies* 3.3.2 (ANF 1:415).

Living the Mystery

God is a communion of persons who created us for communion with himself and with each other. That communion *is* the Church, which is why the second-century *Shepherd of Hermas* can so boldly declare, "The world was created for the sake of the Church."[27] This may seem like a shocking claim, but only if we have a merely functional or institutional view of the Church. God made us for himself, and the Church is the place, the living Body of Christ, where we find communion with God and everyone else who shares that communion.

In Scripture, the term "body of Christ" has three meanings: it refers to Christ's human body, born of Mary, which died and rose again; it refers to the

27. *Shepherd of Hermas* 2.4.1, quoted in CCC 760.

Eucharist; and it refers to the Church. For early Christians, there was a kind of mystical identity between these three that informs how we might live the mystery of the Church. Christ's body was real, not an illusion, and we really become a part of it, for his body, now risen and glorified, is no longer bound by time or space. We belong to Christ in a radical way: we are his very own body. And in the Eucharist, Christ really feeds us with his own flesh so that we might "be transformed into what we consume."[28]

For Augustine, the Eucharist is a mirror in which the Church is able to examine itself. In a beautiful Pentecost sermon, Augustine addresses the newly baptized:

> So if you want to understand the body of Christ, listen to the apostle telling the faithful, *You though are the body of Christ and its members* (1 Cor. 12:27). So if it's you that are the body of Christ and its members, it's the mystery meaning you that has been placed on the Lord's table; what you receive is the mystery that means you.[29]

The Eucharist is the pure body of Christ that shows the Church, the mixed Body of Christ, what it is supposed to be. We can see the unity of the bread gathered from many grains, moistened into dough, and baked into bread. This is meant to show us how we should be: gathered from all parts of the world, baptized into one body, and set on fire with the Holy Spirit. We identify ourselves with the consecrated bread, which is not merely a sign but the true body of Christ that communicates God's life to us. "Be what you can see, and receive what you are," Augustine says.[30] By consuming the body of Christ, we are transformed into the Body of Christ, the only sacrifice pleasing to God.

Having received God's divine life in the Eucharist, we must now communicate that to others. "Go and announce the Gospel of the Lord," we are exhorted at the end of Mass. We have received the gospel of the Lord, the good news of salvation passed on to us through the apostles, which we must share with others. We have been made holy by the holy sacraments, and we must now draw others into that holiness. God entrusts this mission to his people, to us, who, having been given new life in Christ, must go out and bring others into communion with God and his family. This communion *is* the one, holy, catholic, and apostolic Church for which God created the world.

---

28. *Roman Missal*, 487.

29. Augustine, *Sermon 272*, in *Essential Sermons*, trans. Edmund Hill, WSA III/8 (Hyde Park, NY: New City, 2007), 318. See also *Sermon 229* for a similar exploration.

30. Augustine, *Sermon 272* (Hill, 318).

Baptism and Forgiveness

I believe in one, holy, catholic and apostolic Church. I confess one Baptism for the forgiveness of sins	Et unam sanctam catholicam et apostolicam Ecclesiam. Confiteor unum baptisma in remissionem peccatorum.	Εἰς μίαν ἁγίαν καθολικὴν καὶ ἀποστολικὴν ἐκκλησίαν. Ὁμολογοῦμεν ἓν βάπτισμα εἰς ἄφεσιν ἁμαρτιῶν.

OT: Gen. 1–3; 6–9; Exod. 14; Josh. 3–4

NT: baptism, Matt. 3:1–17; 28:18–20; John 3:5; Rom. 6:1–11; Eph. 4:5–6; 2 Pet. 1:4; forgiveness of sins, Matt. 1:21; John 20:23; Acts 2:38

Catechism: one baptism for the forgiveness of sins, 976–87; sacrament of baptism, 1213–84; sacrament of penance and reconciliation, 1420–98

Theological Exposition

The New Testament provides a rich and varied theology of baptism. Drawing on key moments in the Old Testament history of salvation, baptism is presented as a new creation with water and Spirit (Matt. 3:16; John 3:5); as a new flood that destroys wickedness and saves the righteous (1 Pet. 3:20–21); as a new crossing of the Red Sea that liberates us from slavery (1 Cor. 10:2); and as a new crossing of the Jordan River, which leads into the promised land of heaven (Matt. 3:13).

Christ himself is baptized (see Matt. 3 and parallels), and his baptism contains the essential elements of the early Christian understanding of baptism. Jesus is the new Joshua who enters the Jordan River, but instead of parting the waters to enter the promised land of Canaan, he parts the heavens so we might enter the promised land of communion with God. Jesus is submerged in the water, signifying his death and burial, and rises out of the water, signifying his resurrection. The Holy Spirit descends upon him in the water, recalling the original creation of the world, and the Father declares that Jesus is his beloved Son. Christ desires that we all imitate him in being baptized and commands the apostles to baptize all nations in the name of the triune God (Matt. 28:18–20). He also emphasizes the necessity of baptism for salvation: "Unless one is born of water and the Spirit, he cannot enter the kingdom of God" (John 3:5). Our baptism, too, is with water and the Holy Spirit (Acts 2:38), so that dying and rising in Christ (Rom. 6:3–11), we will become adopted children of our heavenly Father (Gal. 4:5–6), new creations (2 Cor. 5:17), who now have access to communion with the Trinity (Eph. 2:18).

The Creed only mentions one effect of baptism—the forgiveness of sins—but the New Testament and the early Church identify a number of other graces that come with baptism. Those who are baptized become members of Christ's body (1 Cor. 12:12–13) and, therefore, "partakers of the divine nature" (2 Pet. 1:4). Baptism sanctifies and justifies us—that is, makes us holy and just or, better, makes us partake of God's holiness and justice (1 Cor. 6:11). We are no longer slaves of the devil, but children of God (Gal. 4:7). We have become sons and daughters in the Son who now can properly call God "*our* Father" (Matt. 6:9; Rom. 8:15–16). And since God is our new Father, we can rejoice that we have been delivered "from the dominion of darkness and transferred

---

LEX ORANDI

The Blessing of the Baptismal Waters

At the Easter Vigil, the priest blesses the baptismal water with this beautiful prayer, which communicates a profound trinitarian theology of baptism:

> O God, who by invisible power
> accomplish a wondrous effect
> through sacramental signs
> and who in many ways have prepared water, your creation,
> to show forth the grace of Baptism;
>
> O God, whose Spirit
> in the first moments of the world's creation
> hovered over the waters,
> so that the very substance of water
> would even then take to itself the power to sanctify;
>
> O God, who by the outpouring of the flood
> foreshadowed regeneration,
> so that from the mystery of one and the same element of water
> would come an end to vice and a beginning of virtue;
>
> O God, who caused the children of Abraham
> to pass dry-shod through the Red Sea,
> so that the chosen people,
> set free from slavery to Pharaoh,
> would prefigure the people of the baptized;

. . . to the kingdom of his beloved Son" (Col. 1:13). Both individually and collectively, we are now "a temple of the Holy Spirit" (1 Cor. 6:19; cf. 3:16).

While the necessity of baptism was universally recognized in the early Church, controversy arose over what constituted a valid baptism and whether "rebaptism" was ever permitted. In this section we will explore why the Creed emphasizes *one* baptism as well as why the forgiveness of sins is highlighted.

One Baptism

The Creed uses the word "one" four times. There is one God; one Lord Jesus Christ; one holy, catholic, and apostolic Church; and one baptism for the forgiveness of sins. This is likely an echo of Ephesians 4, which we have quoted previously: "There is one body and one Spirit, just as you were called to the one hope that belongs to your call, one Lord, one faith, *one baptism*, one God and Father of us all, who is above all and through all and in all" (Eph. 4:4–6). There is one baptism because there is one God and one Lord who founded one Church into which we are baptized. "Is Christ divided?" Paul rebukes the Corinthian Church. "Was Paul crucified for you? Or were you baptized in the name of Paul [or Apollos or Cephas]?" (1 Cor. 1:13).

O God, whose Son,
baptized by John in the waters of the Jordan,
was anointed with the Holy Spirit,
and, as he hung upon the Cross,
gave forth water from his side along with blood,
and after his Resurrection, commanded his disciples:
"Go forth, teach all nations, baptizing them
in the name of the Father and of the Son and of the Holy Spirit,"
look now, we pray, upon the face of your Church
and graciously unseal for her the fountain of Baptism.

May this water receive by the Holy Spirit
the grace of your Only Begotten Son,
so that human nature, created in your image
and washed clean through the Sacrament of Baptism
from all the squalor of the life of old,
may be found worthy to rise to the life of newborn children
through water and the Holy Spirit.[a]

a. *Roman Missal*, 377.

There is one Body of Christ and one baptism in Christ that makes us a part of that body.

But there is another reason why there is only one baptism: our baptism is not to be repeated. In the third century, "rebaptism" (so called) became an existential question. After the Decian persecutions, how were Christians to understand the sacraments that came from apostate bishops and priests? If baptism communicated the Holy Spirit, as Scripture amply attests, how can those who have cut themselves off from the Holy Spirit through apostasy give it? One cannot give what he does not have. The same principle held, so it was argued, for schismatics and heretics. Those who had cut themselves off from the Church could not be the means of bringing others into the Church. Therefore, those who were baptized by an apostate, schismatic, or heretical minister had to be baptized again. Or, to be more accurate, since the original baptism was not valid, one had to be baptized validly for the first time.

This argument was given weight by Cyprian and, in the next generation, by the Donatists who followed his line of reasoning. It was not, however, the argument that carried the day in the Church. In Rome, Pope Stephen disagreed with Cyprian and argued that the worthiness of the minister did not affect the validity of the sacrament. Rather, in every sacrament, it is God who acts and makes it valid. John the Baptist says, "I baptize you with water for repentance, but he who is coming after me is mightier than I . . . ; *he* will baptize you with the Holy Spirit and with fire" (Matt. 3:11). It is Christ, then, who is personally active in every baptism, and the state of the minister's soul cannot obstruct or obscure this grace of Christ. If this is the case, then there really is only one baptism, for there is only one source from which the grace of baptism flows. Whenever someone is baptized, it is God who baptizes.

Arguing against the Donatists a century later, Augustine became the most forceful exponent of this view and set the terms for the Catholic Church's theology of baptism. He writes,

> Although many ministers—whether just or unjust—were going to baptize, the holiness of baptism would not be attributed to anyone but to him upon whom the dove came down, about whom it was said, *This is the one who baptizes in the Holy Spirit.* Let Peter baptize, this is the one who baptizes; let Paul baptize, this is the one who baptizes; let Judas baptize, this is the one who baptizes.[31]

---

31. Augustine, *Homily* 6.7, in *Homilies on the Gospel of John 1–40*, trans. Edmund Hill, WSA III/12 (Hyde Park, NY: New City, 2009), 127.

Because baptism is necessary for salvation, God wanted it to be as available as possible to as many people as possible. Therefore, while it is most fitting for a bishop or priest to baptize, it is the case that anyone—apostates, schismatics, heretics, even nonbelievers—can validly baptize.

Baptism is valid so long as water and the trinitarian formula are used with the proper intention. If these things occur, then one is truly baptized with everything that comes along with it. This baptism is permanent. It leaves what will later be called (but which was always understood as) "an indelible mark," which is another reason there is only "one Baptism." Once one becomes a child of God, one cannot undo one's status as a son or daughter! The baptized is always God's child, even if he becomes a bad child.

This raises one final point that Augustine also helpfully clarifies: a baptism may be valid but not fruitful. Any water baptism using the trinitarian formula can be a true baptism, but it might not bear fruit in the life of the one baptized. If the person remains outside the Church, continues in schism, or persists in a sinful way of life, then there will be no spiritual fruits from the valid baptism.

Forgiveness of Sins

As we discussed above, baptism has a number of effects, so why does the Creed single out "the forgiveness of sins"? One reason, of course, is that this connection is biblical. In a passage worth quoting again, Peter says, "Repent, and be baptized every one of you in the name of Jesus Christ for the forgiveness of your sins; and you shall receive the gift of the Holy Spirit" (Acts 2:38). The reality of sin and its forgiveness in Christ is central to the message of the gospel. The angel tells Joseph that he will call Mary's child "Jesus, for he will save his people from their sins" (Matt. 1:21). Saving us from our sins is not only Jesus's mission but his name and identity. Zechariah, filled with the Holy Spirit, prophesies about his son, John the Baptist, that he "will go before the Lord to prepare his ways, to give knowledge of salvation to his people in the forgiveness of their sins" (Luke 1:76–77). John baptizes those who confess their sins, and Jesus sends his apostles out by breathing the Holy Spirit on them, saying, "If you forgive the sins of any, they are forgiven; if you retain the sins of any, they are retained" (John 20:23).

In the New Testament, Jesus wins forgiveness of sins on the cross, and that forgiveness is effected in our lives by baptism. "Rise and be baptized, and wash away your sins," Ananias says to the recently converted Paul (Acts 22:16). Baptism is also intimately connected with faith and salvation: "He who believes and is baptized will be saved," the risen Christ tells his disciples

(Mark 16:16). At the Last Supper, Jesus says that he will pour out his blood "for many for the forgiveness of sins" (Matt. 26:28). In his crucifixion, he nails our sins to the cross (Col. 2:14). In our baptism, we enter into Christ's death (Rom. 6:3), which releases us from our debt of sin, for "he who has died is freed from sin" (6:7). We also rise with Christ and so are "alive to God in Christ" (6:11) and "walk in newness of life" (6:4).

While the link between baptism and forgiveness reflects a biblical logic, the formula in the Creed likely comes out of the "rebaptism" debate we discussed above. Should those baptized by apostates, heretics, or schismatics be baptized again? Should Christians who commit grave sin be baptized again? No, the Creed emphatically declares, for there is "one Baptism for the forgiveness of sins."

Early Christians discerned that without the forgiveness of sins all other baptismal graces would be futile. "If the forgiveness of sins were not to be had in the Church," says Augustine, "there would be no hope of a future life and eternal liberation."[32] Unless we are relieved of our debt, we cannot be made rich (2 Cor. 8:9). Unless we are freed from bondage to sin and the devil, we cannot be adopted as children of God. Unless we die with Christ, we cannot rise with him. Forgiveness of sins is the foundation of our life in Christ. "Baptism is the basis of the whole Christian life," the *Catechism* says, "the gateway to life in the Spirit."[33] The spiritual life includes growing in holiness but also continual repentance and forgiveness of sins.

If there is only "one Baptism for the forgiveness of sins," then there must be ways for Christians who sin to repent, receive forgiveness, and return to grace. The creedal formula signals that the already-developing theology of postbaptismal penance is necessary. This, as we saw when discussing the holiness of the Church, will also open the door to a very different kind of †ecclesiology. The Church will not be a closed community of the pure who shun the impure from their midst. Rather, the Church, as Augustine says, will be the place where those wounded by sin can practice "the medicine of daily repentance."[34] In the Church, they can encounter Christ, the divine Medic who became Medicine for us in his human nature.[35] The Creed, once again, commits us to a mixed Church in which saints and sinners sit side by side and worship together. We may, as Augustine says, have different ultimate destinies,

32. Augustine, *Sermon* 213.9, in Hill, *Essential Sermons*, 270.
33. CCC 1213.
34. Augustine, *Sermon* 351.5, in *Sermons 341–400*, trans. Edmund Hill, WSA III/10 (Hyde Park, NY: New City, 1995), 124.
35. Augustine, *Sermon* 374.3.

Origen on Many Ways to Receive Forgiveness

Since most Catholics today are baptized as infants, they tend to associate the forgiveness of sins with the sacrament of penance. Writing in the third century, Origen documents the many ways Scripture talks about how Christians can receive forgiveness. His list is a salutary reminder that our Father is rich in mercy:

> For you, the Son of God was killed. How could it please you to sin again? And yet, lest these things not so much build up your souls for virtue as cast them down to despair, you heard how many sacrifices there were in the Law for sins. Now hear how many are the remissions of sins in the gospel.
>
> [1] First is the one by which we are baptized "for the remission of sins" [cf. Mark 1:4]. [2] A second remission is in the suffering of martyrdom. [3] Third, is that which is given through alms. For the Savior says, "but nevertheless, give what you have and, behold, all things are clean for you" [Luke 11:41]. [4] A fourth remission of sins is given for us through the fact that we also forgive the sins of our brothers. For thus the Lord and Savior himself says . . . [quoting Matt. 6:11–14]. [5] A fifth forgiveness of sins is when "someone will convert a sinner from the error of his way." For thus divine Scripture says, "Whoever will make a sinner turn from the error of his way will save a soul from death and cover a multitude of sins" [James 5:20]. [6] There is also a sixth forgiveness through the abundance of love as the Lord himself says, "Truly I say to you, her many sins are forgiven because she loved much" [Luke 7:47]. And the Apostle says, "Because love will cover a multitude of sins" [1 Pet. 4:8]. [7] And there is still a seventh remission of sins through penance, although admittedly it is difficult and toilsome, when the sinner washes "his couch in tears" [cf. Ps. 6:6], and his "tears" become his "bread day and night [Ps. 42:3]," when he is not ashamed to make known his sin to the priest of the Lord and to seek a cure according to the one who says, "I said, 'I will proclaim to the Lord my injustice against myself,' and you forgave the impiety of my heart" [Ps. 32:5]. What the Apostle James said is fulfilled in this . . . [James 5:14–16].[a]

a. Origen, *Homily on Leviticus* 2.4–5, in *Homilies on Leviticus, 1–16*, trans. Gary Wayne Barkley, FOTC 83 (Washington, DC: Catholic University of America Press, 1990), 47–48; paragraphs and numbers added for clarity.

but in this world and at this time, we cannot be sure and we cannot judge.[36] We grow up together in the Lord's field, and he will sort us out in the end.

Living the Mystery

In a famous Christmas sermon, Pope Leo the Great reminds his congregation of their baptism. "Realize, O Christian, your dignity. Once made a 'partaker of the divine nature,' do not return to your former baseness of life."[37] Baptism is a radical transformation of our being. We are changed from being a slave of the devil to being a child of the Most High God. We are changed from being merely dust and ashes to having the seeds of immortality and incorruptibility. We are made, as Leo says, quoting 2 Peter 1:4, "partakers of the divine nature." This radical transformation calls for an equally radical change in our way of life. "There are two Ways," the first-century *Didache* says, "a Way of Life and a Way of Death, and the difference between these two ways is great."[38] Paul exhorts the Ephesians similarly: "Put off the old man that belongs to your former manner of life and is corrupt through deceitful lusts, and be renewed in the spirit of your minds, and put on the new man, created after the likeness of God in true righteousness and holiness" (Eph. 4:22–24 RSV-2CE).

Baptism confers a new dignity upon us. We are like Cinderella, a slave to an evil stepmother whose perverse will we must serve. But a noble prince comes to rescue us, takes us to his palace, and elevates us to the status of royalty. We cannot return to slaving away in the cinders anymore; rather, we must act according to our new dignity as adopted children of the King. Along these lines, Cyprian reminds us that we bear the image of Christ, "the heavenly man" (cf. 1 Cor. 15:47–49), so we must show forth the likeness of Christ in our manner of life. "For this is to change what you had been and to begin to be what you were not, that the divine birth might shine forth in you, that the deifying discipline [*deifica disciplina*] might respond to God, the Father, that in the honour and praise of living, God may be glorified in man."[39] We have been re-created after the likeness of God, and our life must manifest that likeness. By practicing a "deifying discipline," we become integrated by grace, become more godlike, and glorify God by our way of life.

36. Augustine, *City of God* 1.35.
37. Leo the Great, *Sermon* 21.3, in *St. Leo the Great: Sermons*, trans. Jane P. Freeland and Agnes J. Conway, FOTC 93 (Washington, DC: Catholic University of America Press, 1996), 79.
38. *Didache* 1, quoted in Louth, *Early Christian Writings*, 191.
39. Cyprian, *On Jealousy and Envy* 15 (ANF 5:495, modified).

Every time we dip our hand in the holy water font to cross ourselves, we should "remember our baptism and be grateful" (to paraphrase a lovely United Methodist asperges rite). At every Easter Vigil, when we renew our baptismal promises and are sprinkled with holy water, we should remember the gift of salvation we received through baptism. We should thank God for the forgiveness of sins baptism gave us, the new divine life it bestowed upon us, and the holy way of life it has made possible.

Resurrection and the Life of the World to Come

I believe in one, holy, catholic and apostolic Church.	Et unam sanctam catholicm et apostolicam Ecclesiam.	Εἰς μίαν ἁγίαν καθολικὴν καὶ ἀποστολικὴν ἐκκλησίαν.
I confess one Baptism for the forgiveness of sins	Confiteor unum baptisma in remissionem peccatorum.	Ὁμολογοῦμεν ἓν βάπτισμα εἰς ἄφεσιν ἁμαρτιῶν.
and I look forward to the resurrection of the dead	Et exspecto resurrectionem mortuorum,	Προσδοκῶμεν ἀνάστασιν νεκρῶν,
and the life of the world to come. Amen.	et vitam venturi saeculi. Amen.	καὶ ζωὴν τοῦ μέλλοντος αἰῶνος. Ἀμήν.

OT: Isa. 65–66; Dan. 12:2; 2 Macc. 7:14

NT: resurrection, John 11:25–26; 1 Cor. 15; Phil. 3:21; life of the world to come, Matt. 24:35; John 5:24–29; Rom. 8:23; 1 Cor. 13:12; 1 Pet. 1:23; 2 Pet. 3:10; 1 John 3:2; Rev. 21–22

Catechism: resurrection, 988–1019; life everlasting, 1020–65

Theological Exposition

The Creed ends with the end, with our Christian hope that this life is not all there is and that death is not the final word. Based on our belief in all the previous articles of the Creed, we can look forward with hope (for hope is faith directed toward the future) to a life with God that includes not only our soul but our body. The Creed does not go into great detail about this future; it gives us only the barest, though most essential, outline of what believers can hope for.[40]

---

40. For an excellent and wide-ranging survey of early Christian beliefs about the end times, see Brian E. Daley, *The Hope of the Early Church: A Handbook of Patristic Eschatology* (Grand Rapids: Baker Academic, 2002).

These last two articles of the Creed have their roots deep in the New Testament. Jesus had to navigate the Jewish authorities, who were bitterly divided on these questions. On the one hand, the more conservative Sadducees rejected the resurrection, as did the Hellenized Jews of the diaspora. The Sadducees rejected eternal life too: they did not think the soul (let alone the body) survived after death. There was no "life of the world to come," but only this life. On the other hand, the more liberal Pharisees embraced the resurrection of the body, as did Palestinian Jews (Jesus and his disciples among them). This makes Jesus's own views particularly interesting—and shocking. Not only does Jesus believe in the resurrection (siding with the Pharisees), and not only does he promise resurrection and eternal life (How can a man promise that?), but he declares that he *is* resurrection and eternal life.

Before raising Lazarus, Jesus tells Martha, "I am the resurrection and the life; he who believes in me, though he die, yet shall he live; and whoever lives and believes in me shall never die" (John 11:25–26). Those who are grafted onto Christ through faith are united to an almighty God who is the Lord of the living and the dead and has the power to give life. The life we receive in the resurrection will not be more of this life, but a new, transformed, and glorified life—what the New Testament calls "eternal life" (e.g., John 5:24). The raising of Lazarus is an important sign of the resurrection, for it shows that Christ has power over death. But it is only a sign. Lazarus will die again (indeed, the chief priests plot to kill him). Christ's own resurrection provides a vision for what our resurrection will look like: a life that conquers death, a life that has definitively entered into the life of the triune God.

While we do not know the day or the hour of our own death or when Christ will come in glory to judge the living and the dead, over time the Church articulated the final events or stages revealed in Scripture.[41] Most of us will live our lives and die at some point. Upon death, we will receive what is called "particular judgment," which will determine whether our soul will enjoy God in heaven, be purified in purgatory, or suffer punishment in hell. As the soul receives its judgment, our bodies are prepared for burial (unless we die in some way that prevents burial). Our bodies remain where they are and decompose.[42] Our souls experience the "intermediate state" of their particular judgment. All the dead, both the just and the unjust, await the "general resur-

41. What is presented here is the developed form of what Catholics believe. Some of these elements were still being worked out in the fourth century. See CCC 1020–60 for details on these stages.

42. For the problem of how bodies eaten by animals and cannibals will rise, see Athenagoras, *Resurrection of the Dead* 4–9, and Augustine, *City of God* 22.20.

rection," when our bodies will be raised, transformed, and united with our souls again. Some people will still be alive at this time, so they will not die but be transformed "in a moment, in the twinkling of an eye" (1 Cor. 15:52). We call the time when Christ comes "to judge the living and the dead" the "last judgment." He will render ultimate judgment on everyone and everything. We will learn the consequences of all we have done and failed to do and how these have echoed throughout history after our deaths. The just will be vindicated, the unjust will be punished, and the meaning of all things will be revealed. Finally, God will restore creation, bringing about a new heaven and a new earth, where the just will reign with Christ and enjoy communion with God and neighbor, while the wicked will suffer forever.

The Creed does not go into nearly as much detail, but it does briefly assert our hope in our own resurrection and eternal life with God. In what follows, we will try to show what was at stake in these minimalist assertions, what Scripture reveals, and how early Christians navigated challenges to these beliefs.

Resurrection

While much of popular Christian piety today focuses on getting our souls to heaven after this life, the early Christian faith emphasized the resurrection of the body at the end of time. Upon reflection, it may come as a surprise that the Creed says nothing about where souls go when they die, focusing instead on the fate of the body and eternal life in the world to come. Indeed, the word "resurrection" (*anastasis* in the original Greek) means "standing up," an implicit reference to the prostrate body of the dead. We so emphasize "getting to heaven" that it seems we have forgotten that the good news, the gospel, is *Christos anesti*, "Christ is risen!" Christ has conquered death, and this means that even though we cannot escape death, we too will conquer it with Christ. The resurrection of the dead is *the* central hope of the Christian life: "If there is no resurrection of the dead," Paul says, "then Christ has not been raised; if Christ has not been raised, then our preaching is in vain and your faith is in vain" (1 Cor. 15:13–14). Without hope for our own bodily resurrection, there is no Christianity.

Unwittingly, many of us today have adopted a Gnostic or pagan philosophical view of the afterlife in which the goal of life is to escape the material world, which is considered either a burden (pagan philosophy) or evil (Gnosticism). Augustine criticizes Porphyry, the great Neoplatonist philosopher and critic of Christianity, who argued that "the soul must flee from all bodies if it is to attain enduring happiness with God."[43] For both Gnostics and many pagan philosophers, the soul was naturally divine, even identical in some way to God, whereas the body was its prison. The soul's union with a body, then, was an accident, a fall, a punishment, (at best) an opportunity for purgation, and, no matter the cause, certainly unnatural. The soul, then, needed to be free from the body so that it could return to the heavenly realm, where it naturally belonged. Bodies were not saved but went the way of the rest of the material world. While early Christians gradually developed a rich understanding of the immortal soul and of the "intermediate state" of the soul after death, they always fought hard against the Gnostic and pagan philosophical vision of salvation. The focus of Christian hope has always been on the resurrection of the body.

Hope for resurrection is inseparable from faith in an almighty Creator.[44] God has made us as a body-soul unity, and the separation of body and soul—not their union—is unnatural. In Genesis, God creates humans from the dust of the earth and breathes the breath of life into them. On this account, the body is not an accident or a punishment, and neither is the soul equal to God. Both are creations of the good God. The order and integrity of human creation is telling. God is the life of the soul, whereas the soul is the life of the body. There is a clear hierarchy of dependence. So long as humans maintained their union with God, they would not have died. But humans sinned and so separated their souls from God. Once separated from God, their bodies inevitably died, for "the wages of sin is death" (Rom. 6:23). It is kind of like unplugging a laptop computer: once severed from the source of power, the battery will sustain its life for a while, but eventually it will die.

After the fall, then, humans have two fundamental problems that they cannot do anything about: a sin problem and a death problem, or a soul problem and a body problem. Sin separates our souls from God; death separates our bodies from our souls. No matter what we do, we cannot overcome these problems. This is a whole-person problem. Because God cares about his creation, he wants to restore what he made. He sends us a Savior who can reconcile our souls to God *and* our bodies to our souls. By dying on the cross, Christ "died for our sins" (1 Cor. 15:3) and reconciled us to God (2 Cor.

---

43. Augustine, *City of God* 10.29, in *City of God, Books 11–22*, trans. William Babcock, WSA I/7 (Hyde Park, NY: New City, 2013), 340, summarizing writings by Porphyry now lost.

44. We see this especially in two striking passages, 2 Macc. 7:14 and Rom. 4:17, which we quoted in chap. 2 when discussing *creatio ex nihilo*. Both Paul and the Maccabean mother give voice to the biblical logic that the God who has the power to create from nothing has the power to restore what was destroyed.

5:18). By rising from the dead, Christ "abolished death and brought life and immortality to light" (2 Tim. 1:10). We now have a confident hope that "he who raised the Lord Jesus will raise us also with Jesus" (2 Cor. 4:14). Sin and death are a grave affront to God and the human nature he created. By saving both our soul and our body, the God who made us saves us by uniting what sin and death divided.

God wants to save not just a part of us but the whole of us. If God saved only our souls, then death ultimately wins and God is not almighty. But Christ overcame death by his own death, and those who are united to Christ in his death also share in his resurrection. The second-century apologist Athenagoras makes a neat series of arguments about how God made us as a unity and saves us as a unity, meaning there must be a resurrection of the body.[45] God created humans as body-soul composites who could come to know and love their creator. He made us so that we might exist and live and, ultimately, exist and live with him forever.

> We are well aware that God would not have created such a living being and endowed him with all the gifts suited to permanence, if He did not want His creature to be permanent. . . . The reason for [man's] coming to be guarantees his permanence for ever, and his permanence guarantees his resurrection, for without this he would not be permanent *as man*.[46]

It does not make sense, then, that we be annihilated upon death, nor does it make sense that only part of us lives on after death. God created humans to be with him forever—that is, to be with him *as* humans forever, which means that not only our souls but also our bodies must endure forever.

Moreover, Athenagoras argues, we believe that God is just and that we will receive our due—be rewarded or punished—for our deeds. It is obvious that these rewards and punishments do not happen in this life, for many times the wicked prosper and die in comfort while the just suffer unjustly and die in pain. God's justice can only be executed fully in the next life. But since all human acts are the acts of us as humans—that is, they are not the acts of bodies alone or souls alone, but of complete persons acting as body and soul together—then we must be rewarded or punished *as* complete human beings. It cannot be our souls or bodies alone that are rewarded or punished;

---

45. What follows summarizes Athenagoras, *Resurrection of the Dead* 12–24.

46. Athenagoras, *Resurrection of the Dead* 13, in *"Embassy for the Christians," "The Resurrection of the Dead,"* trans. J. H. Crehan, Ancient Christian Writers (Westminster, MD: Newman, 1956), 98 (emphasis original).

rather, it is the whole person, body and soul, who receives justice. Therefore, in addition to an immortal soul, there must be a resurrection of the body, so that the integrity of God's creation can endure and so our just God can fulfill justice to his creatures.[47]

What our risen bodies will be like has always been the subject of much speculation.[48] Perhaps the most we can say with any confidence is that in the resurrection, Christ "will change our lowly body to be like his glorious body" (Phil. 3:21). As we discussed in chapter 4, the risen Christ has the same body that was born of Mary, which died and was buried, but that same body now has new qualities. We, too, will receive our own bodies back, but they will no longer be subject to the changes and ravages of this world. Our bodies, like our souls, will "put on immortality" (1 Cor. 15:53), meaning they will never die again. They will also be "imperishable" (15:53) or, better, "incorruptible," meaning they will never change for the worse in any way. Paul says our bodies will be "spiritual" (15:44), not in the sense that they will be ghostly or ethereal, but in the sense that they will be animated by the Spirit, the Lord and giver of life, who fits our resurrected bodies to a new way of being in the new heaven and the new earth (Rev. 21:1).

The Life of the World to Come

Many philosophers in the Platonist tradition believed that time was cyclical. Just as there is a cycle of seasons, similar cycles could be expected in the universe, history, and individual lives. Part of this belief meant that souls liberated from their bodies would eventually return to other bodies on earth. Some Platonists believed that souls could even inhabit animal bodies, perhaps as a punishment, but others restricted the reincarnation of souls to human bodies. Virgil puts it poetically when he says "that, forgetting everything, they may again behold the vault on high and begin once more to desire a return to bodies."[49] After a time of bliss in heaven, souls forget their time on earth and pine for a body again. The soul must flee the body to be happy, the Platonists thought, but it cannot live forever without a body. Thus, it must alternate between life and death, freedom and bondage, and forever cycle through disembodied bliss and embodied suffering.

47. This argument comes from Athenagoras, *Resurrection of the Dead* 18–22 (Crehan, 105–14).

48. For a comprehensive summary of ancient objections, traditional responses, and a rich, speculative exploration of resurrected life, read book 22 of Augustine's *City of God*.

49. Virgil, *Aeneid* 6.750–51, quoted in Augustine, *City of God* 13.19 (Babcock, 85).

Tertullian on the Resurrection in Nature

One of the early Christian defenses of the resurrection had to do with the witness of nature. Tertullian beautifully articulates how God wrote "resurrection" into the very fabric of nature in order that we might come to believe in Christ's resurrection and our own.

Consider now those very analogies of the divine power. . . . Day dies into night, and is buried everywhere in darkness. The glory of the world is obscured in the shadow of death; its entire substance is tarnished with blackness. . . . But yet it again revives, with its own beauty, its own dowry, its own sun, the same as ever, whole and entire, over all the world, slaying its own death, night—opening its own sepulchre, the darkness—coming forth the heir to itself. . . . Winters and summers return, as do the spring-tide and autumn, with their resources, their routines, their fruits. Forasmuch as earth receives its instruction from heaven to clothe the trees which had been stripped, to color the flowers afresh, to spread the grass again, to reproduce the seed which had been consumed, and not to reproduce them until consumed. Wondrous method! . . . In a word, I would say, all creation is instinct with renewal. . . . All things return to their former state, after having gone out of sight; all things begin after they have ended; they come to an end for the very purpose of coming into existence again. Nothing perishes but with a view to salvation. The whole, therefore, of this revolving order of things bears witness to the resurrection of the dead. In His works did God write it, before He wrote it in the Scriptures.[a]

a. Tertullian, *On the Resurrection* 12 (*ANF* 3:553).

The Christian hope for "the life of the world to come" is very different.[50] Those who are grafted onto Christ through faith and sacrament become united to Life itself and are given the promise of resurrection and eternal life with God. "I am the way, and the truth, and the life" (John 14:6), Jesus says,

50. There is no exact scriptural basis for the Creed's formula "the life of the world [or age] to come." The passage closest to the Creed occurs in the Gospel of Luke, where Jesus says, "Truly, I say to you, there is no man who has left house or wife or brothers or parents or children, for the sake of the kingdom of God, who will not receive manifold more in this time, and *in the age to come eternal life*" (Luke 18:29–30).

so that "he who hears my word and believes him who sent me, has eternal life" (5:24). This life will consist of seeing God "face to face" (1 Cor. 13:12) and therefore becoming "like him, for we shall see him as he is" (1 John 3:2). In beholding God, we will become one with what we behold and receive God's life to the full. For, Jesus tells us, "this is eternal life, that they know you the only true God, and Jesus Christ whom you have sent" (John 17:3 RSV-2CE).

Unlike the Platonist vision, Christ promises us a blessed life in the world to come, with no return to the miseries of this life. The Platonists are correct in their intuition that the soul longs for a body, but the soul longs for its *own* body. Christ promises us our own body back, immortal and incorruptible, which will forever be united to our redeemed and healed soul. While it is true that early Christians came to believe that the saved soul will enjoy happiness with God until Christ comes again, they recognized that this happiness is not complete, because the human person is not complete without a body. The "life of the world to come" is eternal life for both soul and body, which will dwell happily in "the eternal kingdom of our Lord and Savior Jesus Christ" (2 Pet. 1:11).

Eternal life begins now, in baptism, when we are "born anew, not of perishable seed but of imperishable" (1 Pet. 1:23). We live in the "already but not yet" time between Christ's two comings. But even now, the baptized partake of eternal life. Even now, they are new creations living amid the old as they await the renewal of all things at the end of time. Baptism is already the beginning of the new heaven and new earth that Revelation speaks of (Rev. 21:1). United to Christ, the baptized participate in the union of heaven and earth that is Christ himself.

The new heaven and new earth will not be a brand-new creation *ex nihilo*. Rather, it will be a creation *ex vetera*, a creation out of the old, which will renew the creation that already exists. In Romans, Paul famously says, "Creation itself will be set free from its bondage to decay and obtain the glorious liberty of the children of God" (Rom. 8:21). Some interpret this to mean that what was started in us in baptism and brought to completion in our resurrection will also happen to the whole universe. Irenaeus is an early witness to this tradition:

> For neither is the substance nor the essence of the creation annihilated (for faithful and true is He who has established it), but "the *fashion* of the world passeth away"; that is, those things among which transgression has occurred, since man has grown old in them. . . . But when this [present] fashion [of things] passes away, and man has been renewed, and flourishes in an incorruptible state,

so as to preclude the possibility of becoming old, [then] there shall be the new heaven and the new earth, in which the new man shall remain [continually], always holding fresh converse with God.[51]

Irenaeus draws on the prophecies of Isaiah: "For as the new heavens and the new earth which I will make shall remain before me, says the LORD; so shall your descendants and your name remain. From new moon to new moon, and from sabbath to sabbath, all flesh shall come to worship before me" (Isa. 66:22–23). "The world to come" will not be another world; rather, it will be our world redeemed and renewed, where God's "chosen shall long enjoy the work of their hands" (65:22) and "the wolf and the lamb shall feed together" (65:25).

Others interpret the Romans passage to mean that there will be no cosmos anymore, at least not in any form we might recognize: "The heavens will pass away with a loud noise, and the elements will be dissolved with fire, and the earth and the works that are upon it will be burned up" (2 Pet. 3:10). Jesus himself says, "Heaven and earth will pass away, but my words will not pass away" (Matt. 24:35). Athenagoras, for example, believes that "brute nature and all that is inanimate . . . will not remain in being after the resurrection."[52] He argues that the community of the children of God, redeemed and resurrected, will themselves be the new heaven and the new earth. Human beings, as microcosms of reality, contain the material and spiritual within themselves, so that in their resurrected lives creation is finally set free. We will not dwell in a Spirit-filled physical universe, but we will be like the risen and ascended Jesus. Indeed, even now, our "life is hid with Christ in God. When Christ who is our life appears, then you also will appear with him in glory" (Col. 3:3–4). We will be "where" Christ is at the "right hand of God" (3:1), which is not a place but a relationship of glory, honor, and full union with God and each other. On this account, the life of the world to come will not be just a better version of this life, where we happily work and play and love, but an immersion in an infinite communion that defies imagination.[53]

Whichever interpretation is correct, we will not, contrary to the Platonists, escape the world to be in heaven; rather, heaven will come down to us so that there is no longer a separation between heaven and earth. The book of Revelation speaks of the holy city coming down from heaven, "prepared as a

---

51. Irenaeus, *Against Heresies* 5.36.1 (ANF 1:566–67). See also Justin Martyr, *Dialogue with Trypho* 80–81; Lactantius, *Divine Institutes* 7.24; Augustine, *City of God* 20.16.

52. Athenagoras, *Resurrection of the Dead* 10 (Crehan, 91–92).

53. See also Origen, *On First Principles* 2.11 and 3.6 for another witness to this tradition.

bride adorned for her husband" (Rev. 21:2). Heaven will marry earth so that the two will become one. "The dwelling of God is with men. He will dwell with them, and they shall be his people, and God himself will be with them" (21:3). There will be no temple (21:22), which means that God will not be in a particular place, but present everywhere. The sea, that primordial symbol of chaos and dissolution, will no longer exist (21:1). Therefore, there will be no suffering and no death and, importantly, no chance of returning to the miseries in this life (21:4). Christians do not hope for a temporary reprieve from the world; rather, they hope for a permanent transformation of all things in God.

Amen

The Creed ends like the Bible ends: with the word "amen." The word is Hebrew and was so common in the New Testament and the early Church that it has been retained, mostly untranslated, for all of Church history. "Amen" is likely related to the word 'aman, which means "to make permanent or solid" and so "to be certain." If so, it is also related to 'emunah, the Hebrew word for "faith" (which we discussed in chap. 1). In the Hebrew text of Isaiah, the prophet calls God "the God of amen," which is usually translated "the God of truth" (Isa. 65:16). The word "amen" connotes God's faithfulness and trustworthiness. Christ himself is called "the Amen" (Rev. 3:14), which means he is God, he is truth, he is God's faithfulness incarnate.

"Amen" is often used liturgically to express assent to truths proclaimed, which is why Augustine and others in the fourth century interpreted the word to mean "it is true" (verum est). This is how the word is used here at the end of the Creed, which, in a sense, ends in the same way it began. The "amen" affirms the "I believe" of the first line. It proclaims that we commit ourselves to the truths of the Creed and entrust ourselves to the one who revealed them and to the Church, which authoritatively teaches them.

Living the Mystery

Christ died on Good Friday, rested in the tomb on the Sabbath, and rose again on the first day of the week—what we now call "the Lord's day." The Church Fathers understood that this sequence was rich in significance. As a faithful Jew, Christ observed the Sabbath and rose "on the third day," a biblical shorthand for theophany, the fullness of time when God appears (see Exod. 19:10–16). This third day is also the first day of the week, a sign that Christ is inaugurating a new creation. The Church Fathers also understood the Lord's day to be the "eighth day," an allusion to the fulfillment in Christ's resurrection of the Genesis creation story. God creates all things in six days, and each day has an evening and morning, signifying that all things are bound to time. But God rests on the seventh day, the Sabbath, which is never said to have an evening. The Sabbath day opens into an eternal eighth day that will never end. Christ rose on this eighth day, signifying the fulfillment of all things—that is, signifying the taking up of all things into divine life. For those who die in Christ, their souls experience the rest of the Sabbath, union and fullness with God. But they await the fulfillment of this in their bodies when they rise in Christ. Then all things will be fulfilled in them: they will experience God in their souls *and* bodies as fully divinized humans on an eighth day that will never end.

How can we live this beautiful theology of the end times? First, we must recognize that with the coming of Christ the end times have already begun. This does not mean that the world will end in our lifetime (though it might); it means that God's plan has already been fulfilled in Christ and is now being worked out in us, his body. Second, we must realize that "heaven" and "eternal life" are not some destination we head to in the future, but transformations that begin within us now. "Heaven" is union with God, and "eternal life" is sharing in God's own trinitarian communion. If Jesus is "the way, and the truth, and the life" (John 14:6), then "all the way to heaven is heaven," as Dorothy Day was fond of saying.[54] Our own bodies and souls, transformed in God, *are* the destination.

We can live the seventh and eighth days now by allowing God to transform us all the way down. God is rich in mercy, and so he has provided many ways to do this, but let us focus on just two examples of transformative practices that permit eternal life to become manifest in us now.

First, the prayerful reading of and listening to Scripture (especially in the liturgy) can transform us. "The Gospel *is* the body of Christ," Jerome says,[55] and we should feed on it in order to be spiritually nourished. In the Scriptures, Christ is truly present so that by receiving the Word, we can be transformed. Indeed, Augustine says, "for the time being treat the scripture of God as the face of God. Melt in front of it."[56] Scripture is a kind of sacramental heaven,

---

54. See Dorothy Day, *All the Way to Heaven Is Heaven: The Selected Letters of Dorothy Day*, ed. Robert Ellsberg (New York: Image Books, 2010). Day attributes the quote to Catherine of Siena, but the original source is uncertain.

55. Jerome, *In Psalmum* 147 (our translation from the Latin).

56. Augustine, *Sermon* 22.7, commenting on Ps. 68, in *Sermons 20–50*, trans. Edmund Hill, WSA III/3 (Brooklyn: New City, 1990), 46.

a way of seeing God face to face through a created medium. Now, we see God through the pages or sounds of Scripture, but in the next life we will see him face to face. Scripture has the divine power to "melt" us so that we become malleable for God. He can then remake us in the image of Christ and draw us deeper into his divine life.

Second, the Eucharist is the closest we can come in this life to heaven and eternal life. This is why we call it "communion," for the Eucharist *is* communion with God and each other, a true foretaste of life in the world to come. The Eucharist is heaven on earth. Catholics have the beautiful devotion of eucharistic adoration, what many lovingly call "radiation therapy for the soul." We who have a spiritual, terminal illness bask in the presence of God and receive the healing rays of God's light radiating out of the Eucharist. But the Eucharist is meant to be not only adored but consumed. And as our grandmothers often told us, we are what we eat. If we eat Christ, we become Christ. Leo the Great beautifully says, "The participation in the body and blood of Christ does nothing else but that we pass over into what we receive, and we carry everywhere, in spirit and flesh, him in whom we have died, have been buried, and have risen."[57]

When we consume the Eucharist, we truly "taste and see that the LORD is good" (Ps. 34:8). We become permeated "in spirit and flesh" with the life of God. We carry him about within us. He leaves his imprint on our bodies and souls. But more importantly, we are taken into Christ. We course through *his* body and are assimilated into him. And this is heaven: to be fed as children of God with God himself and so become an integral part of God's body, and to belong so intimately to him that we partake forever, body and soul, in the divine nature (see 2 Pet. 1:4).

57. Leo the Great, *Sermon* 63.7 (our translation from the Latin).

Three Creeds Compared

Creed of Nicaea (325)	Nicene Creed from the Council of Constantinople (381)	Apostles' Creed (7th century)
We believe in one God, the Father almighty, maker of all things, visible and invisible,	I believe in one God, the Father almighty, maker of heaven and earth, of all things visible and invisible.	I believe in God, the Father almighty, Creator of heaven and earth,
and in one Lord Jesus Christ, the Son of God, the Only Begotten, begotten from the Father, that is, from the substance of the Father. God from God, Light from Light, true God from true God, begotten, not made, consubstantial with the Father;	I believe in one Lord Jesus Christ, the Only Begotten Son of God, born of the Father before all ages. God from God, Light from Light, true God from true God, begotten, not made, consubstantial with the Father;	and in Jesus Christ, his only Son, our Lord,

Creed of Nicaea (325)	Nicene Creed from the Council of Constantinople (381)	Apostles' Creed (7th century)
through him all things were made, those in heaven and those on earth.	through him all things were made.	
For us men and for our salvation he came down, was incarnate, and became man.	For us men and for our salvation he came down from heaven, and by the Holy Spirit was incarnate of the Virgin Mary, and became man.	who was conceived by the Holy Spirit, born of the Virgin Mary,
He suffered death, and rose again on the third day, and ascended into heaven.	For our sake he was crucified under Pontius Pilate, he suffered death and was buried, and rose again on the third day in accordance with the Scriptures. He ascended into heaven and is seated at the right hand of the Father.	suffered under Pontius Pilate, was crucified, died and was buried; he descended into hell; on the third day he rose again from the dead; he ascended into heaven, and is seated at the right hand of God the Father almighty;
He will come to judge the living and the dead.	He will come again in glory to judge the living and the dead	from there he will come to judge the living and the dead.
	and his kingdom will have no end.	
We believe in the Holy Spirit.	I believe in the Holy Spirit, the Lord, the giver of life, who proceeds from the Father [and the Son], who with the Father and the Son is adored and glorified, who has spoken through the prophets.	I believe in the Holy Spirit,

Creed of Nicaea (325)	Nicene Creed from the Council of Constantinople (381)	Apostles' Creed (7th century)
	I believe in one, holy, catholic and apostolic Church. I confess one Baptism for the forgiveness of sins and I look forward to the resurrection of the dead and the life of the world to come. Amen.	the holy catholic Church, the communion of saints, the forgiveness of sins, the resurrection of the body, and life everlasting. Amen.
However, those who say, "There was when he was not" and "Before he was born, he was not" and "He was made from nothing" or who say that the Son of God is of another substance or essence or that he is changeable or alterable, these are condemned by the Catholic Church.		

The Nicene Creed (from the Council of Constantinople) and the Apostles' Creed are taken from the standard English translations approved by the United States Conference of Catholic Bishops: https://www.usccb.org/beliefs-and -teachings/what-we-believe and https://www.usccb.org/prayers/apostles -creed. In the Nicene Creed, we added brackets to "and the Son" to indicate this was a later addition (see pp. 152–61).

The Creed of Nicaea is our translation from the Greek and Latin texts found in Heinrich Denzinger, *Compendium of Creeds, Definitions, and Declarations on Matters of Faith and Morals*, ed. Peter Hünermann, 43rd ed. (San Francisco: Ignatius, 2012), §§125–26. We have attempted to match the standard language so that the differences in the creeds emerge more clearly.

The Nicene Creed in Latin and Greek

Credo in unum Deum,	Πιστεύομεν εἰς ἕνα Θεόν,
Patrem omnipotentem,	πατέρα παντοκράτορα,
factorem caeli et terrae,	ποιητὴν οὐρανοῦ καὶ γῆς,
visibilium omnium et invisibilium.	ὁρατῶν τε πάντων καὶ ἀοράτων·

Et in unum Dominum Iesum Christum,	καὶ εἰς ἕνα κύριον Ἰησοῦν Χριστόν,
Filium Dei unigenitum,	τὸν υἱὸν τοῦ Θεοῦ τὸν μονογενῆ,
et ex Patre natum ante omnia saecula,	τὸν ἐκ τοῦ πατρὸς γεννηθέντα πρὸ πάντων τῶν αἰώνων,
Deum de Deo, lumen de lumine,	φῶς ἐκ φωτός,
Deum verum de Deo vero,	Θεὸν ἀληθινὸν ἐκ Θεοῦ ἀληθινοῦ,
genitum, non factum,	γεννηθέντα οὐ ποιηθέντα, ὁμοούσιον τῷ πατρί,
consubstantialem Patri:	
per quem omnia facta sunt;	δι' οὗ τὰ πάντα ἐγένετο·
qui propter nos homines et propter nostram salutem descendit de caelis,	τὸν δι' ἡμᾶς τοὺς ἀνθρώπους καὶ διὰ τὴν ἡμετέραν σωτηρίαν κατελθόντα ἐκ τῶν οὐρανῶν

et incarnatus est de Spiritu Sancto ex Maria virgine,	καὶ σαρκωθέντα ἐκ πνεύματος ἁγίου καὶ Μαρίας τῆς παρθένου,
et homo factus est,	καὶ ἐνανθρωπήσαντα,
crucifixus etiam pro nobis sub Pontio Pilato,	σταυρωθέντα τε ὑπὲρ ἡμῶν ἐπὶ Ποντίου Πιλάτου
passus et sepultus est,	καὶ παθόντα καὶ ταφέντα
et resurrexit tertia die secundum Scripturas,	καὶ ἀναστάντα τῇ τρίτῃ ἡμέρᾳ κατὰ τὰς γραφάς,
et ascendit in caelum,	καὶ ἀνελθόντα εἰς τοὺς οὐρανούς,
sedet ad dexteram Patris,	καὶ καθεζόμενον ἐν δεξιᾷ τοῦ πατρός,
et iterum venturus est cum gloria,	καὶ πάλιν ἐρχόμενον μετὰ δόξης,
iudicare vivos et mortuos:	κρῖναι ζῶντας καὶ νεκρούς·
cuius regni non erit finis.	οὗ τῆς βασιλείας οὐκ ἔσται τέλος·

. . . .

Et in Spiritum Sanctum, Dominum et vivificantem,	καὶ εἰς τὸ πνεῦμα τὸ ἅγιον, τὸ κύριον καὶ ζωοποιόν,
qui ex Patre Filioque procedit,	τὸ ἐκ τοῦ πατρὸς ἐκπορευόμενον,
qui cum Patre et Filio simul adoratur et conglorificatur	τὸ σὺν πατρὶ καὶ υἱῷ συμπροσκυνούμενον καὶ συνδοξαζόμενον,
qui locutus est per prophetas.	τὸ λαλῆσαν διὰ τῶν προφητῶν.

. . . .

Et unam sanctam catholicam et apostolicam Ecclesiam.	Εἰς μίαν ἁγίαν καθολικὴν καὶ ἀποστολικὴν ἐκκλησίαν.
Confiteor unum baptisma in remissionem peccatorum.	Ὁμολογοῦμεν ἓν βάπτισμα εἰς ἄφεσιν ἁμαρτιῶν.
Et exspecto resurrectionem mortuorum,	Προσδοκῶμεν ἀνάστασιν νεκρῶν
et vitam venturi saeculi. Amen.	καὶ ζωὴν τοῦ μέλλοντος αἰῶνος. Ἀμήν.

Glossary

adoptionism: The notion that Jesus was merely a human who was "adopted" by God and elevated to a divine status.

Apostles' Creed: Pious legend attributes this creed to the twelve apostles (each one contributing one article of faith), but more likely it developed organically from the **Old Roman Creed** (see below), reaching a final form in the 600s. It is still used by Catholics and Protestants today.

apostolic succession: The way that divine authority in the Church is passed on from one generation of leaders to the next. This includes, among other things, the authority to forgive sins, to offer acceptable sacrifice to God, and to teach faith and morals in a binding way.

Arians/Arian controversy: Followers of Arius who believed that the Son of God is not fully divine, but the first and highest creature of God the Father (a form of **subordinationism**). Arius's teachings gave rise to the controversy that led to the Council of Nicaea in 325.

Athanasian Creed: Piously attributed to Athanasius in the Middle Ages, this creed was likely composed in Gaul in the sixth century. It draws on Augustinian themes of trinitarian theology and reflects Western theological concerns.

begotten: A technical term used to describe how the Son shares the same divine nature as the Father. To "beget" means to pass on a nature; to be "begotten" is to receive a nature. In God, this is an eternal relation between the Father and the Son.

Christology (christological): A theological account of who Christ is, especially of his being both divine and human.

consubstantial (Greek *homoousios*, Latin *consubstantialis*): "One in being" or "of the same substance/nature/essence." The term used at the Council of Nicaea to show that the Son is of the same order of being—that is, equally divine—as the Father.

create (make): To bring into being from nothing; contrast with **begotten**.

deification (divinization, theosis): A Christian doctrine that describes our new life in Christ in terms of our sharing in the life and power of God, both now in this age and fully in the life of the age to come. Deification does not mean that we become God by nature; rather, it means that we share in his life by grace as sons and daughters of God.

Demiurge: "Craftsman" or "artisan," though etymologically it means "public worker." In ancient controversies, it generally refers to a lesser god who created the material universe.

Docetism/Docetists: The teaching that Jesus did not truly become a human being, but only appeared to be human, either as an illusion or as a temporary manifestation (like the angels who appear to people).

doxology (from Greek *doxa*, "glory"): A traditional form of prayer that praises God by recounting his attributes and asking that all "glory" be given to him.

ecclesiology: A theological account of who and what the Church is, taking into account both its human and divine dimensions.

eschatology/eschatological (from Greek *eschata*, "last things"): All that concerns the end of human history: the final tribulations, the coming of Jesus, the last judgment, and the resurrection of the dead. For the New Testament, the end begins with Jesus's passion and resurrection—the transition from the former age to the new and final age of salvation history.

fideism: Literally, "faith-ism"; the notion that faith can operate independently of reason or that faith and reason are opposed.

***Filioque*:** "And the Son," a shorthand for the teaching that the Holy Spirit proceeds from the Father *and the Son*, rather than from the Father alone.

Gnostics/Gnosticism: A category used to describe a diverse group of early Christian sects that generally held to a strict dualism between the good spiritual world and the evil material world. Gnosticism typically entails a belief in a variety of deities who rule these realms, trust in an authority beyond Scripture or the Church, and a belief that salvation comes through gnosis, a secret knowledge revealed to the elect.

homoiousios: "Like in being" or "of like substance/nature/essence." The notion that the Son, while divine, does not share the same order of divinity as the Father. Compare **consubstantial**; **homoousios**.

homoousios: "One in being" or "the same in being"; see **consubstantial**.

incarnation: Literally, "enfleshment"; the eternal Son of God's taking on a human nature—that is, a body and a soul—in the womb of Mary (John 1:14).

kerygma: Literally, "proclamation"; it refers to the heart of the gospel message, the announcing or proclaiming of the good news.

lex orandi: Literally, "the law of praying"; from the ancient formula *lex orandi, lex credendi*, meaning that how the Church prays reflects and determines what the Church believes.

Macedonians: Named after Macedonius, a former bishop of Constantinople, who supported the view that the Holy Spirit was not God.

Manicheans: A Christian Gnostic sect, founded by Mani, that flourished in the third and fourth centuries AD; Augustine was a follower for nine years and later a severe critic.

Marcionites: Named after Marcion, a second-century teacher who rejected the Old Testament as the work of an inferior god.

missions: In theology, a reference to the distinct missions of the Son (Jesus) and the Spirit in the world; the missions of the Son and the Spirit in the world reflect the processions of the Son and the Spirit from the Father.

modalism: The claim that there is no *real* or *eternal* distinction between the Father and the Son (and the Spirit), but that these identities are temporary arrangements that manifest the one God in different "modes" or roles.

nature (substance, essence): Used to designate what is one in God; names *what* something or someone is. Compare **person**.

Old Roman Creed: The earliest written creed, from the city of Rome (produced ca. 175–200), which served as the precursor to the Apostles' Creed.

pagans: A term used by Christians of the ancient world to name those who did not adhere to the monotheism of the biblical God; generally, the non-Christian polytheists of the Roman Empire.

Paraclete: "Comforter" or "counselor"; a name for the Holy Spirit.

person (Greek *prosōpon* or *hypostasis*): Used to designate the real distinction between the persons of the Trinity; names *who* someone is. Compare **nature**.

pneumatology (pneumatological): A theological account of who the Holy Spirit is, especially of the Spirit's divine nature and work in the life of the Church.

polytheism: The belief that many gods constitute the divine being, or the practice of worshiping many deities.

procession: A term used to describe the eternal relation of the Holy Spirit to the Father (and the Son); the Father does not have two eternal Sons, but one begotten Son and one eternal Spirit who proceeds from him. Compare **begotten**.

relation: Used to designate how the persons of the Trinity are distinguished from each other; each divine person is fully God, though each is distinguished by their eternal relations to the other persons of the Trinity.

rule of faith: Short, summary formulas and patterns of speech that capture the trinitarian shape of Christian faith; a measuring stick of what Christians ought to believe.

Septuagint (abbreviated LXX): Literally, "seventy." The Greek translation of the Hebrew Bible dating from the third and second centuries BC, so called because of the tradition that it was the work of seventy scholars. Often quoted in the New Testament, it was the Bible commonly used by Greek-speaking Jews and Christians.

subordinationism: The belief that the Son and the Spirit are inferior to the Father.

***Theotokos*:** A title for Mary that means "God-bearer" or "Mother of God," used to preserve the unity of Christ's two natures. Mary is Mother of the divine person, the Son of God, who unites a human nature (body and soul) to himself in Mary's womb.

Trinity: A summary way of naming God, who Christians believe is a tri-unity: one God in three divine persons.

Suggested Resources

Commentaries on the Nicene Creed

Cary, Philip. *The Nicene Creed: An Introduction*. Bellingham, WA: Lexham, 2023.

Hahn, Scott. *The Creed: Professing the Faith through the Ages*. Steubenville, OH: Emmaus Road, 2016.

Johnson, Luke Timothy. *The Creed: What Christians Believe and Why It Matters*. New York: Image, 2004.

Oden, Thomas C., ed. *Ancient Christian Doctrine*. 5 vols. Downers Grove, IL: IVP Academic, 2009–10.

Wilson, James Matthew. *Praying the Nicene Creed*. London: Catholic Truth Society, 2022.

Histories and Theological Reflections on the Creed

Anatolios, Khaled. *Retrieving Nicaea: The Development and Meaning of Trinitarian Doctrine*. Grand Rapids: Baker Academic, 2011.

Ayres, Lewis. *Nicaea and Its Legacy: An Approach to Fourth-Century Trinitarian Theology*. Oxford: Oxford University Press, 2004.

Barron, Robert. *Light from Light: A Theological Reflection on the Nicene Creed*. Park Ridge, IL: Word on Fire Academic, 2021.

Behr, John. *The Formation of Christian Theology*. Vol. 1, *The Way to Nicaea*. Vol. 2, *The Nicene Faith*. Crestwood, NY: St. Vladimir's Seminary Press, 2001–4.

Hanson, R. P. C. *The Search for the Christian Doctrine of God: The Arian Controversy, 318–381*. Grand Rapids: Baker Academic, 2005.

Kelly, J. N. D. *Early Christian Creeds*. London: Longmans, 1949.

Young, Frances. *The Making of the Creeds*. Harrisburg, PA: Trinity Press International, 1991.

Important Background and Specific Doctrines

Anatolios, Khaled. *Athanasius*. The Early Church Fathers. London: Routledge, 2004.

Congar, Yves. *I Believe in the Holy Spirit*. Translated by David Smith. New York: Crossroad, 1997.

Daley, Brian. *God Visible: Patristic Christology Reconsidered*. Oxford: Oxford University Press, 2018.

———. *The Hope of the Early Church: A Handbook of Patristic Eschatology*. Grand Rapids: Baker Academic, 1991.

Emery, Gilles. *The Trinity: An Introduction to the Catholic Doctrine of the Triune God*. Translated by Matthew Levering. Washington, DC: Catholic University of America Press, 2011.

Ferguson, Everett. *The Rule of Faith: A Guide*. Eugene, OR: Cascade Books, 2015.

Hurtado, Larry W. *Destroyer of the Gods: Early Christian Distinctiveness in the Roman World*. Waco: Baylor University Press, 2016.

Kelly, J. N. D. *Early Christian Doctrines*. 5th rev. ed. New York: HarperOne, 1978.

Levering, Matthew. *Engaging the Doctrine of the Holy Spirit: Love and Gift in the Trinity and the Church*. Grand Rapids: Baker Academic, 2016.

May, Gerhard. *Creatio Ex Nihilo: The Doctrine of "Creation out of Nothing" in Early Christian Thought*. Translated by A. S. Worrall. London: T&T Clark, 2004.

Thiselton, Anthony C. *The Holy Spirit—In Biblical Teaching, through the Centuries, and Today*. Grand Rapids: Eerdmans, 2013.

White, Thomas Joseph. *The Trinity: On the Nature and Mystery of the One God*. Washington, DC: Catholic University of America Press, 2022.

Wilken, Robert Louis. *The Christians as the Romans Saw Them*. 2nd ed. New Haven: Yale University Press, 2003.

Young, Frances M., with Andrew Teal. *From Nicaea to Chalcedon: A Guide to the Literature and Its Background*. 2nd ed. Grand Rapids: Baker Academic, 2010.

Index of Sidebars

Witness to the Tradition

Athanasius on the Term *Homoousios*   94

Augustine on Anthropomorphic Language in Scripture   43

Augustine on the Authority of the Catholic Church   29

Augustine on the Faith of Infants   21

Basil the Great on the Glory of Adoration Given to the Holy Spirit   166

Gregory of Nazianzus on the Holy Spirit   148

Gregory of Nazianzus on the Incomprehensibility of the Begetting of the Son   86

Irenaeus on the Incarnation Leading to Deification   111

Irenaeus on the Oneness of Jesus Christ   78

Irenaeus on the Primacy of Rome   189

John of Damascus on Christ's Ascension   132

Justin Martyr on the Return of Christ and the Final Judgment   137

Maximus the Confessor on the *Filioque*   158

Origen on Many Ways to Receive Forgiveness   197

Pope Leo the Great on Christ's Passion   123

Tertullian on the Resurrection in Nature   205

Lex Orandi

"All Hail the Power of Jesus' Name"   77

The Blessing of the Baptismal Waters   192

Byzantine Hymn to the Holy Spirit   155

Christ as Light from Light   90

Christ's Ascension   131

Christ's Passion   124

The Colossians Hymn   98

"Come, Holy Ghost, Creator Blest"   171

"Come, Holy Spirit"   145

Faith and Works   19

The Faith of Your Church   33

God, the I AM   45

The Holy Church   183

Hymns to the *Theotokos*   113

The Incarnation   109

"O Come, All Ye Faithful"   85

One Church   178

Through the Son   80

A Trinity of One Substance   97

Undivided God   46

The Veneration of the Cross   121

"Veni, Sancte Spiritus"   151

Waiting for Christ's Return in Glory   135

Worshiping with the Angels   64

Contemporary Issues

Creation and Evolution   62

The *Filioque* in Orthodox-Catholic Relations   159

The Inspiration of the Bible   168

The Problem of Evil   68

Stewardship of the Natural World   100

The Uniqueness of Jesus Christ   139

Unity Today   180

Why Is God Called "Father" and Not "Mother"?   54